NOTHING CAN MAKE THEM STUMBLE

The Story of the Stoll/Meinel Family

The German Colony
Haifa, Israel, 2008

Herbert (Herb) E Meinel

Copyright © 2016 Herbert E Meinel
Adelaide, Australia

All rights reserved. No part of this publication may be reproduced, stored in a retrieval system, or transmitted in any form by any means, electronic, mechanical, photocopying, recording or otherwise without prior written permission of the copyright holders.

ISBN: 978-0-9875819-2-1 (Create Space)

Second Edition 2016

Book order enquiries are welcome:
Email: herbmeinel@yahoo.com.au

To my children

Marianne, Philip, Andrew and David

& their children:

Braxton & Bronzyn;

Jake, Kiana & Chloe;

Jack & Beth.

Write down for the coming generation
What the Lord has done
So that people not yet born will praise him.
Psalm 102:18

Acknowledgements

I am deeply grateful for all those who have encouraged me to write this book: my siblings, Werner, Helga and Inge, and cousins, Ted, Gary, Fred, Walter and Herta. Without their help and contributions this book would not be complete. In particular I thank Ted Stoll, who, as the custodian of the Stoll family history, has supplied me with an endless stock of information, photos and stories of life in Palestine.

Thanks to my wife Margaret and daughter Marianne for proof reading the manuscript, and brother-in-law David Bridges and Wendy Noble for their meticulous editing.

My task of researching the history of the early settlements in Palestine has been made relatively easy by the availability of the excellent records of the Temple Society of Australia, and by the books they and other descendants of those early settlers have published. Much of the early source material has come from the following publications:

Marcinkowski-Schumacher, Nelly (1978) *Wenn's aus Blauem Himmel Regnet : mein Leben mit Wladimir Ph. Marcinkowski.* Translation by Martin Stoll (1995)

Sauer, Paul Dr & Temple Society Australia. Regional Council (1987). *The Temple Society : A Brief Historical Introduction.* Temple Society Australia, Melbourne.

Sauer, Paul Dr & Temple Society Australia (1991). *The Holy Land Called : the story of the Temple Society.* Temple Society Australia, Melbourne.

Wassermann-Deininger, Gertrud 1981, *Here we have no lasting City [1995 aka We don't have a permanent home here : history of the family of Gottlieb Deininger in Palestine (1868-1948)]*

I thank God for the privilege of sharing this amazing story with the Stoll/Meinel descendants and all who read it.

Herb Meinel, Hove, Australia, 2016

Preface

Easter Sunday, 23 March 2008, was a day that will always have special memories for me.

My wife Margaret and I were part of a group of 34 Australians and 17 Americans on a two week study tour to Israel. For me the tour had a double significance. I was visiting modern day Israel and the cradle of Christianity. But, even more importantly, I was going to Haifa: the place my parents and grandparents called home, and where I was born 70 years earlier. Now I was back, 68 years later.

It was a beautiful sunny afternoon when our bus stopped in Yefe Nof Street at the summit of Mount Carmel. As we stepped from the bus we were greeted with an amazing panoramic view of Haifa, Israel's third largest city. Immediately in front of us on the slopes of Mount Carmel lay the magnificent Bahai Gardens and Shrine, and below it the Port of Haifa with the azure blue waters of the Mediterranean Sea beyond.

Between them stretched Ben Gurion Boulevard bordered by a patchwork of red roofs within a beautiful green landscape, glowing in the late afternoon sunlight. Our Jewish tourist guide, Yehuda Ashkenazi, said, "You are now looking at what is known as the German Colony, established in 1869".

Although I had no first hand memories of Haifa, I had heard about this place all my life from my parents. I'd seen it in photos, read about it in books and now I was looking at it with my own eyes. What an indescribable feeling! I was looking at part of my heritage. And, somewhere down there was the house I was born in. I couldn't wait to find it.

Why were my parents and grandparents able to call this their 'home'? And why do we find a German Colony in the middle of Israel's third largest city?

To answer these questions I have decided to put on record a short history of the Stoll/Meinel family. In doing so, I want to express my heartfelt thanks to God for my parents, and my Stoll ancestors, for making me the recipient of such a rich and diverse ancestral, cultural and spiritual heritage. I also wanted to ensure that the legacy they have left me, my siblings and cousins, is preserved for our children and succeeding generations of our families.

The story of *Nothing can make them stumble* has its roots in central Europe and traces the lives and experiences of six generations of Stoll family members across five continents over a time span of some 300 years. It is a story of faith, hardship, perseverance and blessing.

The focus of this story is on the family members who were born and lived in the Holy Land: Jakob and Maria Stoll and their children: Wilhelm, Hulda, Maria and Christian. In amongst it you will also read something about my personal story.

Haifa 2008

German Colony 2008

Contents

Acknowledgements iv
Preface v

SECTION I 1

The Stoll Genealogy 3
Political & Economic Environment 7
The Spiritual Climate 9
The Cultural Heritage 13
Dornstetten 17
The Templers 21

SECTION II 27

The Pioneering of the German Colony in Haifa 29
Shaking Foundations 39
Give Me this Mountain 45
Jakob & Maria Stoll 53
A Childhood to be Cherished 61
A Healthy, Happy and Wise Community Life 69
A Troublesome and Uncertain Future 79
Brothers, Sisters and Spouses 89
The Fabulous 1920s and 30s 111
The Winds of Change 119
Behind Barbed Wire 125
The Exchange 135
The End of the Templer Settlements in Palestine 141
The Bigger Picture 147

SECTION III. 161
- White Christmas 163
- Zell u Aichelberg 171
- A Time of War 181
- When the War is Over! 189
- Father returns Home! 197
- A Childhood to Remember 205
- Looking to the Future 229

SECTION IV 235
- Exiled to the Land Down Under 237
- Ebenezer 243
- Barossa Living (1953-1957) 259
- In Search of Purpose 277
- Leaving Home 283
- In Their Footsteps 291
- A Tribute 303

FOOTNOTES 311

Section I.

THE LAND OF MY ANCESTORS

(1700-1868)

Idyll aus der Badgasse

Dornstetten 1960

The Stoll Genealogy

The Stoll genealogy recalled in these pages stretches back to when my great great great great grandfather Johannes Stoll was born in the small rural village of Dornstetten in the south-west of Germany in 1719.

The Stoll/Meinel Family Tree gives a graphic snapshot of the Stoll clan: their names and ages, the places where they were born and the countries to which they travelled and adopted as their homes. From the earliest available record of 1719, the genealogy stretches over almost 300 years to our present day. Embedded in this span of time is the remarkable story of the lives of six generations of my Stoll ancestors. It has been an amazing adventure as I have delved into the past, traced the places where they lived and learned something of the times, circumstances and experiences that shaped their lives.

The early history (1700-1850) is somewhat sketchy. I have not attempted to research any new information other than to make a simple analysis of the statistical information contained in the *Ahnenpass*[1] (Stoll Family Tree) prepared in the 1930's by my uncle, Christian Stoll. Much more information and firsthand accounts are available from the period after 1850.

Johannes Stoll was born in 1719. He was a weaver by trade and married Catherine Margareth Stahl (1722-1744), a local girl from Dornstetten. The life cycle of the first four generations of the Stoll families followed a similar pattern. The Stoll men were all born and lived in Dornstetten; they married girls from Dornstetten or nearby villages, and made their living as weavers in

Dornstetten. Each father passed on the craft of weaving to his son, and he to his, right up to the era of my great grandfather, Christian Stoll (1833-1893).

During those 150 years or so, the economy of Dornstetten was mainly based on agriculture; followed closely by a budding weaving industry. In the second half of the 19th century, weaving became the first trade to be industrialised in this region of Germany.[2] The Stolls would no doubt have made their contribution to the growth and development of this vital industry and the economy of that time.

The family tree statistics reveal other interesting facts. Johannes was the favoured family Christian name. Johannes or its derivative, Johann, occurs five times up to the end of the 19th century. The men married in their mid twenties to early thirties (except one) and children in our direct family line were born when their parents were in their thirties. It was not until the time of our grandparents that some of these fixed patterns started to change. In addition to weavers, members of the Stoll family were bakers, gardeners, station masters and tailors.

It was in the 19th century, also, that the family became more mobile and adventurous. They began to move away from their home base in Dornstetten, to other parts within Germany and outside of Germany to the United States, Russia and Palestine.

The early family tree gives no indication of the number of children born to each family, but we do know that after 1850 the number of recorded children born to our great grandparents, grandparents and parents did not exceed five per family. The infant mortality rate right up to the end of the 19th century was 32% in that part of Germany. The average life span of people living between 1700 and 1900 was 51 years. Our grandparents and parents lived to an average age of 81.5 years.

My ancestors had a love for God. They were faithful members of the *Evangelische Landeskirche* (Lutheran State Church). They were married in the church, their children were baptised and confirmed in the church and they were active participants in the social welfare of the community.

They were also active in the Pietist movement. In addition to attending the church they attended Sunday afternoon meetings (*Die Stunde*) for Bible study, prayer and fellowship. They had an interest in music that, in those days, was largely expressed in singing of hymns and playing musical instruments in church services.

In 1858 at the dedication of a new organ in St Martin's Church in Dornstetten, a member of the Stoll family was part of the brass ensemble specifically formed to accompany the organ in the congregational singing. On this Sunday, and subsequent Sundays, and on special religious days, this brass group was paid a small fee to "play two hymns from three sides of the lofty heights of the church tower"[3]. Their sounds could be heard throughout the town and far into the surrounding countryside.

During that same period, on the other side of the world, another group of church members also formed a brass band to assist in the worship of Sunday services. Lutherans from Prussia and Silesia had left their homeland in search of religious freedom and had settled at Langmeil, in the Barossa Valley, in the newly formed colony of South Australia. The Band was formed in 1858 to play exclusively for church services.

Today, the Tanunda Brass Band is not only known as the oldest brass band but also one of the champion brass bands of South Australia and beyond. The Stoll tradition of brass band playing continued when my brother Werner and I joined the Tanunda Band in 1953. In 2008 the Band celebrated its 150th anniversary and we both attended as past members. One of their legacies is an excellent recording of sacred hymns and spiritual songs.

The times during which our ancestors lived are so far removed from our lifestyle in Australia today that it is difficult to grasp or even imagine what life must have been like back then. For this reason I have chosen to explore the political, economic, spiritual and cultural climate that prevailed in Wuerttemberg, the territory where my ancestors were born and lived during the 18th and 19th centuries. Those times shaped the character and values of my Stoll ancestors and can still be seen in their descendants today, despite the passage of time of over 300 years and the travel across many different countries and cultures.

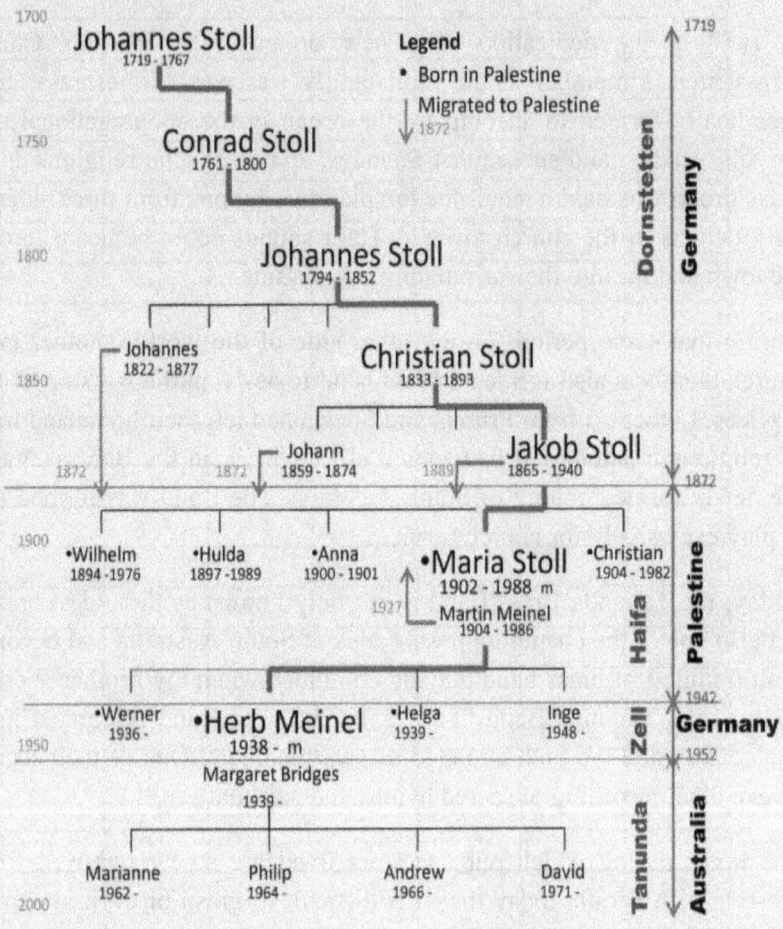

Political & Economic Environment

Our early ancestors lived in a constantly changing political environment. They lived in what is known as the *Hohenzollern Dynasty*: a 500 year feudal system of lords, dukes and kings that tightly controlled the working class people of Wuerttemberg. A constant stream of conflicts and wars within Germany and neighbouring countries characterised much of that time.

In the early 1800s, Wuerttemberg was allied to France during the reign of Napoleon Bonaparte. Compulsory military service forced the local men to enlist in the campaigns against Prussia, Russia and Austria (1812, 13). Casualties were severe. Napoleon's "Grand Army" of 600 000 included 15 800 soldiers from Wuerttemberg, but only 500 returned home. Following the abdication of Napoleon as Emperor of France, the map of Europe was redrawn in 1815. Wuerttemberg became a part of the thirty nine sovereign States of the German Federation.[1]

When King Wilhelm I of Wuerttemberg commenced his reign (1816-1864), Wuerttemberg was a poor and densely populated country. Crop failures in 1816 and 1817 caused much hunger and privation. In 1836 King Wilhelm I married Catherine of Russia and she became the great benefactor of the poor and needy.[2] In the same year King Wilhelm did away with the feudal laws that had suppressed the peasantry, thereby emancipating the farmers. He did much to promote the expansion of agriculture and the infant industry in

Wuerttemberg. It is not surprising therefore that a statue was erected in his honour in the *Schlossplatz* (Castle Square) in Stuttgart, with the inscription:

Dedicated to the true friend of his people, King Wilhelm, the much beloved.[3]

A mass exodus of people from Wuerttemberg followed in the mid 19th century. The main drivers were the crop failures of 1846 and 1847; the political failure of liberalism after the collapse of the internal revolution of 1848 and 1849, and the dissolution of the Frankfurt Parliament. Between 1849 and 1855, more than 70 000 people from Wuerttemberg alone – in excess of 5% of the entire population – emigrated to Southern Russia and to the American West.[4]

In the second half of the 19th century Prussia became the dominant German power, with the "Iron Chancellor", Count Otto von Bismarck, the key figure. A further period of wars followed, which drew Wuerttemberg into an armistice with Prussia (24 July 1866) under the terms of which the people had to pay exorbitant war reparation taxes. In 1870/71 the Franco-German war erupted and the young men of Wuerttemberg were again conscripted.

On 1 January 1871 the kingdom of Wuerttemberg was officially proclaimed a federal state of the German Empire. On 18 January 1877 King Wilhelm I of Prussia became the German Kaiser. During this founding period of 1871 and 1873 money flowed into the German Empire via war reparation from a defeated France, resulting in a major rejuvenation of the economy.[5]

On the 22nd of October 1891 King Wilhelm II ascended the throne of Wuerttemberg. During this time the German Empire was at the peak of its power. It ended with his abdication on the 9th November 1918 and with it some 500 years of uninterrupted rule by the *Hohenzollern* Dynasty had come to an end.[6]

The Spiritual Climate

The religious and church life of the 18th and 19th centuries was as reactionary as the political and economic life. These periods were characterised by a decidedly unchristian culture on the one hand, and some great spiritual awakenings and missions of the Christian church worldwide, on the other.

Historians have called the period from the 1630s to 1780, the "Age of Reason". The Age of Reason

"was a widespread intellectual revolution ... when man began to evaluate God and the world on the basis of reason and scientific principles rather than scriptural revelation"[1].

Enlightenment philosophies began to gnaw at the foundation of Christianity. Many intellectuals abandoned organised religion and embraced instead an outlook called Deism.[2]

Rationalism and Liberalism are the other main enlightenment philosophies that emerged over the next 100 years.

"Rationalism maintained that reason (deductive thinking) was the basis of all knowledge and that man had the ability to discover truth on his own, without relying on divine revelation."[3]

The spiritual awakenings that followed were in part a reaction to the spread of Deism and in part a response to the spiritual deadness of Protestant orthodoxy. For the most part, Lutheran faith and practice had grown formal, cold and lifeless. Awakenings started in Germany and spread to Scandinavia and Switzerland, producing a spiritual movement known as Pietism. Several men of stature led the revivals, including: Philipp Jakob Spener (1635-1705); August Hermann Francke (1663-1727), Professor of Theology at Halle University; and Nikolaus Ludwig von Zinzendorf (1700-1760), who founded *Herrnhut* (1722), a community for displaced Moravian Christians.

Cutting across classes and creeds, Pietism emphasised the basic values of the Bible and the need of a personal experience of Christ as Saviour and Lord. The preaching emphasised repentance and holy living. Pietists were deeply committed to evangelism and missions. The Moravian Church became one of the foremost missionary organisations of its day.

In addition to their missionary training-schools in Halle and Herrnhut in Germany, the Pietists also established missionary schools in Switzerland: the *Basel Mission* and the *Pilgrim Mission of St Chrischona*, with whom our ancestors had a significant connection through several generations.

Pietists believed in a practical Christianity and became champions of social action. Francke founded a series of institutions to support the destitute and deprived people of Halle and environments. He established a school for the poor, an orphanage, a hospital, a widows' home, as well as a teacher training institute and Bible School. Pietists were also keen students of prophecy: the Bible teaching about the end times and the return of Christ.

The influence of Pietism was far reaching. John Wesley, dissatisfied with the coldness of Anglican orthodoxy in Britain and uncertain about his own salvation, encountered a Moravian Missionary during his missionary journey to Georgia, America, in 1735. Challenged to look to Christ alone for his salvation, John Wesley found peace with God in his famous 'heart-warming experience' in London in 1738. John Wesley's 'new birth' served as the impetus for a fresh wave of Gospel preaching in England. In America the first great awakening (1725-1760) began in New Jersey through the preaching of German Pietist Theodorus Jacobus Frelinghuysen (c. 1691– c. 1747), and took root in New England in 1734 under Jonathan Edwards. It reached its zenith when George Whitfield, the associate of John Wesley, toured the American colonies in 1740.

In Wuerttemberg, Pietism had developed strong roots from its inception in 1650. One historian wrote,

"Pietism is widely regarded as the second Reformation within the Lutheran State Church and its influence shaped the beliefs and character of the Swabian (Wuerttemberg) population more than the original Reformation did."[4]

The spiritual heritage of the Stoll family was deeply rooted in German Pietism. While they had disquiet about the coldness and ritualism of the Lutheran State Church, they nevertheless retained their membership and continued to attend Sunday Worship at the St Martin's Church in Dornstetten. At the same time they faithfully attended the Pietist meetings on Sunday afternoons.

During the 19th century ("The Age of Revolution", 1780-1910), neither society nor the church could any longer ignore the sweeping new problems caused by the industrial revolution. There was a dramatic increase in the number of oppressed wage-earners cramped into new industrial centres. The major secular responses to these problems were Socialism and Marxism. Karl Marx (1818-1883), in particular, was hostile to the churches, branding religion as "the opiate of the people".

Other factors emerged that conspired against the long held and treasured beliefs of Christianity. Darwin's landmark works, *The Origin of Species* (1859) and *The Descent of Man* (1871) seemed to draw science and religion further apart and fuelled the rise of theological liberalism. The Bible, historically the sole source for faith and practice, was no longer considered trustworthy. Its critics claimed it embraced errors and contradictions.

"Liberalism reinterpreted Christianity in light of science, philosophy, and contemporary culture. It stripped the historical Christian faith of its supernatural elements, including miracles and the divinity of Christ, espoused the fatherhood of God and the brotherhood of man, and focused on social reform and political action."[5]

In stark contrast to this undermining influence, which attempted to weaken and destroy Christianity, the great Christian awakenings went on around the world. In America the second Great Awakening (1795-1835) spread across the country under the preaching of Charles Finney (1792-1875), the "Father of American Revivalism".

The 19th century also became the great century of Protestant missions. It started with William Carey (1761-1834) and saw the formation of mission societies that included the China Inland Mission founded by Hudson Taylor (1832-1905), and other organisations such as the Moody Bible Institute in Chicago (1886).

These movements in turn influenced the great social reforms, particularly in England. Wilberforce took a stand against slavery (1787); Britain abolished slavery (1807, 1833). George Mueller started faith orphanages in Bristol (1835). Mueller was a graduate of the University of Halle and based his orphanages in England on the principles and practices developed by the Pietist, A H Franke, in his orphanages in Germany.

William Booth founded the Salvation Army (1865). In the late 19th century D L Moody and others drew large crowds to their evangelistic meetings in London during 1873-74 and 1881-84.[6]

Those awakenings in England and America also had their influence in Germany particularly in the Pietism movement, which was now operating under the name of *Reichsbruederbunde* or *Bruedergemeinschaft* (Fellowship of Christian Brethren). Our parents' favourite German sacred song book, the *Reich's Lieder*, was published by that organisation. It has all the most loved hymns and choruses that came out of those revivals, as were made popular by Alexander and Sankey.

The spiritual awakenings in England influenced many parts of the world and have a significant connection with Australia. William Wilberforce secured an evangelical chaplain, the Reverend Richard Johnson, to accompany the first fleet of convicts bound for Australia in 1788. Johnson was the only clergyman on that voyage thus making modern Australia's earliest Christian heritage Evangelical.

The Cultural Heritage

The cultural identity of the Stoll family is unmistakably and unapologetically *Schwaebish* (Swabian). Dornstetten is part of the South-West region of Germany, affectionately known as the beloved "Schwabenland" (Swabia). To this very day its people are called *Schwaben* (Swabians). Whenever members of the Stoll family from my generation get together, it's not long before they lapse enthusiastically into their mother tongue and exhibit their unmistakable Swabian origins.

The following paragraphs of this chapter are an attempt to describe the 'typical Swabian'. The contents are based on the book by Bob Larson, *"Your Swabian Neighbors"* (Schwaben International Verlag, 1981). In 1971 during his third tour of Germany, American Bob Larsen married a Swabian. He had spent almost a decade and a half observing Swabians: their language, customs, history and architecture.

So who are the typical Swabians and what are they like? An old German proverb defines the Swabian;

"As a person who speaks Swabian. That sounds like a magnificent grasp of the obvious until you discover how different the Swabian language is when compared to the standard so called 'High' German."[1]

Whenever and wherever a Swabian opens his mouth he immediately betrays his origin. In moments of tenderness that happens rarely. In moments of anger, it happens often. Asked to make a declaration of love, the Swabian will stammer a few non-committal syllables. Provoked, he will give full vent to his ire with a richness of invectives that would make anyone blush.[2]

Schaffa, butza, schbara (work, clean, save) is the motto of the typical Swabian. There is an old joke that the Swabians were kicked out of Scotland for being too thrifty. Swabians are shrewd, thrifty, inventive and conservative. Swabians have a love for hard work and the acquisition of property. *Schaffe, schbara, Haeusle baua* (work, save, build a house) are the words of a popular song about the Swabian. The shrewd and thrifty house builder (at his best during the post-second world war reconstruction period) will round up as much as he can of the best available talent, plus the skilled and unskilled members of his family, to build his "*Haeusle*" (house). He will build during his vacation, after office hours and on weekends, but never on Sunday or religious holidays. Although he spends a lifetime working and saving for property and houses, even the Swabian knows that he cannot take it with him when he goes to meet his maker. So why does he knock himself out and deprive himself of so many luxuries and pleasures? He claims he is doing it for his children but threatens to cut them out of his will every time they do something out of line.[3]

The Swabian has an obsession with cleanliness. Not only must every part of every room in the house be regularly and meticulously cleaned and polished, but the outside of the house must equally be maintained in sparkling order. As a young teenager it was my job to sweep the footpath and street gutter spotlessly clean every Saturday. All the house owners in the village did the same.

The Swabian has a mind of his own and can often be stubborn about it. He is also well known for his firmness of will, which is a nicer way of expressing stubbornness. But he is equally known for his dogged persistence, his steadfast "stick-to-it-ness" *(Beharrlichkeit)*, especially in saving money to build a *Haeusle*.[4]

The Swabian is noted for his explosive temper and rash anger (*Jaehzorn*), but he is quick to forgive and does not bear a grudge. He has been called, *knitz und derb, aber immer voll menschlicher Waerme*. Loosely translated that means, "cunning, sly and coarse, but always full of human warmth".[4]

The Swabians are known for their particular brand of humour. Swabian humour is dialect humour. It makes it twice as funny, but it makes no sense if you try to translate it. It often displays that trait of enjoying the other guy's misfortune but, unlike the Prussian, the Swabian is able to laugh at himself not just at others. The Swabian humour reflects pride in, and calls attention to, typically Swabian attributes: thrift, hard work, love of domesticity, saying very little (when the occasion might warrant more being said) yet thoroughly enjoying gossip and coarse language.[5]

The Swabians love good food and drink and the dinner table is always filled with deliciously prepared Swabian food. One of the oldest and most famous Swabian specialties is *Spaetzle,* known as 'Swabian noodles', but the word actually means 'little sparrow'.[6] There are lots of jokes and anecdotes about the Swabian's love of wine and his inclination to over consume. The high quality of the Swabian wines is the product of a wine growing industry in Wuerttemberg which goes back hundreds of years.

Wuerttemberg is poor in natural resources but has produced an abundance of skilled craftsmen, perhaps because of it. The Swabian craftsman must take these expensive, imported raw materials – iron, coal, oil – and quadruple their value with his indefatigable industriousness if he expects to make a profit. *Schwaebischer Fleiss* (Swabian Diligence), is a slogan proudly displayed at Trade Fairs. The pride behind all this stems from the pride of a job well done; a pride handed down from generations of solid perfectionist workmen. The true Swabian admires quality in the work of others and sets a great deal of stock in his own. He has no use for junk. Precision instrument making and the building of machinery of all kinds are old Swabian specialties.[7]

Swabians are multi-faceted, often difficult to understand and to see through. On the one hand, Swabians are the little people who, in the last quarter of the 19th century, built up an industry that has become the best and most dependable in Germany, supported solely by the derring-do of the entrepreneur and the high quality of his employees. On the other hand, this Swabian can also lapse into deep introspection - a quite different side which has produced famous men of letters including Friedrich Schiller, Friedrich Hoelderlin, Eduard Moerike, and Herman Hesse.[8]

Throughout its history, Wuerttemberg has produced its fair share of noted Statesmen, Politicians, Scientists, Generals, Poets and Inventors. Here is a sample of just a few:

Generals:	Field Marshall Erwin Rommel (1891 – 1944)
Inventors:	Gottlieb Daimler (1834-1900) founded the Daimler Motor Company in Stuttgart, 1890. Daimler Benz, famous for its cars, trucks and buses. Mercedes Benz, manufacturing plant in Stuttgart. Cuckoo Clocks and Teddy Bears manufacture.
Scientists:	Johannes Keppler (1571 – 1630), First Law of Planetary Motion. Albert Einstein (1879 – 1955), Theoretical Physist, Father of Modern Science.
Poets:	Friedrich Schiller (1759 – 1805) Friedrich Hoelderlin (1770 – 1843).
Statesman:	Theodor Heuss (1884 – 1963), First President of the Federal Republic of Germany in 1949.

This background of the political, economic, spiritual and cultural environment in Wuerttemberg, Germany, sets the scene for telling the story of my heritage in more detail, commencing with my great great grandfather, Johannes Stoll (1794 -1852).

Dornstetten

Our ancestral hometown of Dornstetten is located right on the edge of the Black Forest Region in Germany, approximately 70 kilometres south west of Stuttgart, the capital of present day Baden-Wuerttemberg. This range of mountains was named as the 'Black Forest' as early as the 8th century, because of the dark colour of its pine trees.

It is a charming landscape of diverse character and beauty richly endowed with deep, seemingly endless woods; mountain heights into which enchanting and sometimes chasm-like valleys are carved through which streams and rivers meander; and beautiful little towns where friendly villagers greet visitors. The Black Forest is, in every season, one of the most popular areas in Germany for holiday makers. Not only is the magnificent countryside rich in flora and fauna and full of contrasts but there are also many impressive historical buildings, valuable art treasures and numerous premier health spas, some dating back to the Roman occupation.

Dornstetten itself has a well-documented history. It is a place of ancient cultures, successfully occupied by Celts, Romans and Germanic tribes.

The old town is perched on a hill 730 metres above sea level. One can still see remnants of the old fortified walls and other heritage treasures from the time when the numerous nobles, earls and barons ruled the land. It is a picturesque town proudly displaying its cultural heritage with a medieval market place, classic timber framed houses, a beautiful fountain and St Martin's church, which dates from the year 1499.

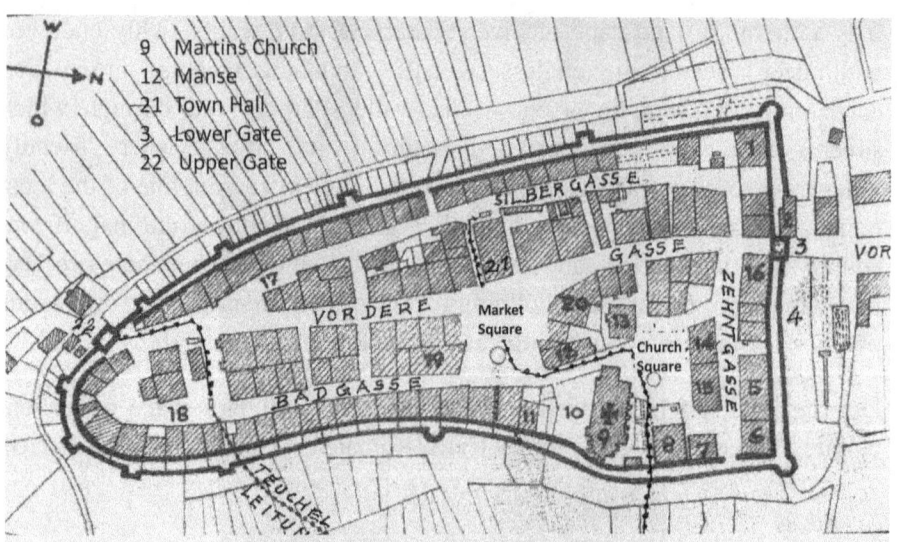

Plan of the Old Town of Dornstetten

In common with many medieval towns, Dornstetten had its share of destructive town fires. In 1415 and 1676 fire reduced the old town to dust and ashes.

When great great grandfather Johannes Stoll was alive (1794-1852) Dornstetten had a population of around 1000 people. It did not escape the economic hardship that ravaged the whole of Wuerttemberg at that time. Extreme hunger, poverty and deprivation characterised those years, as did the decidedly anti-Christian culture. Many looked for opportunities of a better life in faraway places and there was a mass exodus of its population.

The first exodus occurred in 1816/17 when seventy eight people of the Pietistic persuasion (including a Dorothea Stoll), sold all they had and left for the south of Russia. Then, between 1849 and 1855, a further ninety six migrated to Russia; a hundred and ninety eight to America (including a Christian Stoll in 1860 and Eva Maria Stoll in 1885) and later (between 1868 and 1900) eighteen moved to Palestine. These are staggering numbers (390 people over 70 years), considering that the total population of Dornstetten was only around 1000 people[1].

Johannes and his wife Katharina (nee Guehring, daughter of the local butcher) were married in St Martin's church in Dornstetten on the 4th of February, 1821. Johannes was a master weaver (one of nine in the town in 1838) and the family home was situated in the "Badgasse" in the old fortified town. They had five children: three girls and two boys. The first born was a son, Johannes (1822-1877) and because he took his father's Christian name he was called "young Johannes". Eleven years later Christian (1833-1893) was born. Both sons were to have their names recorded in the history of Dornstetten.

The Stolls were devout Christians. Their faith was firmly based on the teachings of the Bible. They sought to live upright and honest lives in their homes, work, church and community. They believed in a personal experience of salvation and were committed to sharing their faith at home and abroad. Their beliefs and values were deeply rooted in Pietism. In addition to going to church they met on Sunday afternoons in what was called *Die Stunde* (the Meeting Hour): a one hour get-together where they would study, share the word of God and pray. It would conclude with coffee and cake, much like a home study group popular in many churches today. The history of the Stoll family is punctuated with many wonderful examples of faith, prayer and dogged determination.

On the 11th of September 1869 a disastrous fire ravaged Dornstetten. It burned twelve houses to the ground and left twenty four families homeless. As the fire moved along the lower "Badgasse" and threatened to engulf the significant buildings in the town square and St Martin's Church, the district fire chief ordered that the house of Christian Stoll be burned down to create a fire break. But Christian retorted firmly, *"My house will not burn down!"* With that he entered his house, fell on his knees and began to pray for God to do a miracle. A little later the fire fighters advanced on Christian's house again to carry out the order of their chief. Christian Stoll stood his ground and refused entrance to the fire fighters.

"Under no circumstances will I tolerate any move to destroy my house, because I know that my house will not burn down."

He went back into the house and continued in prayer. A miracle did take place. The fire was extinguished, at the adjoining house. [2] The record of the history of Dornstetten reads, *"The people of Dornstetten and all those who heard the news of this story from the Black Forest, were amazed at the faith of Christian Stoll – a mighty faith able to extinguish the ravishing flames of a town fire."* [3]

The Stoll family, like many of the Pietists, belonged to a group of Christian believers known as the 'Friends of Jerusalem'. Later they changed the name to the Temple Society. In 1861 the Stoll family joined this Christian community. Johannes, Christian's brother, was a founding elder of the Templers in Dornstetten.

Market Square 1850

Bad Gasse in the 1960s

The Templers

The Temple Society (not connected to the medieval military order of the Knights Templar) owes its origin to the Protestant theologian Christoph Hoffmann, who was born in Leonberg, Wuerttemberg, in 1815. He spent his early years in Korntal in the Community of Brethren founded by his father, the onetime mayor of Ludwigsburg. Here he received lasting impressions of a community organised on strictly Christian principles. He was especially influenced by his father, who had distanced himself from the official church and was dedicated to Christianity in action. Christoph Hoffmann received his theological degree from the renowned University of Tubingen, in Wuerttemberg.[1]

From the early 19th century, living conditions in Wuerttemberg had degenerated to appallingly poor standards. The privation and misery suffered by the majority of the population deeply affected and depressed Hoffmann. While many of the population saw their only hope of a better life in migrating to America and Russia, Hoffmann decided that the situation *"had to be remedied by all means"*[2] at home. He devoted his early life to bringing about reform in both the political arena and the established Church.

Because he was concerned at the growth of an anti-Christian spirit he, with his brothers-in-law, Philipp and Immanuel Paulus, decided to expose this secular spirit in public through the publication of the *Sueddeutsche Warte* (South German Sentinel) in 1845. He wanted to re-establish a Christian State free from modern rationalistic influences and to create a community of believers firmly based on the *"Law, the Gospels and the Prophets."*

After the outbreak of the 1848 Revolution, Hoffmann hoped to gain recognition of his goals in the political arena. He was successful in being elected to the first National Assembly in Frankfurt as a delegate of Wuerttemberg following an intense political campaign against the noted atheist, David Friedrich Strauss. As a Bible believer Hoffmann felt very lonely in the midst of the other delegates and said he was shocked by the *"falling away"* which he witnessed.

Despite his best efforts Hoffmann became disillusioned and after ten months of little fruitful activity as a delegate he completely withdrew from political life. He saw that all the pre-requisites for establishing a Christian society (State), as he envisaged it, were lacking. Further, it became clear to him that the dependence of the Lutheran Church on the State (in Germany the clergy were funded by the State) robbed the Church of dignity and had a highly destructive influence on the message it had to proclaim.[3] A separation of Church and State seemed to him essential at this time.

The following is an extract from an article *Footprints of the Templers,* published by the Temple Society, which states the view of the Templers as seen by its current membership, of the origins and teachings of Hoffmann and his followers,

"The Christian community of the Templers had its roots in mid-nineteenth century Protestant Pietism. Its special concern is to return to the core message of Jesus, to his promise of the kingdom of God and his directive to contribute to the making of a better world through personal action to bring about this kingdom of love and kindness.

In view of the grave social ills of the times and guided by this basic attitude, Hoffmann and his followers saw the renewal of society in line with Jesus' teachings as the foremost challenge facing the Christian community. They perceived such renewal to be achievable through a more profound Christianity, where individuals strive to align their lives and the choices they make with the words of Jesus in the New Testament, and where creeds, dogmas and rituals are of secondary importance in line with the Society's motto: Set your mind on God's kingdom and his justice before everything else (Matth 6:33).

This was to be realised – after the model of the early Christian Church – through the establishment of communities of like-minded people which then, by their example, were to gradually pervade and transform society. In these communities, where tolerance and love of neighbour was practised, individuals would see themselves as living components of a spiritual temple of God, as demanded in the New Testament (1 Cor 3:16)– hence the name Templers.[8]

Consequently Hoffmann made the decision to gather God's people together in a Christian community, exemplary in faith and conduct of life.

Together with many other representatives of Wuerttemberg Pietism, Hoffmann believed that the second coming of Christ to set up his 1000 Year Kingdom on earth was imminent. Because he did not doubt that this would occur in Jerusalem as prophesied in scripture, he called for the bringing together of God's people to be at that holy place.[4] He wanted to prepare the people and the land for the day foretold in scripture when Jerusalem will become the centre of worldwide worship of the one true God.

He found strong support and a like-minded leader in the businessman, Georg David Hardegg, from Ludwigsburg. As early as 1854 they began to register candidates for the departure to Palestine. Many of the Swabian Friends of Jerusalem had already left for southern Russia. Their ultimate destination however was Palestine.

From the early years of the 19th century, within Pietistic circles, there was growing discontent with the State Lutheran Church to which these groups had always belonged. This and Hoffmann's declaration to gather God's people in Jerusalem put Hoffmann at odds with the Church. Soon the conflict between the Templers and the Church intensified and their differences became irreconcilable. The final break with the State Lutheran Church came in 1859.

Earlier, in 1855, Christoph Hoffmann, Christoph Paulus and Georg Hardegg had travelled to Paris to attend the Evangelical Alliance conference to which

Evangelical Christians from all over the world had been invited. The presentation of their ideas to recruit 'people of God' from countries around the world and plans to establish a Christian settlement in the Holy Land found little, if any, support from the conference delegates.[5]

Over time Christoph Hoffmann also began to distance himself from the Pietism movement, particularly when some of their respected leaders, such as the well-known minister Christoph Blumhardt, voiced concerns that Hoffmann's ideas were erroneous and were based on incorrect interpretations of the Bible.

In the meantime, as there was no real prospect of an imminent emigration to Jerusalem due to a lack of political support both from within Germany and the Turkish rule in Palestine, they decided to establish a consolidated model community at Kirschenhardthof near Ludwigsburg. Here they endeavoured to put their beliefs and principles into practice. They also established a school for evangelists, where men like Johannes Seitz and Martin Blaich, the later founders of the Carmel Mission, were trained.

On the 19th June 1861, at a meeting in Kirschenhardthof, the founding manifesto of the Temple Society was signed by sixty four men. It states:

"In view of the general disorientation of mankind caused by the fact that none of the existing churches aspires to making man into a temple of God and to establish the sanctum at Jerusalem for all nations, we, the undersigned, dissociate ourselves from Babylon, that is to say from the existing Churches and Sects, and unite to establish the German Temple, to carry out the Law, the Gospel and the Prophecy." [6]

Some 3000 people, largely from Wuerttemberg but also from other German States including Sachsen (Saxony), joined the community. There were also adherents in Switzerland, North America and Russia.[4] On the other hand, some who had joined the Templers decided to return to the Church, particularly after Hoffmann's confrontation with leaders of the Pietistic Movement.

Today, 150 years later, one can only applaud the stand the Templers took in their time. They denounced the anti-Christian culture of the government and society and the lack of spiritual effectiveness of the State Church. However, their best efforts did not succeeded in rectifying the perceived ailments in the secular and religious world in Germany.

Hoffmann's solution was to make a new beginning. He was passionate about the goal to gather the people of God from around the world in Jerusalem. He was determined to establish a community like that of the first Christians, in readiness for when the Messiah would come to establish his earthly kingdom. He was resolute to make it happen despite opposition and obstacles.

Was Hoffmann's vision too utopian? Were the leaders too ambitious? Were these high ideals inspired by scripture? Or were they influenced by the philosophies of the Enlightenment that were championed by the intellectuals of those days?

On my visit to Haifa in 2008 I was surprised at the level of recognition the Nation of Israel has given to the German Templers. Up and down Ben Gurion Boulevard in Haifa today are displays recording in Hebrew, English, German and Arabic what the Templers believed and why they came to this land.

"Christoph Hoffmann called believers (in Germany) to correct their way of life by returning to the basic values of Christianity. He called for the creation of a new nation, the "People of God" (Das Volk Gottes) that would establish a new, rectified social order that would be deserving of Messianic redemption and would enjoy Messianic rule. It would be incumbent upon the People of God to gather together in the land of God, i.e. the land of Israel, for only there would the Messiah appear. Members of the community would prepare the land for the Messiah's coming and would instruct its inhabitants in the values of Christianity, using self-fulfilment and personal example as their tools. A few thousand supporters adopted Hoffmann's ideas and, little by little, the "Friends of Jerusalem" began to hold meetings. During the 1850s and 60s Hoffmann and his supporters gradually drifted away from the organised Church and established a new religious movement, "The Temple Society", based on the idea of the centrality of the spiritual temple

("Tempel" in German), that would be realised in the Land of God. Hence, the name Templers".[7]

Section II.

THE HOLY LAND CALLS
(1868-1948)

Haifa 1869

The Pioneering of the German Colony in Haifa

In 1868, members of the Temple Society began to follow the call of their leaders, Dr Christoph Hoffmann and Georg David Hardegg, to immigrate to the Holy Land. Haifa was the first Templer settlement on Palestinian soil. Through the mediation of an Arab merchant, the Templers were able to purchase significant parcels of land west of the old town between the foot of Mount Carmel and the Mediterranean Sea.

Haifa in 1869 was a place of about 4000 inhabitants, largely comprised of Muslims but also Jews and Christians. It was not by chance that the Templers selected Haifa. This small town was developing at a rapid pace. It was just then beginning to expand beyond the walls that had encircled it ever since its foundation in 1761 by the Galilee ruler Dahar-El Omar. Haifa's harbor suited the needs of the modern ships that had begun to call at the country's shores.

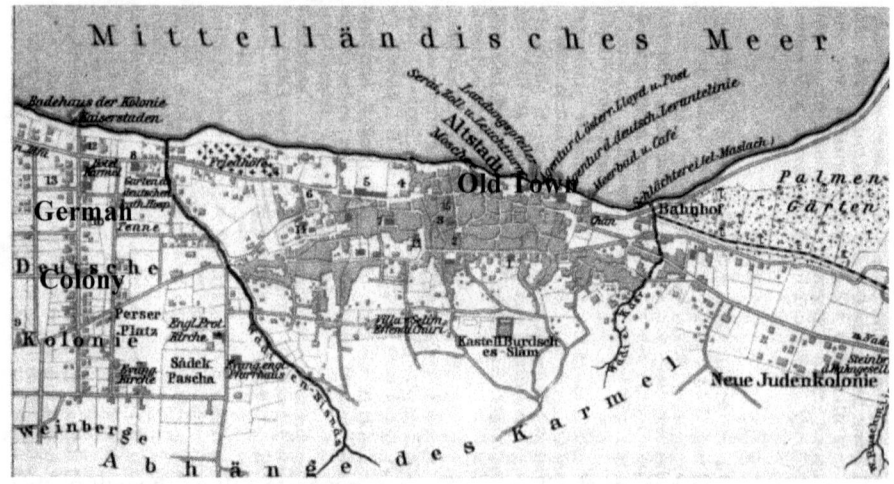

The German Colony in relation to the old town of Haifa

What was the country of Palestine like in the second half of the 19th century? While Jewish communities had existed in the land since Biblical times, the great majority of inhabitants were Arabs. Until 1917, Palestine was part of the Ottoman Empire and had been under the Turkish feudal system for 400 years. Most of the Arab population were Bedouin (nomadic desert dwellers) or Fellahin (peasant migrant labourers) existing under harsh and primitive conditions. Bedouin robber bands terrorized the country. Government corruption permitted tax-farmers to collect monies on behalf of equally corrupt landlords (effendis) to extort poor Arab farmers. Added to these dreadful conditions were frequent droughts that kept the land in a barren state. Famines were frequent.

Lewis French, British Director of Development, in 1913 described the conditions of pre-mandate Palestine as follows:

"We found it (Palestine) inhabited by fellahin who lived in mud hovels and suffered severely from malaria.... Large areas...were cultivated.... The fellahin, if not themselves cattle thieves, were always ready to harbor these and other criminals. The individual plots (of land) changed hands annually.

There was little public security and the fellahin lot was an alternation of pillage and blackmail by their neighbours, the bedouin."[1]

Hardegg, Hoffmann and others had made earlier visits to Palestine and had a good grasp on the conditions that awaited them. In spite of their strong idealism, the founders of the Temple Society were not religious dreamers who in their blind zeal brought ruin on those who entrusted themselves to their spiritual guidance. They established clear criteria for any would-be immigrants and insisted that *"the greater settlement project would succeed only if progress was made step by step, at the rate at which God made it possible."*[2]

There is a German saying, often applied to the first three generations of the pioneering migrant: *Dem Ersten Tod, dem Zweiten Not, dem Dritten Brot* (to the first death, the second dread and the third bread). The settlement's beginnings certainly made enormous demands on the health and working capacity of the first generation of settlers and many did die. Of a group of twenty German settlers, including the Deininger and Appinger families, who settled near Nazareth in the Jezreel valley in 1867, one year prior to the official Templer immigration, fifteen died.[3]

As central Europeans they were not accustomed to the strong sun and some died of heatstroke for lack of appropriate protection. Others succumbed to tropical illnesses foreign to their native homeland: amoebic dysentery, malaria and typhoid. Snakes and scorpions became new hazards and the lack of access to medical help in the early years of settlement helped to contribute to the fragile state of human survival.

In agriculture, too, they had to learn from cruel experience. After planting many vineyards on the slopes of Mount Carmel, vine diseases struck and harvests were small or ruined. In the absence of fences and gates, Arab farmers were able to drive their donkeys and goats into the German fields and vineyards causing harsh loss and damage to crops. Daily bread was in short supply. In time, however, Swabian diligence and innovation brought rewards.

They stuck together and helped each other in all aspects of daily life. They joined forces to build their houses and farm sheds. They consoled each other when death knocked on the door, and they found strength in the truths of God's Word. However, as vignerons and farmers, the settlers in Haifa did not make any lasting progress. So they gradually turned to different types of enterprises. It was in the skilled trades, building trades, hotel and catering trades and in the area of transportation, that the Templers created for themselves alternative and ultimately lucrative sources of income.

By 1873, just four years after the first colonists arrived in Haifa, 250 inhabitants lived in thirty-eight new houses along newly constructed streets and boulevards. These were all laid out in accordance with the town plan designed by Jakob Schumacher, a Templer immigrant from the United States. The town plan was years ahead of its time in the spaciousness of its layout, town zoning and other European landscaping principles. Where else in Palestine at that time could you find a perfectly straight street thirty metres wide?

In planning the development of the German Colony, the Templers first took into consideration the land, its topography, the climate and the distance from town. The plot that was chosen spread from what was then the seashore up into the foothills of Mount Carmel.

Lithograph of the town plan of the German Colony in Haifa 1875

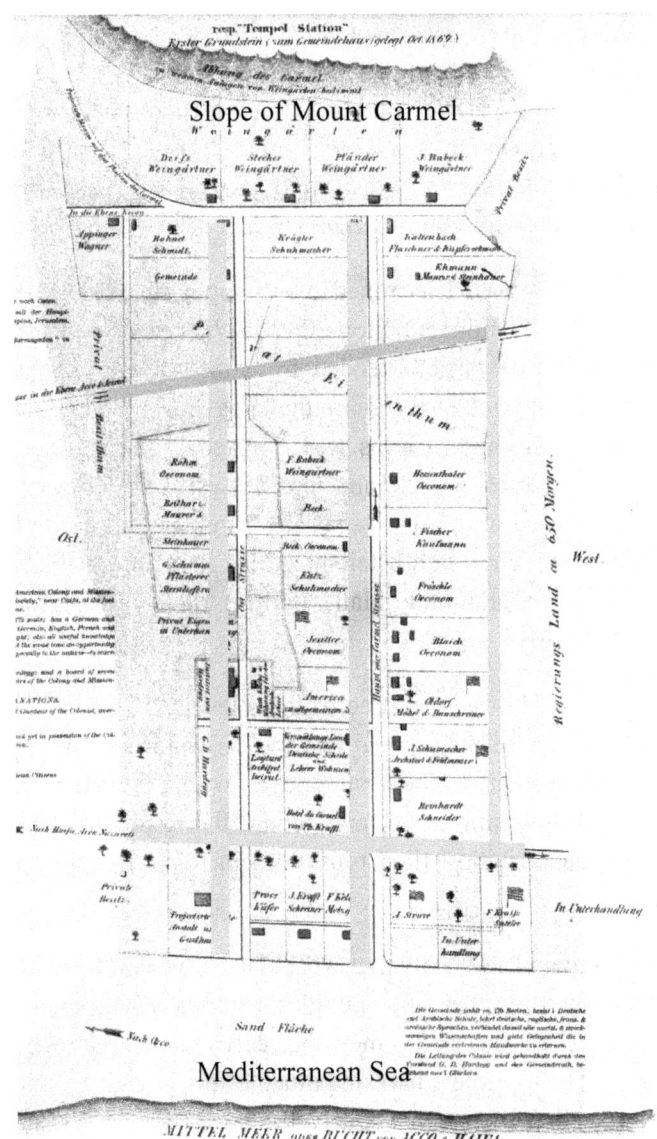

The German Colony Town Plan

Its main thoroughfare, *Die Kolonien Strasse*, (today's *Ben Gurion Boulevard*), ran the length of the Colony. About thirty metres in width, it was joined by two smaller parallel streets: *Garten Strasse* and *Hospital Strasse*, known today as *Haganim* and *Golda Me'ir Streets*. These streets were connected via two latitudinal axes: *Jaffa (Yafo) Road* and the *Carmelite Monastery Road*, known today as *Allenby Road*.

The use of the land was determined by its topography. The vine growers lived at the top of the mountain slope; hence, *Hagefen Street*, which means Vine Street. Their vineyards extended from their homes up to *Panorama Street – Yefe Nof Street* today – in the area now occupied by a Bahai complex. The farmers and artisans were located in the centre opposite the fields. Hotels, factories, shops and businesses were constructed at the junction of Yafo Road close to the sea. The Templers did not build churches in their settlements. They held their meetings in a central building, called *Gemeindehaus,* (the Community Hall), built in 1869. Initially it also served as the School House.

The typical Templer house consisted of three levels. There was a cellar, half of which was sunk into the ground to serve as water storage, food cooling and meat preservation area. The ground level, with a few steps leading up to the kitchen, held the dining room and central living room. The upper level, sometimes combined with a tiled roof, contained the sleeping quarters and guest rooms.

At first the Templers built roofs that were flat but when these started to leak they quickly bought timber and shingles to construct sloping roofs. The construction material was soft limestone, easily chiselled and quarried on Mount Carmel. The Templers invested much effort in giving their homes and streets a modern, spacious feel. Their well-tended gardens had trees for fruit and decoration. They built high fences both of stone and of wood, and trees were planted in such a way as to shade the sidewalks[3]. In their courtyards they dug cisterns for water storage.

Kolonien Strasse with shade trees, fences and side walks

The German settlers soon achieved recognition and a measure of prosperity. The Swabian farmers and tradesmen contributed substantially to the opening up and development of the country, which in 1870 had been very backward and economically neglected. Between 1869 and 1907 the Templers founded seven different settlements in various parts of the land: Haifa in 1869; Jaffa in 1870; Sarona in 1871; Rephaim (Jerusalem) in 1873; Wilhelma in 1902; Bethlehem in the Galilee in 1906; and Waldheim in 1907.

Even though at its zenith the community never numbered more than 1700 adherents, the Templers played an instrumental role in the modernisation of agriculture wherever they settled (Neuhardthof, Sarona, Wilhelma, Bethlehem and Waldheim), including the introduction of new methods of soil management such as fertilization of crops. They operated the first mechanical workshops and factories for the production of soap from olive oil. They were Haifa's first practicing professionals: doctors, engineers, surveyors, builders, merchants, archaeologists, importers and exporters.[4]

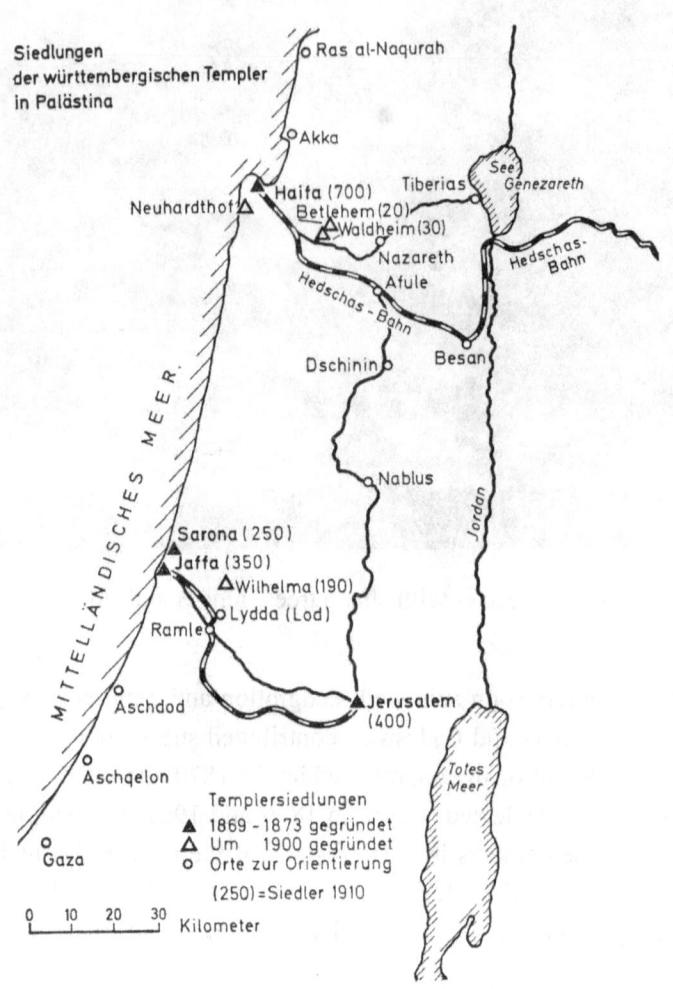

German Settlements in Palestine

They reclaimed malaria infested swamps in the Jezreel Valley and at Sarona (now part of Tel Aviv) and turned them into productive agricultural land by planting eucalyptus trees. They also built roads and bridges and had a strategic involvement in the development of public transport (railways and public transport generally), hotels and the tourist industry[5]. At that time, the political powers of Europe and America had consular representatives in Palestine, in the main staffed by men from the German Colonies. Jakob and Gottlieb Schumacher, and Fritz Keller, were consular representatives of the United States of America and Germany, respectively.

Johannes Stoll, my great great uncle, was the first member of the Stoll family to go to the Holy Land. As a fifty year old widower he migrated from Dornstetten in 1872, accompanied by daughters Katherine and Christiane. His first destination was Jerusalem where he became a founding elder in the newly established Templer Community at Rephaim, not very far from the walls of the Old City of Jerusalem.

The *Dornstetter Heimatsbuch*[6] (History of Dornstetten) records that Johann Stoll, my great uncle (nephew to Johannes and my grandfather Jakob's brother), also migrated to Palestine in 1872 as a thirteen year old. No more is known of him, or of his movements in Palestine. I do, however, remember my mother expressing her concern how a minor was allowed to travel to an uncertain future in Palestine without his parents. The dates cause me to presume that Johann may have been in the party that came to Palestine in 1872 with his uncle Johannes Stoll.

Shaking Foundations

The beginning of the German Colony in Haifa had been tough and challenging. Their success in creating a flourishing settlement in a foreign and impoverished land is in no small measure a testimony to the inherent qualities of the Swabian character: industrious, persevering, innovative, resourceful and sprinkled with a good dose of Swabian humour.

But the driving force behind it all was their unshakable faith in God. They were convinced that God had called them to the Holy Land to establish a Spiritual Temple: a community whose greatest aim was to please God and honour Him in their daily lives, and in their relationships with one another and the people among whom they had come to live. They lived their lives in the expectation that the Messiah could return at any time (1 John 3:2,3).

This was not a Christian community by name only. Every aspect of their lives gave expression of their belief. When the foundation stone of a new house was laid, the whole Templer community assembled and prayed for God's blessing and protection on the new home and its occupants. In the head stone over the front doorway they chiselled a Bible verse that had personal relevance and significance to them. They made Christ the head of their homes.

On Sundays they downed their tools of trade and walked to the *Gemeindehaus* (Community Hall) by families, to attend the worship service. Sunday was set apart as a day of rest and worship. They shared their resources. Each member of the community put money into a common fund to distribute in times of loss and hardship. For example, when a family lost a cow or other livestock, the community helped them buy a new one. They loved one another and gave to anyone who had need (John 13:34, Acts 2:44,45). They got together as a community for picnics and outings to celebrate Christmas, Easter, Harvest Thanksgiving and other public holidays. They were a thankful and joyful people (Nehemiah 8:10).

Hoffmann

Hardegg

But then, within four years of their arrival, the sacred foundation of the Temple movement was to be shaken at its very core. Serious differences of opinion in spiritual matters led to an unresolvable rift between Hoffmann and Hardegg. This, together with a clash of personalities, influenced Hoffmann to leave Haifa in 1870 and move to Jaffa where the opportunity arose to acquire a new settlement abandoned by an American missionary society. The leadership powers of the Temple Society were then allocated to Hardegg to oversee Haifa; Hoffmann managed the settlements of Jaffa, Sarona and Ephraim; while Christoph Paulus was responsible for Germany.[1]

Differences between Hoffmann and Hardegg had already surfaced back in Germany over questions of theology and practice of the Spiritual Temple. Hardegg insisted that scope must be offered to the exercising of spiritual gifts mentioned in the early Christian Church, in particular the gift of healing, which many of the preachers from the Pietist movement practiced at that time. Hardegg's credibility however became somewhat tarnished when an exercise of healing and deliverance proved to be unsuccessful.

In the early 1870s, sections of the original settlers in Haifa developed a growing conviction that the Temple Society was drifting away from some of the fundamental doctrines and practices of the traditional Christian faith. Hoffmann, who in his younger years opposed the teaching of Rationalism, began to embrace liberal philosophies. He expressed doubt about the teachings of the Trinity and the Divinity of Christ, and then dispensed with the practice of infant baptism and Holy Communion.

When Hoffmann questioned the validity of the redemptive work of Christ[2], Hardegg realized that their theological positions were irreconcilable. In 1874 he decided to separate himself from Hoffmann, Paulus and the Temple Society. This resulted in a deep split with about a third of the German community in Haifa supporting Hardegg's position. Those who split from the Temple Society returned their spiritual allegiance to the Lutheran Church. They became known as *Kirchlers*: church goers. The Templers continued to meet for worship in the Community Hall, while the Kirchlers initially met in various homes.

In 1898, the *Jerusalemsverein* (Jerusalem Society), a branch of the Lutheran Church in Berlin, adopted the Kirchler group and sent pastors to Haifa, Jerusalem and Jaffa. They contributed to the building of their churches and manses in Palestine. So deep was the separation in the early years after the split that the Templer and Kirchler each had separate schools for their children, both with teachers from Germany. However, the schools were later amalgamated and all school age children met collectively in the Templer school with only the religious instruction being given separately.

The decision by Hardegg was a painful blow to the community and posed a possible threat to the harmonious co-existence of the German settlers, who were now divided over theological beliefs, not only in Haifa, but right across all the settlements in Palestine. The Templer historians later wrote that this split

"did not destroy its (the Templers) spiritual basis any more than did the internal tensions and splits with which the Temple Society had to contend and which it had to overcome later on"[3]

In 1874 Hoffmann declared himself the sole head and President of the Temple Society in Palestine. The Templer trained evangelists, Johannes Seitz and Martin Blaich, decided to resign from the Temple Society in Germany in 1877. Johannes Seitz wrote after his resignation that Christoph Hoffmann became a *"victim of the enlightenment thinking and taught that man was intrinsically good and capable of redeeming himself."*[4] Seitz emphatically opposed any teaching that upheld Christ purely as a good example to be followed while stripping Him of His real title as the sinless Son of God and only Saviour from sin, death and Satan.

Until his death in 1879, Hardegg remained the spiritual head and pastor of the small band of Kirchlers in Haifa. After his death, Johann Deininger took over prime responsibility and Sunday services were held in his home, and those of other members, until 1898. Hoffmann died in 1885.

In the midst of this explosive church tension, my great great uncle Johannes Stoll arrived in Palestine in 1872. He first settled in Jerusalem where he became one of the founding elders with Hoffmann of the Ephraim Colony.

Shortly after his arrival he contracted a life threatening illness. When all hope of recovery was abandoned he placed himself at the mercy and grace of God. With great determination he asked God, *"If it is your will, please give me an extra three years to serve you in the Holy Land"*. God answered his prayer.

Not much is known of Johannes' activities and movements except that he did return to Haifa. He served there as an elder of the Temple Society together with Jakob Schumacher, Johannes Hermann and Friedrich Lange. On the 12th of May 1877, just four days after contracting cholera and exactly 3 years after his prayer for healing was answered, he passed away.

His dying words were:

"Now I am going home; my work is finished here. Oh, what joy! Please tell the congregation that I am entering eternity at peace because of the cleansing power of the blood of Jesus Christ and his righteousness. Please ask the congregation to think seriously about the purpose of life; to hold faithfully to the word of God and so overcome all obstacles and experience God's abiding peace."[5]

The officiating elders of the Temple Society mourned the loss of their dearest brother and co-worker. They declared that Johannes had only one purpose in life: to seek the salvation of his fellow men, and to pray and work day and night for the work of God through the Temple community.[5]

Johannes, like his brother Christian who faced the fire back in Dornstetten, was a shining example of a man with a deep and practical faith in God. He earned the respect of his fellow believers and was entrusted with leadership roles in the Templer congregations in Dornstetten, Jerusalem and Haifa. He dedicated his life to the extension of God's kingdom in Palestine under the umbrella of the Temple Society from the time he joined in 1861 until his death in 1877. He never compromised his belief in the fundamental truth of the Word of God that Jesus Christ is the Son of God and that *"whoever believes in Him shall not perish but have eternal life"* (John 3:16).

In those early years of divided theological convictions, the question of peaceful co-existence must have lingered in the minds of the settlers. Historically, differences in the fundamentals of Christian belief have been the source of huge conflict, division and outright hatred. What would be the outcome in this instance? Would it lead to the demise of the German community in Palestine, now divided into two religious groups?

Give Me this Mountain

Twelve years after the death of Johannes Stoll and twenty years after the founding of the German Colony, the next generation of the Stoll family arrived in Haifa: my grandparents, Jakob Stoll and Anna Maria Mueller.

By the time they arrived the German Colony had grown and expanded geographically as more people came from the homeland, America and Southern Russia. Those years also saw another development in Haifa: the birth of the Carmel Mission.

Haifa cc 1880

So far the settlement had spread across the plains of Haifa and up the lower slopes of Mount Carmel. The top of Mount Carmel however, remained largely barren and uninhabited except for the lone Carmelite Monastery where Catholic monks had resided for hundreds of years. During the early

1880s, European settlement started to spring up across the ridge of Mount Carmel. Friedrich (Fritz) Keller is the man accredited with the pioneering of the first of these residential developments.

Fritz Keller

Fritz Keller was the German Vice Consul of the Templer colony in Haifa from 1878 to 1908. Born in Calw in the Black Forest region of Germany, a butcher by trade, he was trained as an evangelist by the Templers in Kirschenhardthof in 1862. After four years working in Switzerland in both roles he left for Palestine in 1868 in the company of his close school friend Friedrich Pross. After his marriage, he built his house on the foreshore of Haifa from where he operated his butcher's shop. In 1878, he was promoted to the position of Vice Consul.

Fritz Keller was a close associate of Johannes Seitz and Martin Blaich. They came from the same area of the Black Forest. When these men visited Palestine during the 1870s and 80s, they renewed their friendships. All three originally left the State Church in Germany to join the Temple Society; all three were trained by the Temple Society as Evangelists; and all three withdrew their membership when the Templers began to embrace the contemporary theology of rationalism. Now the three men were about to unite their efforts in a venture that was closest to all of their hearts: the evangelisation of the local people. This decision to start the Carmel Mission in Haifa was to become a pivotal influence in the lives of the Stoll family.

Fritz Keller worshiped with the Kirchlers in Haifa. After the split with the Templers, Seitz and Blaich considered migrating to America. But the leaders of the Pietist movement persuaded them to continue their ministries in Germany. They stayed and founded the *Reichsbruederbund*: the National Fellowship of Christian Brethren of Germany[1].

It was Blaich who had first caught a vision to commence a mission to the Middle East, for the purpose of sharing the good news of God's salvation among the local Jews, Arabs and Turks. As an initial step he envisaged the building of a Mission and Church Centre on Mount Carmel. Because of the favourable location and climate on the Carmel heights such a Centre would also be ideal as an *Erhohlungsheim*: a retreat for missionaries serving in the Middle East.

Blaich wanted to model the Centre along similar institutions in Germany, particularly the centre in Bad Boll, where the well known Pietist preacher, Blumhardt, resided. He had shared this proposal amongst the Brethren Fellowships in Germany and asked them all to pray to discern God's will. During his first missionary journey to Palestine in 1881 - 83 he presented his vision to the small fellowship of believers in Palestine and found enthusiastic support.

In 1882, Blaich attended a series of fifteen lectures conducted by George Mueller, the respected founder and director of the Ashley Down Orphanage of Bristol, England. Mueller spent the last seventeen years of his life travelling the world teaching the great truth and principles of living by faith. This was his only visit to Palestine.

Carmel Hotel

The lectures were held in the dining room of the Carmel Hotel in the main street of the German Colony of Haifa. Blaich heard of what God was doing through the work of Mueller: how through prayer and faith food and shelter was provided to hundreds and thousands of destitute orphans in England without any public appeal for funds whatsoever; how hundreds of schools were established to offer Christian education and of the charitable work of distributing Bibles to those who could not afford them. This greatly inspired Blaich and he felt confirmed in pursuing his plans to start a mission in Haifa, based on similar faith principles

Shortly after Blaich's return to Germany, Keller and a few German colonists purchased some 600 acres of land in a very favourable location on Mount Carmel and work commenced on the construction of a roadway. On hearing this, the Carmelite Monastery immediately sprang into action to sabotage the road works. They physically stopped the construction workers and refused any type of access to Mount Carmel for any further development works. The handful of believers decided to make this a matter of prayer and fasting. They asked God to provide both the approval and the finances to proceed with building a Mission Centre on Mount Carmel.

On one occasion, while they were praying on their knees in the home of Consul Fritz Keller, an Arab funeral procession carrying the corpse of a German nobleman, Herr von Bannwarth, arrived at the front door. Fritz Keller offered the distressed widow assistance and arranged for the burial of her husband in the German cemetery. Frau von Bannwarth was overwhelmed with gratitude and on hearing of the settlers' struggle to build and fund a road up to Mount Carmel, she handed over a very significant gift of 31 000 francs for the project[2].

Three years later, after spending 24 000 francs on fruitless negotiations, and after making representations to the Ottoman Empire in Constantinople and the German Reich in Berlin, and despite an unequivocal ruling of independent consultants that the monastery had no right to deny construction of the road, there was still no resolution. The monastery absolutely refused access.

When Johannes Seitz visited Haifa in 1886 and Keller informed him of the impasse, Seitz and Keller decided to meet for prayer two to three times a day in Keller's office. They asked God to remove all obstacles and by faith claimed an early resolution. God answered their prayer. As a last resort the German Chancellor, Count Bismarck, wrote to the Pope in Rome, who, after making his own investigation, had no hesitation in giving his personal order to the Carmelite Monks to allow the work to go ahead. In 1887 the road works (today's *Ha'nassi* and *Tzionut Avenues*) finally proceeded.

Frau von Bannwarth, who had suffered severe depression since her husband's death, returned to Haifa in 1887 to visit his grave. Consul Keller persuaded her to attend the evangelistic meetings of Seitz. At one of those meetings she prayed to receive the Lord Jesus Christ as her Lord and Saviour and she was completely released from her depression. She then came to understand more fully the vision and purpose of the Carmel Mission Centre and became a voluntary supporter. She declared passionately: *"I will finance and help to establish such a mission retreat on Mount Carmel."*[2]

On 1st November 1890, the first three story house of the Carmel Mission was completed and occupied under the leadership of Martin Blaich. Over the door of the Centre they inscribed the words: "The Lord – He is God" (1 Kings 8:39). These were the very words shouted from this same mountaintop many, many years before (875BC) after the prophet Elijah had the victorious showdown with the false prophets of Baal.

The early years of the founding of the Carmel Mission continued to be fraught with many difficulties and obstacles as if *"all the might and power of hell had been let loose to stop the work of this fledgling Mission on Mount Carmel"*[3]. However, the final outcome was bigger and better than anyone could have believed. The Mission was able to acquire a brand new complex on the top of Mount Carmel, originally built as a state of the art hotel by the Pross family. Once again it came into their hands through prayer in amazing circumstances.

Pastor Martin Philipp Schneider from Saxony, Germany, not only accepted the invitation of Blaich to head up the mission but he also brought with him the necessary funds to purchase the Pross hotel building. He arrived with his family from Germany in 1903 and under his God-ordained leadership the work began to flourish.

Pastor Schneider travelled all over Palestine visiting Jewish settlers. His knowledge of Hebrew learned during his theological studies, together with his stated conviction that the land of Palestine belonged to the Jews, opened many doors and hearts for sharing God's message and attracted many Jews to come and stay at the Carmel Mission[3]. Soon the Mission was able to sell the ex-Pross Hotel for a very favourable price and they established their own custom built complex in an even better location on land originally owned by Martin Blaich.

The Carmel Mission Home

The "Mission Home" was regarded as the pride of Mount Carmel. It served a twofold purpose: a guest house and convalescent home for missionaries and Christian leaders; and an outreach centre for Jews, Arabs and Europeans in Palestine. The Carmel Mission ultimately became the centre of a much greater outreach to the Muslim population throughout Palestine and the Middle East.

From 1933 to 1948, Friedrich Heinrici took over the leadership. A number of other Mission centres were opened in Palestine. By 1939-48, some fourteen European and seventeen local missionaries served with the Carmel Mission as Pastors, Evangelists, Teachers (serving 240 pupils) and Medical Support workers. When the State of Israel was established in 1948 the work of the Carmel Mission was relocated to Lebanon.

During our visit to Haifa in 2008, Margaret and I stayed in the thirty-storey Panorama Centre on Central Carmel, only to discover that it was on the very place on which the Carmel Mission Home had once stood. Just around the corner at 142 Ha'nassi Street, the second Mission House, the old Pross Hotel, has been preserved and refurbished. When the State of Israel was established, the Rothschild Foundation bought the building. Today it is known as the 'Hecht House' and is one of the most prominent centres for culture and art not only in Haifa but the whole country of Israel.

Jakob & Maria Stoll

My Grandparents

Jakob Stoll's name cannot be found among the names of those who have been publicly honoured for their contributions to the pioneering development of the settlement of Haifa. But in his life of seventy-five years (fifty in Haifa) he made the most of his humble beginnings and created a remarkable story of baking and battling, of family, faith, fun and friendship. To him Haifa became a little bit of heaven on earth.

Jakob Stoll was the second of four sons born to Christian and Christine Stoll in Dornstetten, Wuerttemberg. He was 24 years old, single and a qualified baker when he arrived in Palestine in 1889. When he found no work as a baker, Fritz Keller, the German Vice Consul in Haifa, offered him employment as a gardener on his properties, both in the township of Haifa and on Mount Carmel.

It was not by chance that these two men met. Back in Germany in the 1860s the Stoll and Keller families lived in the same Black Forest region and belonged to the same close knit Christian community. Fritz Keller came in contact with Jakob's father, Christian, and his uncle Johannes through their involvement in the newly established Temple Society. They renewed their friendship when Johannes came to Palestine in 1872 with Jakob's brother, Johann. The Vice-Consul, and the settlers in Haifa as a whole, were deeply affected by the sudden death of Johannes just 5 years after his arrival. So it is not surprising to find that Fritz Keller took Jakob Stoll under his wing. It proved to be a providential association.

There surely could not be a better introduction to life in a new country than working in and around the house of the Vice Consul. The Keller house, located in the main street of Haifa, with its constant stream of diplomatic officials, important dignitaries and overseas guests, was the hub of diplomatic relationships, economic negotiations and the centre of communication between the new colony and the homeland. Fritz Keller would be the first to know of the achievements and the complaints or grievances of the settlers and of the local population of Jews, Arabs and Christians.

Not only was the Keller House the centre of political intelligence and friendship but, as we have already learned, it became the battle ground for the defence of Biblical Christianity. In this place Keller stood shoulder to shoulder with Hardegg, Seitz and Blaich to stem the flow of theological rationalism that had crept into the teaching and beliefs of the leaders of the Temple Society. This was also the place where the spiritual battle for the establishment of the Carmel Mission was fought and won.

The insights and opportunities Jakob received while in Keller's employment gave him the best possible start in the fledgling colony that any young man could wish for. But, most of all, it was here in the Keller house that Jakob was re-introduced to the young lady who was to become his wife.

Jakob & Maria Stoll

Anna Maria Mueller had arrived in Haifa in the late 1880s. Jakob had met her previously in Germany when he was employed as an apprentice by her father Andreas in his bakery in Dornhan, a small village not far from Dornstetten. Now, Maria had also found work in the household of Fritz Keller. It appears that Fritz Keller used his considerable diplomatic and match making skills to ensure these two young people got to know each other more closely.

On the 9th of April 1893, four years after Jakob arrived, they were united in marriage. The wedding gift from the Keller's was a large bag of flour. From this flour Jakob made a batch of bread, sold it to the local community and used the proceeds to buy more flour to make more bread. Thus the Stoll Bakery was born in Haifa. The bakehouse was located at No. 21 Hospital Strasse, now Meir Ave. The house is still there today but the bakery is no longer in use.

On visiting the house in 2008 I noticed two inscriptions: the date, 1871, over the doorway of the under croft; and, in the lintel of the front doorway facing the street, the words, *"Grossen Frieden haben die dein Gesetz lieben"*, (Great Peace have they who love your Law). The second half of this Bible verse goes on to say, *"and nothing can make them stumble"* (Psalm 119:165). It was this unshakeable trust in the God of the Bible that was the hallmark of my grandparents.

The inscription over the doorway to the Stoll Home

Their testimony to succeeding generations was that peace is available to all who put their faith in Jesus Christ as Lord and Saviour and that a solid and stable life can be enjoyed by all who love God and faithfully follow God's direction as revealed in the Bible. They regarded the Bible as their blueprint for life and eternity.

The significance and origin of the 1871 date is unclear. It suggests that the original building was constructed prior to Jakob Stoll's arrival. We do, however know with certainty that when Jakob and Anna moved into 21 Hospital Strasse after their marriage, it was a single storey building with an under croft, where the bakery and general storage was located, and the main floor where the family lived.

Soon the house was filled with the sound of children - another generation of Stolls had arrived, the first to be born in the Holy Land. The home became a place of warmth, comfort, refuge, safety, familiarity and joy to the five children who were born there.

The first to arrive was a son, Wilhelm, born in 1894; followed by a girl, Hulda Emilie, in 1897.

Joy turned to sorrow when their third child, a daughter Anna Maria, passed away just twelve months after her birth in 1900. The headstone of the grave located in the German Cemetery of Haifa today simply says, *Auf Wiedersehen,* (till we meet again). The parents were comforted in the sure and certain knowledge that one day they would see their daughter again in heaven.

In 1902 my mother, Maria Magdalena was born, followed by a boy, Christian Andreas in 1904.

Starting a new business and raising a new family in a new country (all in the first eleven years of Jakob and Maria's marriage), is a challenge for any family. For the young couple it proved to be an enormous undertaking but not an overwhelming one. Those early years were tough and Jakob struggled to keep the family clothed and fed. Young Christian recalls how oranges were a delicacy. On the rare occasion when one was in the house, it had to be shared between two or three members of the family. Like the rest of the settlers, Jakob and Maria faced their circumstances head on and overcame the many obstacles through hard work, faith and the fellowship of their Christian community.

An unexpected challenge was the battle for their spiritual allegiance. Jakob's father and uncle had been leaders of the Temple Society in Germany during the founding years of the movement. Both Jakob and Maria were brought up in the Temple community. Since arriving in Haifa they had been embraced with love and practical support by the Kirchlers, the Evangelical Lutheran Community. What my grandparents heard, saw and experienced in the circle of this Church family left an indelible impression on their lives.

These Bible-believing Christians had embraced the vision of Blaich and Seitz to reach out to the local population with the good news of God's salvation and build a Mission Centre on Mount Carmel. God did remarkable things in answer to their persistent prayer and unshakeable faith. Jakob and Maria were there to witness the opening of the first house of the Carmel Mission in 1890, shortly after their arrival. Their hearts were at one with these Evangelical believers, yet they chose to follow the example of their parents to worship with the Templers. They would not have made this decision lightly. It was nevertheless a deliberate choice significantly influenced by William Mader - a godly man who was to become a close friend and inspiration to Jakob Stoll and his family.

William Mader was a gardener and arrived in Haifa in 1885, four years prior to Jakob's arrival. He was humble but influential. His abilities as a spiritual leader and mentor were recognised by the settlers. He became a regular preacher at the Sunday services of the Temple Society and served on their Council of Elders. He was also a generous and active supporter of the Carmel Mission and served as its treasurer for ten years.

William Mader remained in the Temple Society because he was personally convinced that God had placed him there to be a witness for his Lord and Saviour and to proclaim the Good News. He never compromised Biblical truth. Neither was he afraid to express his opinion that *"a Temple Society, which had separated itself from other Christian believers and denominations, could not survive on its own in the long term"*.

Jakob Stoll and his family worshiped with the Templers and Jakob occasionally spoke at their Sunday services. They remained passionate about the work of the Carmel Mission and the whole family became very much involved in its ministry as well as other charitable works supported by the Lutheran Church throughout Palestine and around the world. It was not until the 1930s that Jakob's children resigned from the Temple Society and joined the Lutheran Church officially.

In the meantime the Stoll home and bakery became a busy place. Upstairs, my grandmother had her hands full as a devoted mother to her young and active children, but she still found time to grow vegetables and flowers in the garden of the house and to help in the day to day business of the bakery when needed. In later years she was able to employ local Arab girls to assist with the routine household chores. Specialty cakes and shortbread goodies are a Swabian delicacy, always the domain of the mother of the house, and Grandmother followed that tradition. At Christmas time she would cook up a storm of the most delightful array of biscuits in the most amazing shapes and delectable tastes: *Springerle, Aussteche,* (moulded biscuits), and *Lebkuchen* (gingerbread) etc.

Downstairs, the demanding routine of the bakery was in full swing. Grandfather would rise at 2 o'clock in the morning, six days a week, and light up the wood fired oven to prepare and bake all manner of breads, rolls, pretzels, pastry goods and cakes ready for the first customers before 8 o'clock. By that time the yard outside the shop was alive with the unmistakable sights, sounds and smells of the bakehouse: customers and merchants; donkeys and delivery carts; and at times camel trains with their colourful and animated Arab attendants. When the demands of the workload increased, grandfather started to train local Arab boys to help in the bakehouse.

In front of the Stoll Bakery 1913
Grandpa (Jakob), Maria, Grandma (Anna Maria), Wilhelm, Christian & Hulda on far right. Lady in black unknown

Water was a precious commodity in this dry, arid country and every drop of rain water was carefully collected in cisterns for cooking and drinking purposes. Wells, ranging in depth from ten to fifty metres, provided slightly salty water for general household, garden and animal consumption. The underground cistern was located just outside the bakery shop. From this the precious water would be drawn by bucket, and later by hand pump, and carefully rationed for the daily necessities of the home.

There was no bathroom or toilet inside the house, nor was there any electricity. One of the daily chores was to collect the kerosene lamps each morning, clean the glass shades with a soft cloth wrapped around a wooden spoon and top them up with kerosene.

Most families in the Haifa Colony around the turn of the 20th Century still baked their own bread at home. The fact that the Stoll Bakery was one of two bakeries in Haifa highlights the demand experienced by the growth of the settlement in its local population. There was also the increased number of tourists that had started to flood the many new hotels and guest houses that had been built in Haifa. In a relatively short time the Stoll Bakery began to prosper and as the children grew older, Grandfather began to make plans to expand both the business and the home.

Those plans had to be put on hold abruptly with the outbreak of World War I.

A Childhood to be Cherished

For Wilhelm, Hulda, Maria and Christian, the bakery home in Haifa in the years prior to the 1st World War was a magical place to live as a child. To them it was paradise. Everything was at their doorstep. In addition to the fascination of the bakery, there was the beach and the blue waters of the Mediterranean Sea, the enchanting heights of Mount Carmel and the happy family circle and rich community life.

The beautiful beach was a mere 300m from their home. The sea came right up to the walls of the closest houses of the Colony. During storms the waves lashed against them. When the weather was calm the beach became a child's playground. Swimming was only permissible during summer, strictly segregated by gender and only after Herr Specher had completed his annual task of erecting the bathing shed and beach cabins. A roster placed inside the shed nominated the times when boys and men could go swimming and separate times for the girls and women.

These strict arrangements proved to be no deterrent to the children's fun and exploits at the beach. The jetty and breakwater, built for the arrival of the Kaiser in 1898, stood some two metres above sea level and was the perfect diving board for the more adventurous children. I wonder if my mother was there when her school friend Elfriede (Friedel) Schumacher was enticed to jump off the jetty into the waiting arms of her older sister, Nelly[1]. That was Friedel's first and only swimming lesson.

The Templer School

It took just three minutes for my mother to walk from home to the Templer School. She not only received the best of German education there but she also formed friendships that lasted a lifetime. Among them were Elfriede (Friedel) Schumacher, Kaethe Appinger and Ludwig Beilharz. Besides German, the school taught History, Geography and Arithmetic and a foreign language was compulsory: either French or Arabic. A lot of emphasis was placed on memory work, whether poems, Bible passages or plays. School was highly regimented and retribution for any misbehaviour was instant. Being late for school by just a few minutes resulted in a firm smack of the cane across the outstretched palm of the hand. The same punishment was meted out to any who did not do their homework or whose attention wandered during class.

Ludwig Beilharz did not like school and remarked, *"One had to be extremely lucky if a week of schooling passed with only one caning"* [2]. What he enjoyed even less was detention. This entailed a visit to the headmaster's house during the lunch break, where he was required to sit perfectly still for one hour in the presence of Mr Lange and his family while they ate their midday meal. I am not aware of my mother ever talking about getting into any such trouble while at school. The happiest memories for her were the many school excursions and outings.

During summer the children did not wear shoes, except on Sundays. There were so many natural beauty spots all around waiting to be explored. As transport began to improve, Mount Carmel became an increasingly popular destination for our grandparents and their young family for Sunday afternoon outings and during school holidays. The road to the top was steep and took about an hour to climb, whether by foot or by donkey and cart. Mount Carmel was still sparsely occupied - the Carmel Mission, the Keller and Schumacher houses and the Pross Hotel were the only European buildings then. Native animals roamed freely through the terrain, including partridges, hares, porcupines and sometimes even wild pigs and deer.

Gottlieb Schumacher and his family of nine children had a summer house on Mount Carmel. The boys were keen hunters and they tell of their many conquests and how on one occasion they managed to attract a small gazelle to their garden and tame it to the point where it ate freely out of their hands[3].

Nearby was a place called the Keller's Grove with an open-air nine-pin bowling alley - a special attraction for the young. This Grove could be entered without seeking prior approval from Consul Keller. When one of the Schumacher boys helped himself to some of the fruit from the Kellers' nut and peach trees, his mother sent the culprit straight to the Consul to own up and apologise.

Nelly Schumacher recalls, *"The Consul, an exceedingly kind man who adored children, merely stroked the boy's head and warned him of some very dangerous trap that had been set but only for the purpose of catching thieves of the four legged variety."* [4]

For Jakob and Maria, Mount Carmel held special significance. As they took their children roaming through its cool and beautiful heights, Jakob was able to show them the many trees and gardens that he had helped to plant for Consul Keller and he also took them to the Carmel Mission House. At a young age the children were introduced to the leaders and staff of the Mission – Pastor Schneider, Brother Heinrici and Brother Ibrahim Douany – and they began to learn about the significance of the work that was being carried out there.

The things of yesteryear that we treasure today and pay money for our children to see, such as farmyard animals, quaint horse drawn carriages and vintage cars, were the everyday experience of my mother and her siblings. Donkeys and camels were still the traditional means of transporting goods and people through the streets of Haifa. When these animals came to the bakery the Stoll children were always delighted and excited when the Arab handlers offered them a seat or a short ride on their donkey or camel - always under the watchful eye of a parent.

Personal travelling around the town was generally by foot but later the Arabic *Hantoor*, a horse-drawn carriage cab, provided relatively cheap transport to go shopping in the *Souq*: the Arab market.

There were no transport carriages in Haifa until the colonists introduced the 'American', a six to nine seater wagon designed in America and built by the Germans in Haifa. These were in high demand by the farmers and tradesmen. They proved to be an endless source of fun and adventure for the children, as they were pulled along by two or three horses on one of their frequent family, school and community outings. Donkey driven carts brought similar delights to smaller children when they were offered rides, particularly when the destination was Mount Carmel.

But imagine the awe and exhilaration the children experienced when they saw a motor vehicle for the first time in their lives, right in the main street of Haifa.

It happened in 1903. When Nelly Schumacher saw this amazing contraption she thought she was looking at one of the 'Seven Wonders of the World'. In no time at all a swarm of school children surrounded the car and brought it to a standstill.

When the frustrated driver was unsuccessful in dispersing the crowd he had a bright idea: *"If you step aside I will take you for three laps around the colony"*[5].

Lots were drawn and three groups of seven jubilant children went on the ride of their lives. To Nelly's horror, her name was not among the chosen ones. However, her luck changed when another child's panic stricken mother broke through the crowd and shouted hysterically, *"Stop! My daughter is not going. I will not risk the life of my child!"*[5] Nelly was more than happy to take her place.

Living in a place that was both home and bakery brought lots of fun and enjoyment to all the Stoll children. The bakehouse offered more than enticing aromas; it spoiled them with the delectable tastes of freshly baked breads and cakes and provided a market type atmosphere for them to play in. They roamed freely among the comings and goings of donkeys, carts, pushbikes and camels. Arab handlers and merchants bargained in colourful language with bakers in white aprons and hats, and friendly customers picked up their daily orders. From an early age the children learned to communicate in Arabic and this became the second language of the Stoll children.

Next door they spent many happy hours on the farm with the Beilharz children, playing with their animals and feasting on their mouth-watering watermelons, juicy figs and other fruits and berries.

Sunday was a day of rest - the Lord's Day. No regular business and work associated with the bakery was carried out on Sunday. The hours of Saturday afternoon were taken up doing chores to keep work on Sunday to an absolute minimum and to make Sunday as relaxed as possible. That meant cleaning the house, polishing shoes, making sure that their Sunday clothing was clean and ready to wear, and the preparation of the Sunday meal were all completed by Saturday night.

Entertainment was rarely scheduled for a Saturday night. Sunday was the most important day of the week and going to Church was not a meaningless ritual. They saw it as a divine appointment with their Saviour, Sovereign Lord and King. As such it required the same preparation, respect and honour one would offer the Kaiser or other important dignitary. To approach him frivolously would show a lack of respect and sincerity. When they walked to Church they wore their very best Sunday attire. After the Sunday meal, the rest of the day was spent in rest and relaxation with family and friends. As often as possible they also had an hour of Bible study and prayer in the Mission House on Mount Carmel in the tradition of their Pietist forbears.

The Christmas Eve Church service was always a highlight. But even more beautiful and exciting, particularly for the children, were the Christmas celebrations that followed in the family home after the Service. The children queued excitedly outside the lounge room. When mother Maria gave the signal they started singing *Ihr Kinderlein Kommet* (Oh Come all you Children) and marched single file into the room. They were asked to sit very still around the beautifully decorated Christmas tree. Their father, Jakob, led in the singing of more Christmas carols, read the Christmas story from the Bible and then prayed. Finally the children received their presents, always practical gifts for everyday use, such as clothing, shoes and socks. The loving parents found a way to make Christmas Eve a very special occasion, filled with fun and laughter and a deep appreciation of the true meaning of Christmas.

Central to family life was the Bible. At the end of each day the whole family sat around the kitchen table. At the end of the meal father Jakob reached for his Bible. He read a short portion, explained its meaning and then he prayed. He knew the importance of parents teaching the Bible to their children (Deuteronomy 6:4-9). Eternal truths are most effectively learned in the loving environment of a God-fearing home. Church and Christian schools, though important, cannot replace this parental responsibility.

Around this table Wilhelm, Hulda, Maria and Christian learned the amazing stories of the Bible: the great things God did for the children of Israel in the Old Testament; the miraculous birth, life, death and resurrection of Jesus in the New Testament; and the incredible exploits of the apostles and disciples of Jesus in taking the message of God's salvation to the whole of the then known world.

Jakob knew that retelling the stories of what God had done in their personal lives would keep the memories of God's faithfulness alive in his family. So he told them how God answered the prayer of his father Christian and saved the family home in Dornstetten from destruction by fire when he was just four years old. He recounted how God raised up his Uncle Johannes from the deathbed and gave him an extra three years to work for God in Palestine. He told how God removed many obstacles and provided the finances to start a Mission on Mount Carmel. Finally, he told them how God gave him a godly wife, their mother Maria, and provided for all their family and business needs.

But Jakob Stoll also shared with them the scriptures about God's plan for the Jews and about the land they as a family were privileged to live in. He taught that God had willed this land, not to the Turks, and not to the Swabians, but his chosen people Israel. He told the children that Israel lost its statehood over 1900 years ago, and its people were scattered to many countries of the world. He also taught that one day the Jews would return from the dispersion and become a nation again in their ancestral homeland. He told them that there was a day coming when the eyes of all Israel would be opened and they would recognise Jesus of Nazareth as the Messiah. Then the Lord will commence his reign of peace and Israel will be rid of the yoke of the nations.

Jakob counted it an amazing privilege to be living in this land, the land of the Bible. But he reminded his family that, as Christians, they were mere pilgrims and strangers there. Their ultimate home would be their eternal home, the one prepared for them in Heaven. In the meantime their aim was to love God and serve him with all their strength in their daily lives, work, among their community and among the local population.

The counsel to his young family was:

" Whatever you do or say, let it be as a representative of the Lord Jesus ... work hard and cheerfully at whatever you do, as though you were working for the Lord rather than people. Remember that the Lord will give you an inheritance as His reward and the Master you are serving is Christ." (Colossians 3:17, 23-24).

In the knowledge of such truth the Stoll family learned to be generous to others and to hold lightly to material possessions.

A Healthy, Happy and Wise Community Life

At the turn of the twentieth century, the German Colony in Haifa was one big family of approximately 500 people including children. Everything was shared: births, weddings, funerals and the celebration of special days and occasions. It was a unique community with a seamless and finely balanced mix of spiritual, social, family, church and national celebrations. These celebrations became an essential ingredient to their survival and unity and they were an unfailing source of their joy and strength.

In 1977, after years of just lip service by the homeland, the Templer colonies in Palestine began to enjoy some tangible national support from the German Reich. The Temple Society in its book, *A Brief Historical Introduction*, relates the following background to these changes in relationship.

"In 1877, the Temple communities in Palestine came under threat when the Russian/Turkish war broke into open conflict. The German Reich under Chancellor Bismarck sent several warships to the Mediterranean and engaged in diplomatic activities. For the first time, the Templers discovered what it meant to belong to a powerful nation: they could rely on the strong arm of the homeland for protection and assistance in times of danger. All previous attempts by the Templers in Germany to gain recognition and support at local and national government levels had been spectacularly unsuccessful, up to then.

"The support of the homeland gave their, as yet, economically unconsolidated enterprises the necessary impetus. The building of the spiritual temple in Jerusalem was now seen as a national task. Germany had to fulfil not only a spiritual and cultural mission but also an economic function in the Middle East. They regarded themselves as pioneers leading their nation as they established an exemplary spiritual and social community life. From the financial years of 1879/80 onwards, the Reich granted an annual financial subsidy to the settlers towards the running of the schools they had established, which then, as later, enjoyed an excellent reputation."[1]

20th October 1898 became one of the most celebrated occasions in the history of the German settlements in Haifa, and my grandparents were part of it. Kaiser (Emperor) Wilhelm II, the highest representative of the German Reich, came to Haifa.

When it became known that the Emperor was planning to visit Palestine to participate in the ceremonial consecration of the Lutheran Church of the Redeemer in Jerusalem, and that he was disembarking at the Port of Haifa, the settlers began preparations for an appropriate reception for the sovereign. By order of Sultan Abdul Hamid II, who was on friendly terms with Wilhelm II, the building firm of Christian and Fritz Beilharz, using the plans of Gottlieb Schumacher, constructed a jetty. It was later called the *Kaiserdamm*: the Emperor's break water and jetty, as an extension to the main street of the German settlement.

Kaiser Wilhelm Reception 1898

On arrival the Turkish dignitaries prepared a splendid reception for the Imperial Couple. This was followed by addresses of welcome from the German Consul Fritz Keller and the Templer community of Haifa. The festivities continued into the next day when the Emperor granted an audience to the settlers. As he did in Jerusalem, he praised the German character of the settlements and the outstanding contribution the settlers had made to the economic development of the country.

"You have won a name for yourselves here and abroad," he said, *"and have shown how to make barren fields fertile again...."*[2]

For the Templers, the Emperor's praise was a great honour. For the first time their efforts towards the economic development of the Holy Land had been recognised and their exemplary conduct had been praised by the highest representative of the German Reich.[3]

While in Jerusalem, the Emperor also met with Theodor Herzl, the leader of the recently founded Zionist movement. Herzl was impressed with the work of the Templers and told the Emperor that he saw Haifa as the 'Town of the Future' in Eretz Israel.

Emperor Wilhelm II's visit to the Holy Land had made the Templers' work widely known. In the press, numerous articles praised their great cultural and economic achievements. The Emperor's praise of the Swabian settlers for bringing honour to the German nation found an approving public echo in Germany, particularly in Wuerttemberg[3].

This festivity was just one example of the rich and varied community life that was deliberately cultivated and enjoyed by the settlers. They were patriotic and devoted to the Kaiser and faithfully celebrated his birthday on the 27th of January each year. In fact it was extremely doubtful that the homeland celebrated the Kaiser's birthday as passionately as they did.

On those anniversaries the school was in recess. The festivities commenced at 7am with the raising of the flag and a bugle call, followed by a thanksgiving service in the Community Hall. General celebrations commenced at 2pm and concluded in the evening with a torchlight procession through the colony by the young people[4].

Harvest Thanksgiving in autumn was another highlight on the community calendar. The Community Hall was decorated with homemade multi-coloured paper garlands. In front of the hall, produce from the farms and fields was piled up high on tables: pomegranates and water melons, bananas and sheaves of corn, a huge array of vegetables and everything that autumn yields. It was a feast of thanksgiving; an acknowledgement by the settlers of God's blessing and provision for their daily needs. Prayers were offered, hymns sung and any children born during the past twelve months were dedicated to the Lord. The front row of seats was reserved for the ten to twelve parental couples. As the couples stepped forward, the Community Elder placed his hand on the head of each child and prayed for them and the parents[5].

Among the colonists in Haifa there were some forty five to fifty Swabian settlers with American citizenship. They held their own picnic on the 4th of July to celebrate American Independence Day in Palestine, in honour of the land that had welcomed them so freely when they migrated there in the first half of the 19th century.

Wedding ceremonies were held in the Community Hall or the Evangelical Church, followed by the reception usually in Wagner's Hall or the open air if numbers were large. On most of these occasions the whole community was invited to join in. Speeches spiced with Swabian humour were given and children recited poems or presented short skits. All enjoyed a simple meal of sausages and potato salad, a huge assortment of homemade cakes and local fruit of water melon, oranges and bananas.

Who could forget the glorious community excursions? On special holidays, such as Pentecost Monday, children and adults piled onto the six and nine seater horse-drawn wagons filled with straw, and drove into the *Haradijje* forest, the oak covered hills near the settlements of Bethlehem and Waldheim.

On arrival they made themselves comfortable under the hundred year old oak tree and passed the day away with singing, recitations, games and speeches as well as good Swabian food and drink.[6]

Everyone was encouraged to be actively involved in this Christian community. They were encouraged to exercise their God-given gifts and talents by joining one or more of the many clubs and societies that had been formed.

Brass Band 1908

By the turn of the century they included a Men and Women Society, a Male Choir (the *Lorelei*), a Mixed Voice Choir, a Young Men's Association and a Brass Band. These groups, together with the programmes of the school children, offered a huge variety of education, fun and entertainment at their many community functions.

The cornerstone of community life was the corporate worship of God. All the settlers, with their whole families, attended the Sunday morning service. The Templers met in the *Saal* (the Community Hall), and the Kirchlers in the Lutheran Church.

The Temple *Saal* was very plain. There was no altar, no candles, neither were there any images of saints sparkling with gold or silver. Ludwig Beilharz recalls the order of service of a typical Sunday meeting of the Templers.

"While it was not specifically prescribed it was expected that the seating arrangements be observed on a strict gender basis. Men sat on one side of

the central aisle and women on the other. The school children were seated right at the front, near the pulpit and at right angles to the congregation. The youngest children sat in the front rows in direct view of the adults. The teenagers that had finished school and the single adults sat behind them. As soon as the Church bell stopped ringing the service started with the gentle playing of the harmonium, followed by a congregational hymn and prayer. The message would normally be presented by the chief elder, Friedrich Lange, but on occasions also by other men, such as Herr Mader, Herr Stoll and Herr Paetzner. The service concluded with prayer and another short hymn. The general notices were given before the congregation dispersed."[7]

Christmas Eve and New Year's Eve celebrations held the fondest memories for our grandparents and parents. On Christmas Eve the large pine Christmas tree at the front of the Community Hall was aglow with brightly burning candles. It was decorated with oranges, gold and silver nuts; an array of German Christmas biscuits and other shiny handmade objects. The congregation arose and the excitement built as the school children (Wilhelm, Hulda, Maria and Christian among them) led the procession into the Church. The congregation sang Christmas carols and the children recited the Christmas story from Luke 2. They were dressed in bright costumes representing the angels, the shepherds, the wise men, Mary and Joseph and the child lying in the manger. The officiating Elder then stood to share the significance of the coming of Christ as a babe in a manger some 1900 years ago, in the very land in which it was now their privilege to live. At the end there were small presents for the children prepared by the congregation.

Christmas Eve Service

The Haifa Community had its own unique way of celebrating New Year's Eve. Nelly Schumacher remembers how her grandfather, Friedrich Lange, the Community elder of that time, led proceedings.

"Five minutes to twelve. A crowd of young men and women stand on the road in front of the Community Hall. Grandfather holds his watch in his hand. At the stroke of twelve the Community bell rings above us. As its sound ebbs away, the Community elder starts to sing in a bright and clear voice, Nun danket alle Gott, (Now thank we all our God) and young and old join in with great enthusiasm. The procession marches up the Colony Street with the aged, but sprightly figure of Friedrich Lange at its head. One hymn of thanks follows another. We pause and sing an extra hymn from our endless repertoire whenever we come to a house with someone sick in bed inside. Many, many New Year Eves have come and gone but none of them equals those when our dear grandfather led his community through the streets of the German Colony of Haifa into another year.[8]

By the beginning of the 20th century, Haifa was no longer a place of misery and persistent hardship. Considerable progress had been made. An informative insight into the social and economic circumstances of the Haifa settlement can be gleaned from the following statistics, selected from a survey prepared on 1st August 1898.

There were 517 inhabitants (101 families), including:

- 360 Templers (70 families)
- 145 members of the Evangelical Community (29 families)
- 4 members of the Roman-Catholic Church (1 family)
- 2 bakers
- 1 brewer
- 3 consuls
- 2 engineers
- 16 farmers
- 1 gardener
- 1 Lloyd's agent
- 8 merchants
- 4 millers
- 1 pastor
- 1 physician
- 1 postmaster
- 3 restaurateurs
- 2 soap manufacturers
- 5 teachers (males and females)
- 33 tradesmen, and
- 23 winegrowers.

The settlers had built 92 buildings and 95 outbuildings; cultivated 150 ha of arable land in the plain, 35 ha of vineyards, several olive groves and they owned property on Mount Carmel and possessed 458 heads of live stock comprising horses, cattle, donkeys, pigs, goats as well as poultry.[9]

On Mount Carmel, once overgrown with thorns and scrub, there were now woodlands, gardens and vineyards and a beautiful residential area, which had a strong attraction for tourists. As already noted, many of these new trees and landscape gardens were planted by our grandfather while in the employ of Fritz Keller. The settlers called the mountain range by its original name: *Karem-El* (The Garden of God). This was a truly remarkable achievement and evidence of God's blessing on the work of the settlers.

In 1900, King Wilhelm II of Wuerttemberg, the highest representative of the settlers' Swabian homeland, awarded Vice Consul Keller and Christoph Hoffmann with the highest possible distinction: the Knight's Cross (First Class) of the Order of Friedrich. It was in recognition of the contribution that they had made to the German settlements in Palestine.

The University of Haifa also established the Gottlieb Schumacher Institute for 'Research of the Christian Presence in Palestine' on Mount Carmel. Since 1993 the Institute has conducted its research activities in the historical site of the first residential building erected on Mount Carmel in the late 1880s. This was the residence of Fritz Keller and is today named the Keller House in his honour. The street where it is located also bears his name.

Keller House 1900

Keller House today

Jakob and Maria Stoll considered Fritz Keller as their mentor, benefactor and friend. While Keller held the respected office of German Vice Consul in Haifa, and was influential and well-to-do, he was also a humble man with a compassion for people and a generosity of heart, offering material and spiritual help to many in need. My grandparents remained grateful to God for the Keller influence on their lives.

A Troublesome and Uncertain Future

The 20th century started with huge optimism and hope of a brighter and more secure future for the Swabian settlers in the Holy Land, both in terms of spiritual outreach and economic and national development. But by 1920 the settlements had been brought to their knees and the work of the Temple Community stood in danger of total collapse.

The residential development on Mount Carmel had been expanding at a steady rate. On the 29th of May 1904 Pastor Martin Schneider with his wife and two children arrived from Saxony in Germany and took up residence in the Carmel Mission Home. Under his leadership, the work of the Mission began to grow significantly and the influence of its ministry reached out to the local population and became more effective[1]. As the work began to grow, more workers joined the Mission, including a young Swiss national by the name of Gottfried Meyer. In 1908 he was sent by the Tent Mission organisation, *Patmos-Geisweid*, to work as gardener. Gottfried Meyer and his family were to develop a special connection with the Stoll family.

Carmel Mission Staff 1912

In 1909, at the age of 50, William Mader, as treasurer and field representative of the Carmel Mission, went on a four months mission trip to Germany visiting Christian friends, leaders, missionaries and pastors. He attended conferences and spoke in many places about the Templer settlements and the work of the Carmel Mission. He came back to Palestine with renewed enthusiasm and a passion to spread the Good News of God's salvation throughout the Middle East and beyond. He taught that this was possible through people, irrespective of denominations and nationality, who had crowned Christ as Lord and King of their life.

"A Christendom based on selfish, denominational and national interests," he said, *"cannot succeed but for the power of a new life, which has been made available to us through Jesus and a commitment to serve Him in total obedience. 'Everything for Him and His Kingdom' that must be our slogan. God expects nothing less!"*[2]

This statement takes on extra significance when considered in the context of the Templer movement of which he was a member. William Mader saw that a Temple Society, with its forthright rationalism, its ambition for national statehood and its isolation from other Christians and denominations, would probably not become the means of fulfilling the 'Great Commission' (Matthew 28:18,19) to extend God's kingdom on earth. In the Carmel Mission he saw an organisation that gave him the opportunity to reach out to a needy world the way God intended it. He devoted himself to this cause unconditionally.

Soon after his return the third and final Carmel Mission Centre was opened in 1911 on land owned by the original founder, Martin Blaich, and at the spot where the Panorama twin towers are located today. This magnificent mission building provided accommodation for forty guests and included a large meeting room. The Mission's long term vision was brought to a temporary halt with the outbreak of war in 1914.

By the early 1900s a second generation of settlers had grown up in Haifa. When it became increasingly difficult for them to gain a livelihood in the existing settlements, because of its limited agricultural area, two new settlements were founded to meet those needs: Bethlehem in 1906 by the Templers, and Waldheim in 1907 by the Kirchler community.

They were both located near Nazareth in the Jezreel valley, twenty five kilometres from Haifa, and just two kilometres apart. Both became model agricultural settlements. The young men of the Lutheran congregation in Haifa pooled their resources and, with financial assistance from the Stuttgart Society, acquired land from *Sirsouk*, a Lebanese landowner. They called the new town Waldheim (Forest Home) because of the many stands of small Tabor oak trees. The two colonies combined to transport their produce, including milk, eggs, fruit and vegetables, to Haifa. They established a buying and selling co-operative, *Kopro*, which sent a horse-drawn wagon to Haifa twice a day. This "milk wagon" also served as transport for passengers and as a mail courier[3].

The Lutheran congregations of Haifa and Waldheim shared the same pastor and established strong community links and friendships. The eighteen properties at Waldheim spread along two main roads laid out in the form of a cross. The Lutheran Church was prominently located at the intersection of the roads.

Some of the original settlers included the families of Deininger, Aimann, Blaich, Unger and Staib. After the First World War, the Meyer family also settled in Waldheim. In addition to running a small farm, Gottfried Meyer started a school for some thirty girls belonging to the Arab families who were employed by the Waldheim settlers. Had it not been for his efforts these children would not have received any schooling. The children received not only a good education but also heard the good news of God's salvation from the Arab missionary, Ibrahim Douany, during his regular visits. Later the

Stoll/Meinel families also came to live in Waldheim, under circumstances not of their choosing.

Jakob & Maria Stoll at Home in 1914 with Hulda, Christian & Maria

In the year 1914, Wilhelm was twenty years old, Hulda seventeen, my mother, Maria, twelve and Christian, ten. As they grew up, all the Stoll children learned to do odd jobs in the bakery. From a young age they had to deliver bread to customers before school started each morning. During winter that happened while it was still dark. Later the boys took a donkey saddled with bread baskets to deliver to Jewish homes and Arab families.

Wilhelm, as the eldest son, followed in his father's footsteps and was now a fully-fledged baker busy helping to run the family business. As part of his apprenticeship his father had sent him to Geneva, Switzerland, to hone his skills and gain overseas experience. Hulda was assisting in the shop and doing household chores in the home. Maria and Christian were still at school.

At the outbreak of the 1st World War in August 1914, all the young men of the Templer Colonies in Palestine who held German citizenship were called up for military service. As Palestine was a Turkish territory, and the Turks had allied themselves with Germany, the inhabitants of the Templer colonies did not feel in any imminent danger. But the outbreak of war did have an immediate impact on the Stoll family.

Wilhelm Stoll was still in Switzerland when he was enlisted in the Infantry Regiment 126 of the German Army on the 26th December 1914. He was ordered to serve on the Belgian front. The parents now had lost a son and their main worker in the family bakery to the dangers of war in a far-away country. But this was just the beginning of what proved to be a very uncertain future for the life of the Stoll family and the German settlers as a whole.

A famine struck Haifa in 1915. On Palm Sunday of that year thick swarms of locusts overran Haifa and surroundings without warning, almost blocking out the sun. It also rained a little on that day and the locusts began to lay eggs. The whole community was ordered to collect these newly laid eggs. School came to a virtual standstill as children joined the adults in this hunt for locust eggs. Eggs were burnt by the bag-full but the whole exercise made little impact on the spread of the plague.

When the young locusts, known as 'hoppers', hatched, they crawled by the millions everywhere to devour everything green in their path: all the leaves of the trees, bushes, corn and whatever was growing in the fields. The fowls, which fed on the locusts, laid eggs with red yolks and the people soon lost their appetite for eggs[4].

Christian was eleven years old. He helped to chase the freshly hatched locusts that could not yet fly with palm branches on to a ten meter square hessian rug. The rug had a hole in its centre and, when they had gathered a sufficiently thick layer of locusts, they simply lifted the four corners and discharged the offending pests into a large drum for their disposal. Eventually a strong wind swept the locusts out to sea but the damage caused was devastating and the countryside took some years to recover. It was a blessing that the barley and wheat had already been harvested so at least there was enough bread. Otherwise it would have been a more tragic situation[5].

By autumn 1917, British troops under General Edmund Allenby occupied Palestine, advancing from the south.

On 31st October 1917 Beersheba fell into the hands of Australian troops, the 4th Light Horse Brigade.

On the 9th December 1917 the Allies occupied Jerusalem. The Templer settlements in the south – Wilhelma, Sarona, Jaffa and Ephraim in Jerusalem – were all in the hands of the British by the end of the year.

On 3 August 1918 all Germans from the south were interned as prisoners of war in Egypt at *Helouan* in a complex called *Al Hayat*.

Since the Germans in Haifa feared the same fate of deportation, many sold their homes in an attempt to salvage their money. While most of the men were away at the war, for those remaining, money and food were scarce. Wheat and barley became increasingly difficult to obtain. The Stoll bakery simply could not supply enough bread for the population, now teetering on the verge of starvation. Even though the Arabs tried their best to bribe grandfather, whatever food was available was rationed carefully within each family.

School-aged children like my mother, Maria, and her brother, Christian, barely noticed that times were tough. But they did have vivid memories of the adventure and excitement of those war years.

A small contingent of the German military was stationed in the north of Palestine. When one of their army trucks appeared in the streets of Haifa, Christian was one of a group of young boys and girls that chased the vehicle and hassled the driver until he offered them all a ride. Christian was ecstatic. What an adventure: a joy ride with German soldiers.

Those in the truck were blissfully unaware of the French frigate on the distant horizon patrolling the coastline, until they heard an explosion and saw cannon fire coming in their direction. Two more volleys, aimed at the German Consulate, flew over their heads and crashed into the lower slopes of Mount Carmel. In total panic, the driver dodged for cover and the young people ran for their lives, convinced they were the target of this enemy attack[6].

On another occasion the residents sought shelter in the safety of their cellars after they had been warned of an imminent attack from a French warship. Fortunately this did not eventuate. Just thirty years later, history was to repeat itself when I, as a seven year old, also had to retreat to a cellar under threat of artillery fire and aerial bombardment. But more of that later!

The Turkish army, including a small contingent of German airmen, were stationed near Waldheim. As they retreated from the advancing British troops, they commandeered all of the settlers' horses and horse-drawn vehicles. The settlers in Haifa feared that the English would confiscate their properties. While this did not eventuate, except in a few cases, for those remaining it was nevertheless a frightening experience.

During the night prior to the arrival of the British troops on the 18th of September 1918, starving Turkish soldiers broke into many houses and ate all that was edible; even the chickens were not spared. When the British army (mostly Indian soldiers) arrived, many residents had to evacuate their homes and live in their stables or workshops for a short time.

The Stolls did not have to leave their home but Wilhelm Mader and his family did. They were thankful that they were allowed to stay on their garden property. The younger German men still living in Haifa, some holding American citizenship, feared incarceration. They fled the town on the night of 22nd and 23rd September and headed for Germany. This made life even more difficult for those left behind; mainly women, children and older people. Food and money were in short supply. Some found work with the British military. Mrs Deininger did the washing for English officers. Besides their payment for the washing they also gave her soap and food, which she could use for her small children. She later told her daughter, Gertrud, how grateful she was to her Heavenly Father for the assistance she received from the English officers[7].

On the 11th November 1918, a ceasefire was declared.

The presence of the English military soon helped to improve the living conditions in the Colony. It also did not take long for mutual respect to be developed between the English and the Germans. The English brought employment and commercial trading opportunities to the settlers. The Germans opened up their homes, and offered friendship and social activities to the young English soldiers, many of whom suffered from loneliness and home sickness.

Jakob and Maria Stoll were one of a number of families that invited the soldiers to their home on Sunday evenings for hospitality and hymn singing. Christian Stoll remembered how he, as a teenager, enjoyed singing the revival songs of Alexander and Sankey with many of these fine English Christian soldiers. For the Stoll teenage children, this was a living example of how the bond of Christian love breaks down all barriers of language, race and colour.

Meanwhile, Wilhelm Stoll experienced the horrors of all that we know of the brutal trench warfare in Belgium. He served on the front for the duration of the conflict and was not released until 12th September 1918. In rare leave breaks, Wilhelm was able to return to Germany where he visited his grandmother, Christine Stoll, his aunty in Dornstetten and Christian friends at the Liebenzeller Mission in Bad Liebenzell and other towns.

On the 25th of April 1917, Wilhelm was struck in his face by flying shrapnel and sustained a serious injury. In an effort to save his life he was operated on in an ill-equipped and understaffed field hospital, but was left with permanent damage to his face. Several more operations had to be carried out over a period of ten months in Germany, to remove all fragments of steel and bone splinters.

In the early recovery period the wound ruptured and, despite medical attention, the bleeding could not be stopped. As he weakened and felt at the point of death he pleaded with God to save his life. He reasoned that he was too young to die and still had so much to live for. Finally he prayed, *"If it is really best for me to die now, I am willing to accept your will"*.[8] Wilhelm said, that at that point the bleeding stopped and he began to recover.

Even though the doctors declared him unfit for military service, the army required him to work as a guard in prisoner of war camps in various places across Germany from March to September 1918[8].

Wilhelm was part of a major successful military offensive in August 1915, which earned the Regiment the highest praise from General von Deimling and a congratulatory telegram from His Majesty King Wilhelm II. On the 31st October 1918, Wilhelm was presented with the Iron Cross, 2nd Class, for outstanding military service[8]. Wilhelm never spoke of his military decorations, as he did not want to be associated with anything that celebrated the senseless killing of soldiers and innocent civilians.

During his life time Wilhelm did not talk about his war time years but he did keep a detailed diary. It offers an amazing insight into the horrors and brutality of that war and how Wilhelm was protected and survived. It also paints a picture of a man totally surrendered to God and His sovereign will.

The loss of sight in his left eye and the stigma of a disfigured face was the 1st World War legacy that Wilhelm Stoll carried with him. However, becoming an invalid at the age of twenty three was not an impediment to Wilhelm living a full, long and successful family and business life. He knew that the grace of God, which had spared him from death on the battlefield of Belgium, would be sufficient for whatever circumstances life would throw up at him.

The end of the war in November 1918 brought no relief for the 850 Palestinian Germans interned in Egypt. These, mainly women, children and older men, remained behind barbed wire. The Allies considered deporting them to Germany and confiscating their property for reparation purposes. For many months, this threat hung like the sword of Damocles, not only over those who were interned in Helouan in Egypt, but also those who had remained in the settlements of Haifa, Bethlehem and Waldheim.

Back in Europe, a number of organisations had begun to fight for the right of the Palestinian Germans in internment in Egypt, and for those soldiers still residing in Germany, to return to Palestine. It took until 1921 before the majority were able to return to reclaim their homes, land and businesses. Those in the south found their properties in a much neglected and partially ravaged state. Fortunately, the British Mandate Government showed understanding of the needs and problems of the settlers and paid approximately 50% restitution for their livestock and other property losses.

The inhabitants of the northern settlements were more fortunate but while they were able to remain in their settlements, they had to make some of their houses available to the occupying forces over a long period, particularly in Haifa[9]. The Carmel Hotel served as the residence of the city's British military commander and a number of other properties were occupied by military officials on a permanent basis.

The 1st World War brought the 400 year rule of Palestine by the Ottoman Turks to an end and ushered in the era of the British Mandate. What would this change of political rule mean for the German settlers in Palestine? They had pioneered seven new settlements and achieved much after fifty years in the land, including the respect of the Jewish and Arab population for their contribution to the modernisation of the country.

Was this the end of their dreams to establish a German Christian community in Palestine or merely a temporary setback?

Brothers, Sisters and Spouses

Wilhelm, Hulda, Christian & Maria (front right)
With parents Maria & Jakob

Now, let me introduce the adult children of Jakob and Anna Maria Stoll: Wilhelm, Hulda, Maria, Christian and their spouses. These pages provide a brief snapshot of their early adult years: their careers, marriages, faith and values in life. They would regard the seventeen years between 1922 and 1939 in Palestine as the happiest and most rewarding years of their lives.

Palestine was the land of their birth. Haifa was their home town. The Temple Society was their Swabian community in which they grew up, where they went to school and church, and in which they forged their careers and families. One thing they never took for granted was that the land they called home was the 'Holy Land': the land of the Bible, of Abraham, Isaac and Jakob, of Kings and Prophets of the Nation of Israel. And, it was the land where Jesus was born, lived, died and rose again from the dead.

During those years the Stoll siblings took time to discover the roots of the Judeo-Christian heritage. They travelled far and wide across Palestine and stood in many of the historic places of the Bible. They realised how privileged they were to see with their own eyes the places that they had read about in the Bible since they were small children. The photo albums they left behind are evidence of their travels and of their appreciation and thrill to be in Palestine at that time.

Wilhelm Stoll

Wilhelm was the eldest of the four siblings. He followed in his father's footsteps, became a baker and worked in the family Bakery. In 1913 he travelled to Geneva to complete a course in *Konditorei*: pastry cooking and specialty cake decoration. From 1914 to 1917 he fought in the German Army in Belgium during the 1st World War. He did not return to Palestine until 1920. The two years after the end of the war he spent with Stoll relatives and friends in Germany recuperating from his war injuries and visiting many of the Christian leaders and mission organisations his father-in-law-to-be, Wilhelm Mader, had made him familiar with.

In Bad Liebenzell, in the northern area of the Black Forest, he met Herr Wilhelm Heinsen. Mr Heinsen was a lecturer and later a field representative of the Liebenzeller Mission. A strong friendship developed between Wilhelm Stoll and Wilhelm Heinsen and proved to be the beginning of a lifelong connection between the Stoll family and the Liebenzeller Mission. Heinsen subsequently visited Haifa in 1928 and 1930.

The Liebenzeller Mission is an interdenominational organisation which trains candidates for missionary service around the world. It was formed on the 30 November 1899 at the request of the founder of the China Inland Mission organisation, James Hudson Taylor of England, and by Pastor Heinrich Coerper of the Lutheran Church in Hamburg, Germany. In 1906, the Mission transferred its headquarters to Bad Liebenzell from where they sent many young missionaries to many parts of the world, but particularly to China. Through the passage of time this German branch of the China Inland Mission not only cared for the blind in the province of Hunan but they also established hospitals, schools and orphanages. Today the Liebenzeller Mission has some two hundred and thirty missionaries working in twenty five countries around the world. Their motto is *Mit Gott von Menschen zu Menschen* (with God, by people for people).[1]

Hudson Taylor had an indirect influence on the Stoll family through the Liebenzeller Mission. Back in the 1880s, Hudson Taylor also captured the attention of another young man by the name of C T Studd, an all-England cricketer and member of the so-called 'Cambridge Seven'. C T Studd went to China as a missionary and in 1913 he founded WEC (World Evangelisation Crusade) in the Belgian Congo. Some fifty years later the Meinel family established a strong link with WEC when my sister, Helga, served with that Mission in West Africa and the Middle East.

After an absence of seven years, at the age of twenty six, Wilhelm returned to Haifa and resumed his work as a baker in the family business. He did this with some reluctance. He had set his heart on becoming a missionary but his father wanted his eldest son to continue the family bakery. Jakob felt strongly that Wilhelm was needed in the bakery, particularly after the difficult post-war years.

By the early 1920s, the bakery began to grow again and saw the employment of a growing number of Arab bakers and assistants. This period also saw a significant extension to the family home with the addition of a second floor.

On the 16th March 1928 thirty four year old Wilhelm married Katherine (Tine) Luise Mader, the eldest child of William Mader, in the Community Hall of the Temple Society. They were married by Tine's father and the reception was held in the Wagner Hall where two hundred and seventy guests from near and far joined in the celebration with this very popular couple. Mr Heinsen was a special invitee from Germany and he accompanied the couple on their honeymoon on a guided tour through the Holy Land. They could not have had a more qualified guide: a Bible College lecturer!

Wilhelm & Tine Wedding 1928

Wilhelm and Tine had five children: Ruth (1930), Wilhelm (1931), Theodor (1932), Gerhard (1935) and Siegfried (1937). Up until 1935, all of the Stoll siblings, with their spouses and children lived with their parents in the *Hospital Strasse* (now Me'ir Street) home.

By the 1930s the bakery was doing well and Wilhelm wanted to free himself from the day to day running of the bakery so he could pursue other business and ministry interests. He recruited a young man, Martin Meinel, from Germany to help him run the bakery. In 1932 Wilhelm purchased several acres of undeveloped land near Acre. He put down a bore, found water and developed a new plantation growing oranges, mandarins, bananas and vegetables.

Meanwhile Jakob and Maria, now in their early 70s and late 60s, had built a new two storey home in *Garten Strasse* (now Haganim Street). They lived on the lower level and Wilhelm and family moved into the top floor during 1935.

Jakob & Maria Stoll's new Home

By this time the political condition in Palestine was changing for the worse and Wilhelm had the foresight to predict the possible demise of the German Colonies in the British-controlled Palestine. He was looking for an opportunity to invest in real estate in Germany for the relocation and education of his family, should this become necessary. In 1936 he travelled to Germany and bought a run down two storey house with a disused bakery that had been listed for demolition, in a small farming village called Zell unter Aichelberg. This was in contrast to his fellow Germans from Palestine who bought property in Stuttgart where the financial returns promised to be much more attractive.

Wilhelm put the property in the care of 'uncle' Otto Mader, a church deacon of the Lutheran Church in Zell, and a Christian friend. When he returned to Haifa, Wilhelm acknowledged that this was probably not the best investment deal he had ever made but he remained confident that God had guided him in making the right decision. He could never have anticipated the far reaching effects of his decision and the good fortune it was to bring to the Meinels and the whole village of Zell.

What was it that attracted Wilhelm to Zell? Wilhelm always had a passion for serving God in outreach and mission. If circumstances had prevented him from being a full time Christian worker, he wanted to make sure that his future home in Germany was within close range of a Christian organisation that shared his beliefs and offered him opportunities for hands on involvement.

He found such a work in the Bad Boll *Erhohlungsheim* (Christian Retreat) and health spa resort. For almost 70 years Bad Boll was the headquarters of two of the best known leaders of Swabian Pietism: Johann Christoph Blumhardt (1805-1880) and his son, Christoph Friedrich Blumhardt (1852-1919). Following the death of Friedrich Blumhardt the Christian retreat came under the umbrella of the *Herrnhuter* Brethren. Wilhelm knew these organisations well and their close association with Seitz and Blaich. Zell was located just three kilometres from Bad Boll.

Bad Boll Christian Retreat 1870s

Wilhelm, as the eldest in the family, enjoyed the respect and admiration of his sisters and brother. He had a profound influence on them. In so many ways he was their role model; they respected his example and in years to come they were to follow his call to come and join him in Australia.

Like his father and father in law, Wilhelm was passionate about the work of the Carmel Mission. The foundations of his Christian faith were laid in the parental home but it was the influence of the Carmel Mission that consolidated his beliefs and gave him a vision for missions. The Carmel Mission gave him the tools and opportunities to reach out to the poor and needy, both in Palestine and other parts of the world. He became a faithful and sacrificial giver to God's work but, because he strongly believed that financial giving was a matter between God and the giver alone, few knew of the extent of his giving. One example typical of his generosity emerged from the writings of the Carmel Mission staff worker, Herr Heinrici, who conducted a prison ministry in Acre. He writes:

"One day a case of 100 Bibles in Arabic arrived anonymously from Beirut. Sometime later I found out that a German colonist had ordered these Bibles for distribution among the prisoners. Now that he and his family are living in

Australia I can disclose his name: it was the baker Wilhelm Stoll from the German Colony in Haifa. To this day I remain grateful for his generous missionary service. Through the reading of the Bible Muslims have come to faith in Christ."

Wilhelm loved all true believers and enjoyed their fellowship irrespective of creed, denomination, race or colour.

For many years Wilhelm wrestled with the question: Is my personal Christian belief compatible with my membership in the Temple Society, whose leaders he considered had drifted away from sound biblical Christianity? Out of genuine respect for his father-in-law who had chosen to stay and work within the Temple Society, he retained his membership. After the death of Wilhelm Mader, on the 28th of February 1929, Wilhelm Stoll felt at liberty to hand in his resignation and to officially join the Lutheran Church but did not do so until 1936. It is a matter of record that despite the theological differences between the Templers and the Kirchlers both enjoyed each other's respect and lived in harmony throughout their stay in Palestine.

Hulda Stoll

Hulda was the second child and eldest daughter in the Stoll family. She, like her siblings, received her primary education at the German Templer School in Haifa. From a young age she helped her mother in the home and her father in the bakery shop. Helping and caring for members of the family was to be her life's calling. It was also very much the role expected of the eldest girl in the family.

Unlike her brothers and sister she did not travel overseas, she never married and she never owned or lived in her own house. All of her life we see Hulda in a servant role. As a teenager she was a willing helper in the home and the bakery. When her siblings married and had children, and they all lived under the roof of the family home, she enjoyed being an Aunty and voluntary nanny, when one or the other of the parents was out of town or overseas.

When Christian took his wife Christel (neé Appinger) to Germany in 1934, for urgent medical treatment, their children Herta (3) and Walter (1) were left behind in the care of Hulda and *Oma* Appinger.

Like her siblings, she credited the influence of the family home, the Lutheran Church and the Carmel Mission for her strong values and Christian convictions. She sang in the church choir, taught in Sunday school, financially supported missions and helped in the ministry to the poor in the community.

When her parents shifted to their new house in *Garten Strasse* around 1935, Hulda went with them and cared for them in their retirement years. When all the Germans in Haifa were interned in the agricultural settlement of Waldheim at the outbreak of the Second World War, she became a full time carer for her ageing father and ailing mother until their deaths in 1940 and 1945, respectively. Hulda was one of just a handful of Germans left behind in Waldheim in 1945, after all the others had been transported to Australia and Germany. Hulda, once again, found herself caring for others, this time a couple in their 80s, Mr & Mrs Wurster.

Hulda lived a quiet unassuming life in the shadow of the other family members. However, in 1948, just a few days prior to the declaration of the State of Israel, she found herself catapulted to centre stage. Her name became etched in the history of Waldheim and the plight of the German settlements in Palestine. This story is reserved as the subject of another chapter.

I got to know aunty Hulda after our arrival in Australia in 1952 when she lived with her brother Wilhelm, and his family, in the Barossa Valley. When Margaret and I were looking to buy our first home after our marriage in 1962, Aunty Hulda (and Uncle Wilhelm) gave us a generous interest free loan. To me, Aunty Hulda will always remain a wonderful example of the benefits and obligations that come with belonging to a loving extended family. She served the family all her life and the family provided her with shelter, safety and security.

Maria Stoll

My mother, Maria Magdalena, was the 3rd child of Jakob and Maria Stoll, born on 18th June 1902 in Haifa.

She assisted in the day to day chores of the family home and worked in the bakery after she completed her primary schooling. Through her activities in the church and the Carmel Mission, she came into contact with a number of deaconesses. A deaconess belonged to a particular order of 'sisters' who dedicated their lives to serve God in Church and Mission organisations in Germany and other countries: usually as teachers, nurses and carers. My mother felt drawn to these sisters and befriended many of them in Palestine through the Carmel Mission, the Syrian Orphanages, the Pilgrims Mission *St Chrischona* and the *Kaiserswerther* Deaconesses Institutions. She struck up a special friendship with Sister Annchen, the daughter of Pastor Heinrici.

In 1924, as a 22 year old, Maria travelled to Germany. For the next seventeen months she visited many of the headquarters of the Christian Missionary and Deaconess organisations she knew of during her childhood in Palestine. She worked in a children's home called *Sonnenland* (Land of the Sun), managed by a group of deaconesses. In Bad Liebenzell Bible College she attended a ladies' conference and in Malche she graduated from a cooking class. She visited the Stoll families in and around Dornstetten and made many special friendships. In 1925 she returned to Haifa now equipped with the specialised skills of child care, household duties and cooking, and a new appreciation of the life and ministry as a deaconess.

Sister Annchen & Mum

In 1927, a young man from *Sachsen*, (Saxony) Germany, by the name of Martin Meinel, came to work in the Stoll bakery in Haifa. He became part of the Stoll family. Maria tells how she resisted Martin's romantic approaches for a long time. But, on her second trip to Germany in 1931 she made time to meet Martin's parents and his brothers and sister and their families in Schneeberg, Saxony.

Many British officers and diplomatic officials had made their headquarters in Jerusalem and Haifa when Palestine became a British Mandate. Their presence offered the German settlers new employment opportunities.

Mum with Allan   Mum with Pat & Helen

Maria worked as a Nanny from 1929 to 1932 for one of those English officials and his wife in Jerusalem, caring for their young boy Allan. In 1932, she was recruited into the home of an English doctor, Dr Soh, and his family in Haifa. My mother looked after their two young children, Helen and Pat and they spent many hours in the Stoll home and joined in the family celebrations. It was not long before *Schwaebisch* became the children's second language.

In 1934 Maria was invited to join the Soh family on a visit to their home in England. Maria relished every day of the ten months in England and Europe. On their travel through Germany, Switzerland and Italy she saw many of the iconic tourist attractions Europe could offer including Lake Luzern, Mount Pilatus and Rome with its St Peter's Square.

Back in Haifa, love had overcome Maria's earlier resistance. She told how during one of her meditations she was given an unmistakable conviction from God that Martin was to be her future husband. She needed that assurance because Martin was still in a relationship with a girl from Schneeberg at that time. True love and respect conquered both of their hearts and after a short engagement Martin and Maria were married on 17th October 1935 by Pastor von Oertzen in the Lutheran Church in Haifa.

Martin & Maria 1935

Their first three children – Werner (1936), Herbert (1938) and Helga (1939) – were all born in Haifa. Inge, their fourth child, was born in Zell in Germany in 1948.

Much of the above information I did not learn from the lips of my mother but through searching the family records, particularly her photo albums, after her death. That in itself says a lot about my mother. By any standard, hers was a remarkable life in the age in which she lived. She was the product of a working class Christian family, trying to make a living in difficult circumstances in a pioneering settlement in a foreign country. Yet, before she married at the age of 33, she had traversed the length and breadth of the Holy

Land; trained in a number of the foremost overseas Mission and Church organisations in Germany; been to England as a nanny; travelled all over Europe, and spoke fluent German, English and Arabic. Yet, I never heard her boast or talk about those events.

When Margaret and I did our first overseas trip in 1983 to Europe and we talked excitedly about our time in Switzerland, and our climb in the steepest railcar in the world to the top of Mount Pilatus, she casually remarked, "I have been there!" I had no idea. But that was my mother.

She never drew attention to herself. She was capable, fearless in tough situations, didn't wear her emotions on her sleeves and she had a deep reservoir of faith and scriptural convictions. She didn't tolerate fools lightly. When a situation demanded, she was quite capable of giving her opinion in the best of Swabian fashion, whether you asked for it or not. She was a remarkable cook. Besides her bakery know-how, she was able to serve up the best of German, English and Mediterranean cuisines. How many mothers in Australian homes in the 1960s could dish up the best of Middle Eastern food? It took another thirty years before these recipes were introduced to menus in Australian restaurants. I have always marvelled at the competence and confidence with which my mother conducted the routines of everyday living.

Christian Stoll

Christian was the youngest child in the family. Jakob Stoll had a firm expectation that Christian would become a baker and, like his older brother Wilhelm, work in the family business. Christian had other ideas. He did not want to be a baker and pleaded with his father to let him pursue a different profession. It was Wilhelm that eventually was able to persuade his father to release Christian from the bakery obligation.

Christian decided to become a gardener. In 1923, aged nineteen, Christian went to the agricultural Templer settlement of Sarona, (now part of Tel

Aviv), to do an apprenticeship with Hans Orth. After spending two very happy years in Sarona, Christian pursued his love of gardening overseas by working in Nurseries in Fellbach and Degerloch in Wuerttemberg and a Florist Shop in Frankfurt, Germany. He also made time to visit friends and relatives in Dornstetten and parts of Switzerland.

While Christian was in Germany his brother Wilhelm wrote to him and offered to pay for him to attend the Christian Endeavour World Convention in London in 1926. Christian tells how this experience and the fellowship of so many like-minded Christian young people from around the world, left a deep and lasting impression on him.

In autumn 1926, at the age of twenty two, Christian returned to Palestine. With the encouragement of his father, he started his own small nursery on land in Haifa, some of which he rented and some he bought. As the business grew he acquired ten hectares of land, three kilometres north of Acre. Christian's nurseries became legendary for the quality and variety of roses he cultivated. In the flowering season he employed up to eight Arab workers and grew 10 000 rose bushes and many thousands of carnations, in addition to vegetables and fruit trees. When they were in season, he gave away bunches of roses and flower arrangements to the local hospitals and to his regular customers, who were mainly English clients. This generous gesture was not only greeted with great delight but also helped to spread the good name of the Stoll Nursery far and wide.

On the 8th July 1930, Christian married Christel Appinger in the Lutheran Church of Haifa. Pastor von Oertzen officiated. Christel was the daughter of Gottlieb and Katherine Appinger (nee Unger), who were both born in Palestine during the founding years of the Temple Society.

Christian & Christel Wedding 1930

Christian and Christel had two children: Herta born in 1931 and Walter in 1933. Immediately after their marriage they lived in the home of Jakob and Anna with the rest of the Stoll family. Eventually they built their own two storey home at their Nursery in Haifa, at the corner of *Garten Strasse* (now Haganim St) and King George Ave (now Hameginim Boulevard) in about 1934.

While all the Stolls held membership with the Temple Society, Christian was the first in the family to officially resign from the Templers and to join the Lutheran Church. Christian credits the Carmel Mission with the influence that brought him to an assurance of personal salvation. Specifically it was the meetings at the Mission House on Mount Carmel and at which either Pastor Schneider or Herr Heinrici led the Bible study, which cultivated his spiritual interest and nourished his Christian life. Christian Stoll also broke with both Templer and Lutheran tradition when he asked to be baptised in the Kishon River as an adult, by immersion[2].

One feature that was common to all the houses where my Uncle Christian and Aunty Christel resided, whether in Palestine, Germany or Australia, was their 'out of this world' gardens. Their home, both inside and out, was a four season kaleidoscope of living colour and texture; pots and pans dripping with flowers and plants of every variety, all lovingly tended and addressed by their unpronounceable botanic names. Their front-of-house gardens were like outstretched arms bidding a warm embrace to all who came to visit them; a powerful symbol of their lives and of their love for family and friends.

Christian's life remains a testimony for our generation that the Bible can be trusted and that its truth will guide us into making wise choices in life: in our work, career, families and spiritual destiny. He studied Hebrew and was a keen student of Bible prophecies. On many an occasion, my brother, sisters, cousins and I would sit with him to explore what the Bible said about the end times.

Martin Meinel

My father, Martin Gottfried Meinel, was the youngest of six children, born in 1904 to Ernst Wolfgang Meinel (1865-1942) and Amalie Ida Werner (1866-1940), of Schneeberg, Saxony.

Schneeberg was a mining town in a scenic mountain range called *Erzgebirge* (mountain containing ore) in the north-east of Germany. Ernst (my grandfather) was a professional musician. His musical talents were evident from his early childhood and his parents nurtured him to become a violinist. They made sure that young Ernst did not become a miner or farmer. He was not allowed to use a hammer lest an injury to one of his fingers should stop him from playing the violin or ruin his promising musical career. The eldest son, Walter, died in the First World War. The next son, Max, followed in his father's footsteps. He could play many musical instruments and became a director of music in the Lutheran Church in Schneeberg. The three other sons, Erich, Rudolph and Martin, became bakers. The only girl in the family was Martha.

Back Row: Martin, Rudolph, Martha, Max, Erich
Front Row: Ida & Ernst Meinel

Martin did his apprenticeship as a baker with his older brothers (Rudolph in Schneeberg and Erich in Wittgendorf) between 1922 and 1926. He also gained valuable experience in Berlin and in Wuerttemberg in the bakery of Gottlieb Weiss in Bad Liebenzell. Although he only stayed for 3 months, Martin loved Bad Liebenzell. He spoke with great enthusiasm of this beautiful place in the Black Forest, the Christian fellowship he enjoyed there and the teaching he received at this branch of the China Inland Mission. He remained grateful for his association with his colleague and mentor, Gottlieb Weiss, and the opportunity of getting to know Wilhelm Heinsen and other staff members of the Liebenzeller Mission.

Martin's parents became Christians in their adult years: Ida through the preaching of Martin Seitz, and Ernst through the godly influence of his wife. They attended the *St Wolfgangskirche* Lutheran Church in Schneeberg. At the same time, Martin's mother developed close ties with the *Bruedergemeinschaft* (the Fellowship of Christian Brethren). She knew Blaich and Seitz and was a supporter of the Carmel Mission in Palestine. One of its directors, Martin Philipp Schneider, came from Saxony. It was her connection with these Christian leaders and organisations that enticed Martin to Wuerttemberg during 1924.

Martin spoke often about the prayerfulness of his mother and the godly influence her life had on her family and the community. Ida became a founding member of the *Frauen Missions Gebetbund*, a women's prayer meeting for missions in Schneeberg. This prayer group is still in existence to this day and has provided prayer and financial assistance to many missionaries and mission organisations around the world. My sister, Helga, a missionary in Africa and the Middle East, has been a beneficiary of their love and sacrificial giving for some fifty years.

Ernst Meinel supported his family by playing and teaching the violin. A major part of his income was derived from performing in hotels and bars. Ida was deeply saddened that her husband had to spend so many nights playing in what she called the *"devil's den"*. She pleaded with God to bring about a change. She prayed for years but nothing seemed to change.

One night, Ernst, then in his early fifties, came home in the early hours of the morning, put his violin in the corner of the bed room and said to Ida, *"I have just played my last gig in the pub!"* He never went back. Ida was overjoyed that God had answered her prayer. Then the reality hit her. How were they going to live? Ernst was not a handyman. He had never worked in the mines like the majority of men in Schneeberg! But, they found a way. Ernst continued to teach music to his limited number of pupils and he installed a weaving machine in the loft of his house. Together, he and Ida began to learn the art of weaving, making bobbin lace, tapestry and rugs for sale.

There are two more significant influences for which I remain indebted to my Meinel forbears from Schneeberg. Sadly it is not something that I was able to experience firsthand. I never did meet my Grandmother Ida and I only met Grandfather Ernst very briefly, just days before he died; he was 77 and I was 4. But, my dad spoke glowingly of a parental home filled with warmth, love and affection overflowing with the sound of beautiful music. The Meinel home, and village life, reflected the rich culture and customs for which Schneeberg remains a favourite tourist destination today: mining, regional folk art and the *Weihnachtsland* (Christmas Land).

Making Music at Home – Dad 2nd from right

Imagine family and friends squeezing into the family lounge room. Uncle Max takes his seat at the piano. *Opa* (grandfather Ernst) tucks the violin under his chin, another player leans over his cello, bow drawn, while others raise their wind instruments to their lips. The music flows and the rest of the family and friends listen with rapt attention or join in song from their repertoire of German Lieder and hymns. Needless to say, the music that our father taught us to listen to came from the same classical composers his father and family enjoyed: Bach, Handel, Mozart, Beethoven, Hayden and Schubert.

Schneeberg is best known for its Christmas tradition. In the Erzgebirge this is intrinsically linked with centuries of mining, wood carving and turning and making bobbin lace. The first snowflakes descending from the sky evoke that 'Christmas feeling'.

When the first weekend of Advent is near everyone begins to rummage in chests and cupboards and display their treasures which have often been gathered over many generations. Angels, miners and nutcrackers have their rightful place. The candle arch and the illuminated stars in the windows shine brightly into the night. The whole family work together to assemble the pyramid, or the Christmas 'mountain', and to decorate the Christmas tree. The smoking man is finally smoking his pipe again, imbuing the air with incense. Miners and bands, dressed in their ceremonial costumes, march through the narrow streets. An evening walk around one of the many Christmas markets captivates this unique atmosphere of togetherness and hospitality[3].

From a young age, all of the Meinel family were participants in the presentation of the miners' cantata: *Glueck Auf!* (God speed!). On the stroke of midnight on Christmas Eve, the choir and brass band enthusiastically sang and played from the lofty heights of the spire of the St Wolfgangskirche to usher in Christmas day, followed by the church service.

My dad would sing those songs and relive this Erzgebirge Christmas all of his life, whether in Palestine, Germany or Australia. It was not until late into our adult lives – when my siblings were able to visit Schneeberg during Christmas – that we could understand and appreciate his passion for this unique cultural tradition.

Schneeberg Christmas Market

Miners Church Parade

Back in Haifa, Wilhelm Stoll was making plans for the future of the family bakery. In 1926 he placed an advertisement for a baker in the Christian Endeavour publication in Germany. Martin, being young and adventurous, applied and became the successful applicant. He took up his new position in 1927, at the age of 23.

Many years later Martin asked Wilhelm how and why he chose him for the job. Wilhelm told Martin that his was the last of over thirty written applications he had received. With tongue in cheek he said, "Rather than study each one in detail, I picked you on the basis of the scripture, *"Those who are last shall be first!"* I am not sure whether Martin understood this brand of 'Swabian' humour at the time but I do know that Wilhelm was an astute business person who did his homework thoroughly. He would have prayed about it and consulted his good friends Heinsen and Weiss in Bad Liebenzell, to confirm Martin's trade skills, his character and most of all, his Christian credentials. Wilhelm must have been satisfied with what he learnt about Martin.

Martin, Wilhelm and Jakob enjoyed a wonderful partnership working together in the bakery for many years. In 1934, just prior to his marriage to Maria, Martin returned to Zittau in Germany for seven months to complete his apprenticeship, and to gain further training and experience in the latest baking trends and skills before Wilhelm handed the Stoll bakery over to him.

Martin spent eight happy years as a bachelor in Palestine. He was energetic, full of life, fun and adventure. His extensive photo collection shows him front and centre in photos in and around the bakery and the many Biblical destinations all over Palestine. When I and my sister Helga visited the Schumacher Institute of the University of Haifa on Mount Carmel in 2008 and introduced ourselves as the children of Martin Meinel, the researcher responded with a broad smile, *"Martin Meinel? I know him!"* She opened up one of her research folders and pointed to our father in dozens of photos in her collection.

Behind this zest for life, Martin had a deep personal relationship with Jesus Christ as his Lord and Saviour. He had dedicated his life to honouring and serving God in his work and missions. He always spoke with great affection of his mother. She led by example and took her children to Church and Sunday school. She introduced them to *"Die Stunde"* (The Meeting Hour) for Bible study and encouraged them to attend the Christian Endeavour meetings and conferences in Germany. She also encouraged them to support missionary organisations who were involved in world evangelisation.

When Martin and Maria married in 1935, they were determined to do it on God's terms. Before they even considered marriage they wanted to make sure that they shared similar convictions about what was most important to them in life. They wanted to follow God's counsel and took note of what the Bible taught. *"Do two people walk hand in hand if they aren't going to the same place?"* (Amos 3:3, The Message). They came from families with similar backgrounds in faith, work, values and interests, which certainly put them on an equal playing field. They were determined to follow God's instruction, *"Do not be yoked together with unbelievers"* (2 Corinthians 6:14). To them the most important ingredient in marriage was to be one hundred percent united in their faith.

There was, however, one aspect of their relationship in which they differed. When Martin arrived in Haifa he was a German among Germans, a Christian among fellow believers, a baker among his peers, but he was a lonely Saxon among a crowd of Swabians! He came to Palestine from the middle-east of Germany. The Stolls came from the south-west of Germany. Martin brought with him the dialect, culture and customs of Saxony, which were so different to those of the Stoll family from Wuerttemberg.

This not only created bemusing banter and friendly rivalry – akin to the colloquialism often seen between South Australians and Victorians – but also the occasional irritation and frustration. Adjustments had to be made to reconcile the forthright, 'no nonsense' demeanour of Maria Stoll, with the more emotionally sensitive personality of Martin Meinel who came from a home where love and affection was expressed much more warmly and openly.

The Fabulous 1920s and 30s

It took a few years for the German settlers in Palestine to recover from the loss and consequences of the 1st World War. So much had changed. German nationalism had been dealt a severe blow. The Germans in Palestine felt the stigma of a defeated nation. The Turkish rule had come to an end and the new regime of the British Mandate was in its infancy. The population of the country was increasing rapidly, mainly because of the large number of Jewish immigrants. The German settlers, now reduced in number, went on with the business of rebuilding their lives, homes and enterprises. But the land of Palestine was on the move. Everywhere there were signs of a new awakening.

In its effort to bring European principles of order to the administration of Palestine, the British Mandate Government made fundamental changes in the political, judicial and economic spheres within a few short years. They extended the school system; encouraged construction work; created a useful network of roads and railways; built electric power installations; and promoted agriculture as well as crafts, trade and industry. Economic development was also accelerated by the enormous financial resources that were made available by the large number of Jews pouring into the country[1].

The German settlers, after the initial set back, quickly adjusted to these new circumstances. There was an increasing demand for their agricultural produce and their skills of crafts and industry. The quality of their work in the various occupations was a decisive factor in the success of their enterprises and formed the basis of many successful business dealings with Jews, Muslims and the British. This in return enabled their settlements to enjoy renewed growth and prosperity.

Templers established new business premises, factories and farming properties, and were able to buy more land and to extend their orange orchards. In December 1925, a total of 1324 Templers lived in Palestine. They owned 321 residential buildings and 176 other buildings, as well as 2397 ha of fields, vineyards, orchards, forests, gardens and building sites. Of those gainfully employed 54 were farmers, 174 tradesmen, industrialists and engineers, 55 business men, 18 teachers, 13 civil servants and 7 independent professionals, including 2 doctors.[2]

Jakob Stoll and family also benefited from these good economic times. Jakob was pleased and thankful to God that he had the means to support his children as they started to commence their adult lives, careers and marriages. He made generous extensions to the family home that provided much needed space for his expanding family.

The home also provided the setting for the friendships, engagements and marriages of his children and the arrival of the first grandchildren. At one time, Wilhelm and Tine, Hulda, Christian and Christel and Maria and Martin, all lived together with Jakob and Maria in this house in Hospital Strasse: an extended family of nine adults and four grandchildren.

Street front of the Stoll Family Home 1930s

Back of Family Home - Bakery 1930s

The home extended endless hospitality to friends and strangers. The pastors from the Lutheran Church – von Oertzen and Berg; the missionaries and evangelists from the Carmel Mission – Schneider and Heinrici; from the Liebenzeller Mission – Heinsen, and travelling friends from Germany, were all welcomed in the Stoll home. The English soldiers came for the regular Sunday evening hymn singing, and the children to whom my mother was nanny, and their English parents, were regular visitors and joined in with the family activities.

Haifa Mission House & Library

By the 1930s, the Stolls all worshiped in the Lutheran Church and became actively engaged in its work and ministry. They sang in the Church choir, taught in Sunday school and were involved in outreach to the poor and needy. The Carmel Mission now also owned a house and library in the Colony of Haifa under the care of Mr Heinrich Heinrici. They started a school for Arab children and through them made contact with many poor and needy families. Twice a week between 200 and 500 people stood in line up to two hours waiting patiently for a free meal. While they were waiting, one of the mission staff would share a message or read to them from the Bible. In addition to their involvement with the Carmel Mission, they prayerfully and financially supported a number of other missionary organisations overseas, including the Liebenzeller Mission and the Pilgrim's Mission, St Chrischona.

These were exciting times. The Stoll siblings were part of a close knit circle of friends, all singles in their mid-twenties to early thirties, and they enjoyed life to its full. They travelled extensively through the Holy Land and drew great inspiration from seeing and experiencing the many historic sights of the Bible. The advent of the car and bus made these places more accessible as they explored the upper regions of the Jordan River, walked the shores of the Sea of Galilee, climbed the heights of Mount Tabor, visited the ruins of Caesarea, swam in the Dead Sea and walked the streets of old Jerusalem. In their travels they visited many of the Christian welfare organisations supported by their Church and learned about their work. Among them were the Syrian Orphanage in Tiberius, the Leprosy mission in Jerusalem, and

Talitha Cumi – a mission school for Arabic girls run by the Lutheran deaconesses in Jerusalem.

When Margaret and I did our tour of Israel in 2008 we stood in the same places my parents stood. We recognised them from the photos my father had taken some eighty years earlier. We had a taste of what they enjoyed and gained a new perspective of what it meant to them. We came as overseas tourists; they lived here for twenty years of their adult lives. No wonder they remained so enthusiastic and described that short period of their lives in Palestine as 'the fabulous years'.

By 1935, the Stoll children, except Hulda, were married and they all forged ahead with their own independent careers. Wilhelm, with his young family, had moved into the top floor of our grandparents' new home in *Garten Strasse* and was well established in his various business interests. They had 5 children: Ruth (1930), Wilhelm (1931), Theodor (1932), Gerhard (1935) and Siegfried (1937).

Hulda lived on the lower floor, to care for her parents in their retired years.

Christian Stoll House

Christian and his family occupied his new home just a few houses further down the road, in *Garten Strasse*, from where he managed a successful nursery and florist business. They had two children: Herta (1931) and Walter (1933).

My parents lived in the old family home, in *Hospital Strasse*, (now Me'ir St) with dad in charge of the busy Stoll bakery, which he now leased from Jakob and Wilhelm Stoll. In our family there were 4 children: Werner (1936), Herbert (1938), Helga (1939) and Ingeborg. Inge was born in Germany after the war, in 1948. My mother had a governess/nurse, Hedwig, and Arab employees worked in the bakery and garden.

What was life like for this generation of the Stoll and Meinel families in Haifa? Regrettably as I was just 23 months old when we had to leave Haifa, I have no first hand memories of the family home and the bakery, but my older cousins do. Wilhelm (Bill) Stoll, the second oldest grandchild, has left a wonderful description of what he remembers about life in the family home, the bakery and Haifa in general.

Dad with Werner & Camels at the Bakery

"It was a wonderful time all around. As a child, one felt secure. The family was reasonably well off. The home was a fascinating place for growing and curious children, with all that was going on in the adjoining bakery. There were its many goodies and snacks, its carts, delivery horses and bikes with baskets; friendly Arab bakers and workers; delicious smells, chocolate Easter eggs; a garden at the back; a gravel driveway in front to the shop door, and almost unceasing activity. Then there were the Sunday walks up to Mount Carmel; coach rides to the German agricultural settlement of Waldheim; teasing and having fun with Uncle Martin Meinel; sitting on my father's knees listening to Bible stories, and having formal lessons in Arabic taught by my mother".[3]

My own insights come largely from my parents' word of mouth accounts, and the excellent photographic records of the family. There are pictures of dad with the Arab workers in front of the bakery oven; of my brother and me standing with dad in front of the bakery shop; Werner, Helga and me on the front steps of our house; horses, donkeys and carts in the bakery courtyard; family pictures with Mum, Dad, Grandfather and Grandmother, and the whole extended family.

But the winds of change were once again about to sweep over the German settlers in Palestine. And, this time, with consequences of more catastrophic proportions.

Dad, Herbert & Werner

Donkey with Bread Basket
Dad, Werner & Mum

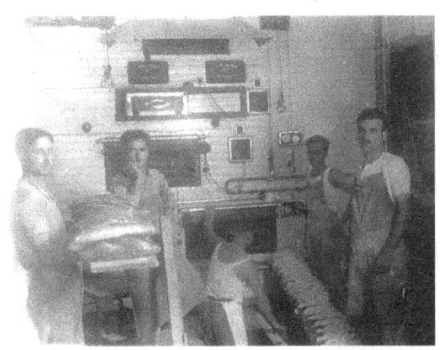

Bakery Oven, Dad with
Arab Workers

The Extended Stoll Family

The Winds of Change

During the difficult post World War I years of reconstruction between 1920 and 1925, good relationships between the German settlers and the British administrative authorities had been established. This improved further with careful cultivation on both sides and lasted until the outbreak of the Second World War.

"The German settlers are a valuable part of the population of Palestine and are appreciated as such".[1]

These words by the British High Commissioner for Palestine are high praise for the presence, efforts and achievements of the German Community. In their annual reports the British District Commissioners often commented very favourably on the conduct and the economic achievements of the German settlers[1]. In recognition of this fact, the High Commissioner appointed Templers to the Agricultural Board and the Harbour Board of Haifa.

The Germans were also on good terms with the indigenous Arab population and the Jews, often going beyond mere business contacts. Numerous Arabs and Jews were employed in German enterprises, or were representatives of German firms. Jakob Stoll and family enjoyed wonderful relationships with the Arab bakers and workers they employed. They made every effort to include them in their family gatherings, such as weddings and other special family events. Arabic was the predominant local language. My mother loved it and spoke it fluently. She always spoke affectionately and enthusiastically about the beauty and richness of the Arabic language.

Friendly co-existence and mutual co-operation with the minority Jewish population was also a hallmark of the early 1900s. Many of the construction and infrastructure projects undertaken by the Jews were designed and constructed by the architects, engineers and builders of the German colonists. This co-operation was also seen across many agricultural projects. The Waldheim experience is one of many.

In the late 1920s, many new Jewish settlements were established in the plain of Jezreel. The German farmers from Waldheim were invited to visit these nearby settlements where they discussed the latest European agricultural machinery and practices. At the end of the day they enjoyed Jewish hospitality. As these Jews were mostly from Poland or Russia and spoke Yiddish, the German settlers could understand them and converse with them freely. On Saturdays, these young Jewish settlers returned by droves to the Waldheim colony and observed the work practices of German farmers there. Much friendly dialogue was continued over *Kaffee und Kuchen* (coffee and cake). In later years the friendly relationships cooled before they eventually ceased altogether[2].

The Jewish population of Palestine was constantly increasing in size, economic importance and cultural influence, and it is true to say that the German settlers became increasingly dependent on them. The coexistence of Jews and Christians over many years had given rise to many close and friendly ties. On both sides there were, of course, also business rivalries, conflicts of interest and personal differences. But these hardly surfaced, as the Germans were an insignificantly small minority compared to the Jews or the Arabs.

The Germans had achieved a disproportionate importance only because of their high qualifications in the intellectual, technical and economic fields. In any case, remaining on good terms with the Jews was necessary for the survival of the Templers, as well as that of the other Germans in Palestine. They were at home in Palestine and, in order to retain this home for themselves and their children, they had to respect the laws and customs of that land and observe its interest. Certainly they had no occasion for anti-Semitic behaviour in the daily dealings with Jewish neighbours, friends, business partners and employees[3].

On the other hand, the tensions and conflict between the Jews and Arabs did spill over into the day to day life of some of the German colonists. The early Arab riots of 1920 and 1929 developed into bloody confrontation between 1936 and 1939 and exposed some of the German settlers to uninvited danger.

On the 8th July 1938 my Uncle, Christian Stoll, was returning by car from his nursery in Akko (Acre) with his five-year-old son, Walter. As they approached Haifa they drove headlong into a riot. Just a few minutes before their arrival a bomb had exploded in the Arab market. In an instant, Christian's car was surrounded by an enraged, rock-throwing mob of fanatical Arabs, bent on taking revenge on any Jew they could find, or his property.

Shots were fired, the car windshield smashed and Christian, cradling his young son Walter protectively in his arms, was struck on his forehead by a rock as he tried to disembark from the car. As he saw the rioters bear down upon him, barely conscious and bleeding profusely, he called out, "*I am German, not a Jew!*"

An Arab rioter recognised Christian, placed his huge body in a protective mode in front of him and with arms raised above his head yelled at the top of his voice, "*Leave this man alone, he is German!*"

His fellow rioters withdrew instantly and Christian was ushered into the nearby police station. When he was given first aid treatment a young Arab policeman asked, "*Who did this to you?*" To which Christian replied, "*Your brothers!*".

On hearing this, the policeman offered a heartfelt apology and asked, "*How can I be of service to you?*"

Christian, his shirt drenched and stained with blood, politely suggested, "*A clean shirt would be nice*". The young man disappeared and after a few minutes returned with a freshly ironed shirt, which Christian gladly accepted. Christian made a good recovery, grateful to God for sparing his life and that of his son. Others on that day were less fortunate. The Jewish driver travelling just in front of Christian's car was shot through the head and an estimated thirty others lost their lives on that tragic day[4].

In general the Arabs were well disposed towards the Germans in Palestine but, by the late 1930s, any person with European dress was regarded by the Arabs as a Jew. Christian Stoll recorded that the only safe way for Germans to mix with the Arab population was to wear an Arab head scarf.

Wilhelm Stoll became the victim of such a mistaken identity. He was travelling home from his vegetable garden in Acre by car - a little later than usual, near dusk. The next morning on returning to work, his Arab workers approached him in agitated distress.

"Last night," they said, "you were an inch away from becoming a child of death".

They told him how they left work the previous night and hid behind bushes, intending to fire at any Jewish vehicle that came along the road. The only reason he was not dead was because they recognised Wilhelm's car at the very last minute. To ensure that their hands remained clean of his blood they made him strap a vegetable crate to the roof of his car as identification[4].

The rise of the National Socialists (NSDP) in Germany, in 1933, was greeted by the majority of Templers in Palestine with enthusiasm equal to that of their countrymen living in the Reich itself. They hoped and wished for a national resurgence under Hitler's regime, which would enhance Germany's reputation in the world, increasing its cultural and economic influence on other nations, and thus strengthening their own position as a small national minority group in a foreign country.

As ardent patriots, although with a very incomplete picture of the internal conditions of Germany, they were understandably attracted to Hitler's idea of an ethnic community, as this idea fitted in with their own perception. The promise of peace by the Fuehrer and his oft repeated, loudly proclaimed profession of a 'positive Christianity' were eagerly welcomed by them. However, apart from a small minority, they had little interest in anti-Semitism which the Nazi regime had central to its ideology.

Nevertheless, the NSDP gained a number of members from the ranks of the settlers who had retained their German citizenship. In August 1939, the proportion of party members among the German population in Palestine was about 17%. It was good that the settlers were successful in preventing non-resident Germans from gaining a controlling influence in the local Palestine branches of the NSDP, as there was a danger that their anti-Semitic attitude would provoke the Jews, or that their taking sides in the Jewish-Arabic conflict would threaten the country's peace. In hindsight, it is easy to make the accusation that the settlers, especially those who were party members, were not only blind towards National Socialism but also derived profit from it. The settlers obviously did not expect a war, despite the tensions steadily increasing since 1938[5].

The Stoll/Meinel families did not join the NSDP. Nevertheless, they cherished their homeland and were enthusiastic about the national resurgence of Germany after the First World War. There was great jubilation among all Germans when the airship *Graf Zeppelin* flew over Jerusalem in 1929 and Haifa in 1931. To welcome the airship and celebrate the occasion they had written in large letters on the ground, *Hoch Zeppelin* (long live Zeppelin).

But, slowly, the Stolls started to hear reports from within Christian circles in Germany about Hitler's regime and his treatment of the Jews. They learned in disbelief about the boycott of Jewish shops and businesses in 1933. They were horrified to hear mixed reports of the targeted destruction and vandalism of Jewish synagogues and shops in 1938 (*Kristallnacht*). Later, history would record that 7500 businesses were destroyed, 267 synagogues burned and 91 Jews killed, on that night[6].

The Stoll/Meinel families were now alarmed. It became clear to them that such anti-Semitic actions by the Hitler regime could only bring national disaster to Germany and its people. That conviction was based on their understanding of the Bible and, in particular, the promise that God had given to the founding fathers of the nation of Israel: *"I will bless those who bless you and whosoever curses you I will curse"*. (Genesis 12:3)

The goodwill so carefully cultivated with the Jews in earlier decades was now dissipating rapidly. Personal and business relationships began to suffer as more and more Jews labelled all Germans as Nazis and Arab collaborators. A number of Jews remained loyal customers of Wilhelm and Christian Stoll and my father Martin, despite threats by their fellow Jews not to do business with Nazis. When Wilhelm delivered a load of vegetables to one of his Jewish customers, a Jewish neighbour poured petrol over the produce. As he walked away he barked at his fellow Jew, *"There! Now go and do business with the Germans!"*[7]

The British Mandate administration found it increasingly difficult to maintain stability during the Jewish/Arabic conflict. They struggled to manage the immigration of the huge numbers of displaced Jews from Europe and Arabic countries. In 1939 they issued the 'White Paper', limiting Jewish immigration to 15 000 per year and stopping it thereafter. The British pursued this immigration ban with a vengeance. The Zionist organisations brought illegal immigration from Europe but the British would not let them enter Palestine. Boatloads of Jewish immigrants escaping Nazi persecution were caught and the immigrants interned in various destinations. One of those was Atlit, located on the coast some thirty kilometres south of Haifa. It was built by the British Army in the 1930s and saw more than 122 000 people (known as *Ma'apilim*, illegal immigrants) detained there between 1934 - 1948. Today the Atlit 'illegal' Detention Camp is a museum telling the story of the Jewish history of that time[8].

None of the Stoll/Meinel families living in the 1930s could ever have imagined that in just a few short years Atlit would become part of their history as well.

Behind Barbed Wire

"**R**eport *for departure at 6 pm!*"

This written order was placed into the hands of my father by a German war official, just two days prior to the outbreak of the Second World War in August 1939.

It was a sad day. Two family members – my Dad and Uncle Christian Stoll, both aged thirty five – together with all eligible men under the age of fifty, were conscripted into the German Army. Wilhelm Stoll was exempt on account of his First World War injuries. They had just a few short hours to pack their bags. *"We will be back in 3 to 4 weeks!"*[1] they shouted optimistically, as they waved their goodbyes to their young families.

From Haifa they travelled to Athens by boat and from there by train to Germany. After receiving his three months basic training my father's deployment for military action was delayed by seventeen months. During that time he was allowed to work in his profession, as a baker, in Aue and Ueberschlema in his home state of Saxony. Finally he was dispatched to the Russian front in April 1941.

Christian, who spoke good Arabic and English, first attended a course for interpreters at a language school in Potsdam in order to hone his Arabic language skills, before he was assigned to the Interpreters Corps and posted to the Arab Liberation Corps, destined for Bagdad, Iraq[1]. Germany by that time had entered the war in North Africa and had established diplomatic relationships with Iraq and by May 1941 had commenced arms shipments to the Iraqi army.

The German families in Palestine had been urged by Germany to leave the country just a few days prior to the outbreak of war. That advice came too late for most but some three hundred and fifty persons did manage to leave in the last days of August. The majority however decided to stay[2].

The British quickly took military control. Soon after the start of war they converted the four German agricultural settlements of Sarona and Wilhelma in the south, and Bethlehem and Waldheim in the north, into internment camps for German nationals. The Stolls, Meinels and a number of other Kirchler families, who had been living under house arrest in Haifa, were interned in Waldheim in December 1939. The Templer families went to the internment camp in Bethlehem. They were only allowed to take the bare necessities of their belongings with them. In Waldheim, the Stolls were among their friends and fellow Christians who found room for them in their homes and farms. Even though it meant living together in very cramped quarters, everyone found shelter and all remained thankful, despite the great distress and uncertainty of the time.

Werner, Herbert, Helga & Mum

Jakob and Maria Stoll and Tine with her 5 children ranging in age from two to ten, together with Hulda Stoll and the Cluss family, all moved into the Staib home. Wilhelm, who was initially interned in Acre, later joined them. Christel Stoll, Herta (8) and Walter (6) found accommodation with the Sus family. Lydia Sus (nee Appinger) was Christel's Aunty. Kaethe Weberruss (nee Appinger) with Elfriede (four months) also lived with them. My mother, Werner (three), Helga (six months) and I (twenty three months) found shelter with Gottfried Meyer and family. Gottfried cleaned out a room above the chicken shelter and this became our home for the next 3 years. My mother was very grateful to be taken in by this beloved Christian brother and former full time worker of the Carmel Mission.

All of the people with German citizenship living in Waldheim were declared 'Alien Subjects'. The British secured the whole village with a barbed wire fence and put the compound under the supervision of two English police sergeants and the Jewish auxiliary police, many of whom had grown up in Germany or Austria and spoke German. Most were friendly but not all. All internees were allowed to move freely around the compound and could continue to do their farm work but only within the confines of the compound. Initially the Arab workers had to move into quarters outside the fence and were not allowed into the village until after 1941. That meant the settlers had to do their own work in the farmyards, stables and the community dairy but they were allowed to supervise the Arab workers on their fields outside the camp provided they had a pass or were accompanied by a guard[3].

I have often wondered how our parents and grandparents felt when they were labelled 'Alien Subjects'. According to the dictionary that made them 'foreigners, not in harmony with the land or country'. By nationality they did belong to another country but their heart and soul belonged to this land. They and their ancestors had come to this land some seventy years before. They were pioneers who had established a Christian community and built contemporary homes and strong families. They turned barren wastelands into flourishing gardens and fostered industrial and rural development when such concepts were still in their infancy in Palestine.

How did my mother feel to be called a foreigner? She and all of the Stoll children were born here. This was their home. They knew no other. I never did ask them those questions. But I do know that reason and logic go out the window in times of war. War is no respecter of people, race or creed. They had no time to be philosophical or introspective. They were concerned with living, with surviving, taking care of their children and creating hope for a better future. They did this by instinct and with their unshakeable confidence that God was in control.

It did not take long for the internees to come to grips with this new order of community life. A school was organised in Bethlehem for all primary school aged children and teaching responsibilities were assigned to qualified adults. A small kindergarten was inaugurated for the preschool children in Waldheim, freeing more adults to help with the orderly running of this overcrowded community.

All hoped that the war would soon be over. Instead, the war in Europe was just beginning. Bad news led to more and one death followed another. The number reported missing or killed in action climbed higher with every passing day and few escaped the grief of a lost or missing family member. Elfriede's father was one of the early war casualties.

In the summer of 1941, when Hitler attacked the Soviet Union and General Rommel achieved great military success in North Africa, the British authorities moved most of the younger settler families out of Palestine to an internment camp in Cairo, Egypt[4]. Wilhelm Stoll and his family, and a number of other families from Waldheim, were among the 655 people expelled from Palestine, now classified as war refugees. From there they were put on board the *Queen Elizabeth*, which had been converted into a troop carrier for Australian soldiers destined for the war in North Africa. They sailed down the Red Sea to an unknown destination. On the 23rd August 1941, the *Queen Elizabeth* dropped anchor in Sydney Harbour. From 1941 to 1947 these Germans from Palestine were interned in a camp at Tatura in the State of Victoria, under the care of the Australian Government.

The 655 people transferred to Australia represented the majority of the Germans from Palestine. Those now left were a few men, too old for military service, the elderly, and women and children, including my Grandmother Maria (Jakob had died in 1940), Aunty Hulda, my Mother and Aunty Christel. They were allowed to stay in Waldheim for the time being. Living conditions and life generally now improved and the pre-war goodwill established between the Germans, the British and Jewish authorities resulted in more relaxed supervision and less restrictive control. In fact, life for most returned to a reasonably normal routine.

For me, Waldheim will always be special. It is the place where I spent three years of my childhood. My first and only memories of Palestine come from this time. Even though those memories are sketchy, they nevertheless formed a very significant part of my life and provided me with a very tangible link to the land of my birth. This land, which is Palestine to the Arabs, Eretz Israel to the Jews and the Holy Land to Christians, I am privileged to call the land of my birth and the home of the Stoll ancestry since 1889.

Main Street

Today I can still recall walking up and down the main street between the tall, green poplar trees. I remember playing on the wide verandah of our makeshift home, with the backdrop of the snow covered peak of Mount Hermon in the far distance, and listening to the menacing howls of the hyenas at night fall. For my brother and me, aged four and two, there were endless temptations to wander away from our mother's protective eye, to look for new adventures that this exciting farming community offered around every corner. There were birds and insects, donkeys, horses and cows, tractors and farming equipment, all waiting to be discovered and played with. Snakes and scorpions were plentiful but held no fear for the innocent.

When I spotted an insect-like creature, tail raised and scurrying across the floor boards of our veranda I began to chase it with wild enthusiasm. My excitement turned to tears when my mother snatched me away just as the creature was within my grasp. What I thought was a 'little birdie' turned out to be a deadly scorpion!

Gertrud Deininger was my kindergarten teacher during our stay in Waldheim. Some of our school activities spilled across into the Lutheran Church located directly opposite the kindergarten. In the middle of our boisterous play on the balcony of the Church, Gertrud hushed us into deathly silence after she spotted a snake sunbaking on one of the window sills inside the Church. The only way out of the Church was down a flight of stairs located within touching distance of the snake. Our instructions were to remain calm and tip toe past this dangerous reptile without making a sound.

Fortunately the snake decided to ignore us all and we escaped to safety. What I remember most about this incident is a sense of adventure and heroism for outwitting the snake. It certainly did not leave me with a life crippling fear of the creatures.

My most vivid memory of Waldheim is a ride in the milk truck. The milk truck had replaced the horse-drawn wagon for carting milk from Waldheim to Haifa. Driven by our spirit of exploration, Werner and I had wandered down to the co-operative milk dairy located at the other end of the village. As we stood there admiring the truck, the driver offered us a ride back to the town centre, no doubt wondering what these young boys were doing here on their own. We hopped into the back of the truck and made ourselves comfortable among the huge milk cans. The trouble was, the driver forgot to let us off at the agreed destination and drove out through the secured gates of the barbed wire enclosure and on to the next village on his way to Haifa, 25 kilometres away.

Werner soon realized that something was amiss but there was no way we could alert the driver to our dilemma. The small window of the driver's cabin was out of our reach and our knocking on the truck wall was drowned out by the noise of the engine. Our banging, kicking and screaming soon turned to panic and tears. Then, suddenly, the truck screeched to a halt. Apparently the absent-minded driver woke from his dreaming and remembered that his precious human cargo was still on board. Full of apologies, he turned around and delivered us back to Waldheim into the waiting arms of our very relieved mother.

Waldheim Lutheran Church

Among my childhood memories of Waldheim there are also the images, ever so faint, of just a few adult personalities. Gottfried Meyer, our host, was a very kind and caring person. He tells the story of my captivation with the harvesting machine and how he had to use his best diversionary tactics to keep me away from the dangers of this equipment while in full operation.

Pastor von OertzenGertrud Deininger 1943

Pastor von Oertzen looked more like an ancient patriarch but behind that white hair and long flowing beard was a very approachable man who was totally devoted to his church family.

I remember, most clearly, Gertrud Deininger, my kindergarten teacher. We maintained contact with her when we all lived in Germany. She and her husband became full time Christian workers in Germany, and then returned to the Middle East as leaders in the Carmel Mission when it was relocated to Lebanon after the war.

Then there was Frau Frieda Unger. While I have no direct memories of her, her name was often spoken of in our family for her incredible hospitality. Any visitor to Waldheim, whether business people, missionaries, officials or tourists would be offered the best of her home cooking from *Kueche und Keller* (kitchen and cellar).

For some reason, I have no vivid memories of my interaction with my grandparents while we were all in Waldheim, other than viewing the coffin when my grandfather was buried.

Later, many of the residents from Waldheim came to settle in the Barossa Valley in Australia. I was able to get to know them more personally, including the Unger, Weigold and Weinmann families. I went to High School in Nuriootpa with their children.

Grandfather Jakob died on 11 April 1940, aged 76 and Grandmother Maria on 29 September 1945, aged 77. Both were buried in the German Cemetery in Waldheim. In the 1970s the remains from the graves of the Bethlehem and Waldheim cemeteries were relocated to a mass grave in the German Cemetery in Haifa.

Jakob & Maria Stoll Graves in Waldheim 1945   Relocated Mass Grave in Haifa 2008

We left Waldheim in late 1942 but the German history of this wonderful agricultural village was to continue for several more years yet.

The Exchange

As early as 1940 negotiations to release German Nationals held in internment camps in Palestine in exchange for displaced Jews in concentration camps in Germany were conducted by the British Mandate through the US Embassy in Berlin. On the 10th December 1941 the first contingent of sixty two women and children left Palestine for Germany.

My mother, who had applied to return to Germany, was advised in late September 1942 that she was in the next group of 110 women, 99 children and 8 men in the exchange programme. On the 2nd October 1942, my mother with her three children, aged six, four and two said goodbye to Waldheim.

I remember waiting for the bus to arrive. Our earthly possessions consisted of what we could carry as hand luggage: two suitcases and a small backpack for each of the children. Among the group leaving Waldheim were my Aunty Christel Stoll with her children Herta and Walter, Kaethe Webberuss with Elfriede, and Gertrud Deininger. The only Germans remaining in Waldheim were a few younger families with sick children, some widows and the men who were too old for military service, together with their wives. Aunty Hulda Stoll stayed to look after her mother, now in her seventies, as well as some members of the Deininger families and the Meyer family who held Swiss citizenship.

The bus took us to Atlit on the shores of the Mediterranean Sea some thirty kilometres south of Haifa. Our stay in this transition camp was intended for only a few days but, due to some unexpected delays in the exchange negotiations, we remained there for four weeks. Atlit had been purpose built by the British for so-called illegal Jewish immigrants who were fleeing war torn Europe and were looking for a new home in Eretz Israel. Now it also became a camp for us Germans who were being displaced from our home in Palestine and on our way to making a new start in troubled Europe.

The Atlit Camp 1942

I remember Atlit as a cold and wet place. The women and children were accommodated in one set of barracks and the men in another. Rows of slab beds were cramped into each long barrack, with barely enough room to store the suitcases out of which we lived. The detainees found extra space by suspending their clothing, washing and other personal belongings from the roof rafters.

Lice infestation, dysentery and other gastric illnesses were rampant, and rest and sleep were hard to find with so many children, including myself, being sick and crying. When bed bugs were discovered the women went to work and scrubbed the barrack from top to bottom. Never before had so much disinfectant liquid been consumed on the barracks for cleaning!

Every adult was required to help with the cooking and serving of food in the camp kitchen[1]. I also remember the excitement rush when my brother and I watched in awe as a giant tornado like water spout roared across the sea right in front of our eyes.

Finally, with injections and all paper work completed, we left Atlit by bus on the 5th November 1942, bound for Germany. It proved to be a most eventful journey.

At Affule in the Jezreel Plain, and under the tightest police control, we boarded the train and travelled north towards Damascus, with periodic stops for meals served by the British military along the way[2]. The train also stopped for toilet breaks in the open country. This was not to my mother's liking and she made sure to be the last to disembark from the train. Werner, Helga and I watched in horror as the train started to move with our mother still stranded on the embankment outside. Our screams alerted other passengers and the English soldiers, and a chorus of frantic voices cried out, "*Stop the train! Stop the train!*" But still the train kept rolling with our mother scrambling to catch it.

By now the three of us were shedding uncontrollable tears, terrified at the thought of our mother being left behind. It took a super human effort for my mother to scramble after the train before she reached the strong clasp of the outstretched hands of the soldiers hanging off the steps of the train. Totally exhausted, in great distress, and propped up by a hefty soldier, she staggered towards us. Oh, it felt so good to feel her comforting embrace again.

The train ride in war conditions was risky. It travelled very slowly and during the night a full black-out was strictly enforced. We were tightly cramped inside one of the compartments with other passengers. A British soldier stood guard at the door.

In the middle of the night my mother woke, startled to find Werner's head bathed in perspiration. Alarmed, she alerted the soldier to the plight of her sick boy.

When he lit a candle, she discovered in horror that what she thought was sweat was in fact blood pouring from a wound on Werner's head. My mother quickly assessed the situation and realized that the soldier's rifle had accidentally slipped from his grasp and struck Werner on the head. A very protective mother gave the frightened soldier a piece of her mind in fluent English and demanded that her boy get immediate medical attention. When this was not forthcoming to her satisfaction she insisted in a no uncertain manner that the train be stopped and a doctor be found to attend to him. The train was stopped, a doctor was found and Werner was patched up to the satisfaction of a very relieved mother.

Our next stop was Aleppo, in present day Syria, where the Orient Express was waiting and we were transferred from British to Turkish authorities.

The official exchange between displaced Jews from concentration camps and national Germans took place at *Haida Pascha*, the Istanbul railway station. There was no official ceremony, no fanfare, just two trains parked on different platforms at a railway station in the middle of the night, travelling in opposite directions. My mother, together with the rest of the German group on the train, had little or no knowledge of the plight of the passengers on the other train, and the suffering and persecution they were fleeing from.

On that train was a young Jewish boy, named Henry, and his mother. Henry lived with his parents in the Netherlands when the Nazis took control of their country. His father was taken away and they never heard from him or saw him again. For months Henry and his mother had been able to remain in hiding but eventually they were hunted down by the Nazis and taken to Bergen Belsen concentration camp. There they became part of the program to free Jews in concentration camps in Germany, in exchange for German Templers held in captivity by the British in Palestine. Henry arrived safely in Eretz Israel with his mother in 1942 and they were present at the birth of the Nation of Israel in 1948. Later Henry migrated to America where he pursued a successful professional career[3].

Another young lady on that train vividly recalls the day when, as a teenager in Bergen Belsen, her name was listed on the exchange program. Now aged 87 and living in Israel, she passionately declares, *"I thank the Templers for saving my life!"*

At the time, the Germans from Palestine did not know of the existence of a concentration camp in Bergen Belsen. Bergen Belsen was a Prisoner of War camp near Hannover in Germany. Initially it was built as Stalag XI-C, partly for French and Belgian and, later, Russian prisoners of war, and partly as a Jewish transit camp. It was designed for 10 000 prisoners but eventually held up to 60 000. Conditions were good by concentration camp standards and, initially, prisoners were not subjected to forced labour. But by 1943 it was operating as a fully-fledged concentration camp. Although it contained no gas chambers, some 35 000 prisoners died there of hunger, cold or disease. It was the first concentration camp to be liberated by the Western Allies on the 15th April 1945. Today it is known that very few exchanges were in fact made, except for the 500 Jews that were part of the Templer exchange and some 1500 Hungarian Jews to Switzerland[4].

After crossing the *Bosphorus*, (Istanbul Strait) our train journey continued through the Balkans. While travelling through Greece we noticed increasing numbers of children along the railway tracks with hands outstretched, hungry and begging for food. Some of the passengers on the train wrapped pieces of bread from their own war rations into small paper parcels and threw them out of the train window. I can still see the smiling faces of children as a parcel fell within their grasp.

At Istanbul, Sofia and Belgrade railway stations we were warmly welcomed by the local German communities. There, each family received a small gift from these complete strangers: a parcel containing tooth brushes, hazelnuts and other useful things. We were surprised and bewildered by these expressions of kindness until we learned that there was no prospect of obtaining such essentials in Germany, our chosen destination[5].

On the 14th November 1942, the train arrived in Vienna. We were given a celebratory reception in the town hall, two nights of accommodation in a hotel and during the day we were shown the sights of Vienna. My mother decided to take us to the Vienna Zoo.

Our nine day train journey from Palestine to Austria had been safely completed. Palestine and over sixty years of Stoll history lay behind. My mother, with her three small children clutching to her side in the streets of

Vienna, now stood at the threshold of another chapter of her life. What lay ahead for them in their national homeland of Germany, a nation in the middle of the Second World War?

Before I answer that question I need to record a little about the last few years of the Stoll dynasty in Palestine, from 1942 to 1948.

The End of the Templer Settlements in Palestine

The few Germans left behind in the four internment camps of Sarona, Wilhelma, Bethlehem and Waldheim tried as best they could to keep the agricultural enterprises going. They were able to do so with the help of so-called 'illegals' – Germans, Italians and Hungarians – all of whom had been interned in the camps, and the Arab workers previously trained and employed by the German settlers. After the war, in 1945, the internment ceased but the four camps remained enclosed in order to protect the settlers from the Jewish extremists. Following the atrocities committed by the Nazi regime towards the Jews in Europe during the war, they wanted to attack all that was German with *"fire and the sword"* [1].

Just a handful of mainly older German settlers still remained in Waldheim. Aunty Hulda was living in the Staib house with the Aimann family of five and Mr & Mrs Wurster, a couple aged eighty four and eighty five, for whom aunty Hulda was caring following the death of her own parents in 1940 and 1945. The house was located just inside the secured gate leading to Bethlehem in Galilee.

The Zionist organisations wanted to evict all German citizens from the Jewish Homeland as early as 1945. But it was not until 1947 that an agreement was reached by Great Britain, the Mandate Government of Palestine, and Australia, allowing the remaining Germans in Palestine to travel to Australia to join their relatives there. This scheme also provided for the liquidation of the settlers' properties in Palestine and the transfer of the proceeds to Australia to cover resettlement costs[2]. However, before this agreement could be carried out, open war broke out between the Jews and Arabs just before the end of the British Mandate and the founding of the State of Israel.

War came to Waldheim with a vengeance. On 17th April 1948, the Jewish military (Haganah), equipped with automatic rifles and machine-gun-mounted armoured vehicles, completely surrounded Waldheim and at 4 am they opened fire on the village.

The first casualty was Mrs Katharina Deininger, aged 67. She was seriously wounded from a shot to her head while she was milking the cows in her milk shed. When the gun fire started, the Arab sentry at the Bethlehem gate supposedly returned fire. The Jews assumed the shot came from the Staib house, which adjoined the gate. They stormed the house and shot Mr & Mrs Aimann dead, at point blank range, in front of their three children aged nine, four and three.

On hearing the shooting Aunty Hulda ran into the kitchen only to be confronted by the point of the gun of the soldiers standing over the bleeding corpses. With typical Stoll determination she demanded to know what was going on. She ordered the oldest Aimann boy to get a drink of water for his father who appeared to be still alive. The gunman refused her request. She looked him straight in the eye and said, *"Surely you are not thinking of killing me too, a defenceless old woman? (She was fifty one years old)."* She bellowed, *"Go and get a doctor!"*

Her life was spared and she, together with all the women in the village, was herded into the co-operative dairy where they spent the rest of the day and night. The men were also rounded up, interrogated and locked up in the British Mandate barracks built in Waldheim in the early 1940s. The injured Mrs Deininger was eventually taken to a hospital in Nazareth and survived[3].

On the next day, everybody was given just twenty minutes to return to their homes to pack whatever essential personal belongings they could carry. They found their houses in a sorry state, thoroughly ransacked with the best of their belongings stolen or vandalised. Aunty Hulda not only had to pack her own things but also assist in packing for the Aimann children and Mr & Mrs Wurster.

On the 18th April 1948, the English military escorted the Waldheim residents by trucks to a military camp near Acre. The English treated the Germans well. They gave them basic necessities of food and hygiene and took them to the military cinema that evening for a film show. After the horror and trauma of the last 24 hours this proved to be a pleasant diversion[3].

From Acre they were taken by boat under British protection to the temporary refugee camp of "Golden Sands" in Famagusta, on the island of Cyprus[3].

'Golden Sands' Refuge Camp

In January 1949 Aunty Hulda was transported from Cyprus to Australia where she joined her brother Wilhelm Stoll and family, who had paid for her fare. For the next 27 years she lived with her brother and family. Her last 13 years, until her death in 1989, she spent in the Tanunda Lutheran Home.

I was ten years old when news of the Waldheim shooting reached us in Germany and I distinctly remember how proud I was to have such a brave aunty. I couldn't wait to meet her.

At the time of the founding of the State of Israel on 14th May 1948, there were still about fifty Germans within its borders. These later left their old home of Palestine; some voluntarily, while others were evicted by the Israeli authorities. The Regional Council of the Temple Society in Australia recorded the end of the Temple Society in Palestine with the following words:

"Thus, about 80 years after the founding of the first settlements and 63 years after the death of the founder of the Temple Society, Christoph Hoffmann, the highly successful settlement project of the Wuerttemberg Templers in the Holy Land which had been carried out with such admirable religious fervour and personal commitment, came to an end".[4]

"But the forced abandonment of the Templer settlements in Palestine was not the end of the Temple Society. It merely led to a new phase in the history of this small religious community. Not only in Germany, but particularly in Australia, the Temple Society developed new spiritual life. The two widely separated regions of Germany and Australia were united under one leadership, as had formerly been the custom between Germany and Palestine. In 1962, there were 1300 Templers in Australia. In Germany there were 750, including those who had always lived there."[5]

While living in Palestine there were religious differences among the German colonies. The last phase however – the deportation and loss of home and the life's work of three generations – was the lot of all German colonists. There was no difference between the Templers and the Kirchlers; all shared the same destiny. Together they experienced the final and most devastating episode of their time in Palestine. The grandparents came as one to the land and now their children and grandchildren left the land as one[6]. The spiritual allegiance of the Stoll/Meinel families living in Australia and Germany remained with the Lutheran Church, but they maintained very close ties with their many friends in the Temple Society in both Germany and Australia.

For many years the German settlers received no compensation whatever, with the exception of the Sarona settlement which had been sold by the British Mandate Government to the city of Tel Aviv in 1947. (Ben Gurion, the first Prime Minister of Israel, made his headquarters in one of the houses of the Sarona settlement.) Not until 1st June 1962 was an agreement reached between the Federal Republic of Germany and the Israeli Government, whereby Israel committed itself to pay DM 54 million compensation to the Germans from Palestine. This was far below the commercial value of the German property seized by the State of Israel according to the independent valuers. However, more favourable terms of settlement could not be secured and Israel finally fulfilled its obligation by the end of 1963, after an earlier advance payment of DM 22.8 million during the years 1956 to 1961. The Israeli payments were set off against the reparations which the Federal Republic of Germany paid to the State of Israel for the assimilation and rehabilitation of the half million survivors of Nazi persecution. Thus, twenty years after the end of the Second World War, the dispossessed or their heirs received a partial financial compensation for the property they had lost in Palestine[7].

My grandparents, Jakob and Maria Stoll, lived to the ages of seventy six and seventy seven. They toiled for some fifty six years in this ancient land of the Bible. Befittingly, their bodies were laid to rest in the soil of their adopted country, first in Waldheim and later in the mass grave in the cemetery of the German Colony of Haifa.

By 1943, the four children of Jakob Stoll, aged between thirty nine and forty six, with their spouses and ten children, all born and raised in the Stoll home and bakery in Haifa, found themselves dispersed from their homeland as war refugees or prisoners of war in four different continents of the world:

- Wilhelm Stoll, his wife Tine and their five children: Internment Camp, Victoria, Australia.
- Hulda Stoll: Internment Camp, Waldheim, Palestine.
- Maria Meinel and her three children: war refugees, Germany.
- Martin Meinel: POW, USA.
- Christel Stoll and her two children: war-refugees, Germany.
- Christian Stoll: POW, USA.

They had lost or left behind their homes, businesses and personal possessions in Palestine. Now they faced an uncertain future, separated from one another by huge distances, with no guarantee of being reunited in the foreseeable future, if ever.

What did the end of the German settlements in Haifa mean to those families? How did they cope in the face of such loss and human tragedy? It would be unrealistic to pretend that these circumstances did not take a heavy toll on the physical, mental and emotional stamina of each and every adult member of the Stoll/Meinel families. But as a child, and later as an adult, I never saw any bitterness or heard a harsh complaint from my parents about their loss and forced expulsion from Palestine.

Underpinning their remarkable attitude was their faith in a sovereign and faithful God. It remained unshakeable. They understood and experienced the truth of God's promise chiselled in stone above the Stoll bakery doorway: "Great peace have they who love your law, nothing can make them stumble".

It was their testimony that God had led them to Palestine to serve him through the Christian community in Haifa. In the process God had blessed them both spiritually and materially. They did it out of love for all that Christ did for them in giving them eternal life through his death and resurrection. Whatever had been accomplished was by God's grace and for his glory alone. The hymn, *Nun Danket Alle Gott*, (Now Thank We All Our God), was a genuine expression of their gratitude to God.

> Now thank we all our God, with heart and hands and voices.
> Who wondrous things hath done; in whom his world rejoices.
> Who, from our mother's arms, hath blest us on our way,
> With countless gifts of love and still is ours today.
>
> O may this bounteous God through all our life be near us,
> With ever joyful hearts and blessed peace to cheer us.
> And keep us in his grace, and guide us when perplexed,
> And free us from all ills, in this world and the next.
>
> All praise and thanks to God the Father now be given.
> The Son and Him who reigns with them in highest heaven,
> The one eternal God Whom heaven and earth adore,
> For thus it was, is now and shall be evermore. [8]

The Bigger Picture

So far the main subject of this book has been the story of the Stoll/Meinel family in the context of the settlements by the Wuerttemberg Templers in Palestine, between the years 1848 and 1948. As amazing as this story is, it was to be completely overshadowed by other events that transpired during those same one hundred years in the same land. When the German settlers came to Palestine their numbers barely exceeded two thousand. This chapter tells the story of other peoples who came from around the world by the hundreds of thousands to find a new home and resurrect a nation.

The Birth of a Nation

The question of who has the right to make the land of Palestine their national home has been hotly debated over many centuries. Jews, Muslims and Christians have all argued their case, made claims and fought wars to secure a stake in this very special piece of real estate in the Middle East.

In this section of the book I have drawn from the writings of Randall Price's book, *Fast Facts of the Middle East,* which deals with the biblical basis and historical facts relating to this issue, from the conservative theological perspective.

The Jews as well as many Christians believe that the land of Palestine belongs to the Jews. Both groups base this on the record of the Bible, which states that God established a covenant with Abraham in 2100 BC and with the three generations succeeding him. The covenant was specifically established with Isaac and Jacob, and not with Ishmael, Isaac's half-brother. On this basis the Abrahamic covenant and the land promise contained within it (Genesis 15:18-21) is exclusive to the Jewish people as the sole descendants of Isaac[1].

This promise, in turn, was selectively passed on to Isaac's son Jacob (who was renamed Israel), rather than to his son, Esau (Genesis 28:13-15, 35:12). Moreover, the Abrahamic covenant was unilateral and unconditional, which means its fulfilment depends upon God, not man. Even Israel's sin and their dispersion from the land cannot keep the promise of God's own covenant from being fulfilled in the 'last days'. It will be at this time that the full territorial aspects of the Abrahamic covenant will be fulfilled[1].

According to the Bible (Genesis 17:8 and Deuteronomy 4:40) Israel's possession of the land was not meant for a limited period, ended by sin, as Muslims understand the Koran to teach; or by spiritual substitution, with Israel being replaced by the Christian Church, as some Christians interpret certain statements in the New Testament; but forever[1].

The Jewish people claim an uninterrupted settlement in the land from the time of Joshua around 1406 BC. *"Despite a forced exile of the northern kingdom by the Assyrians (721 BC) and another forced exile of the southern kingdom by the Babylonians (605-596 BC), a remnant of the Jewish people returned to the Land to re-establish their national existence. The Romans ended Jewish rule, yet Jews continued to live in parts of the Land under pagan Roman rule (AD 135-391) and the Roman Byzantine Christian rule (AD 391-636). Islam invaded the Land in AD 638 but many Jewish communities remained resident and lived under Muslim rule up until the creation of the modern State of Israel."*[1]

Muslims do not agree with this interpretation of history. *"They accept only that which is preserved in the Qur'an. They regard the Jews as having forfeited their chosen status and right to the land through sin, and the Jewish Torah (and the New Testament of the Christians, which agrees with the Abrahamic account in the Jewish Torah,) has having been lost and corrupted"*[2]. From the Muslim viewpoint, the land is desecrated by infidels and must be cleansed by blasting Israel off the map, or pushing Israel into the sea. They do not believe Israel has any right to exist and therefore do not acknowledge her existence or legitimacy[3].

In the 1870s and 1880s anti-Semitism was rife in Russia and pogroms (organised attacks) on the Jewish communities threatened their existence and demanded a safe refuge for the preservation of the Jewish people. This gave rise to Zionism: a secular, political movement, to defend the rights of Jews. Theodor Herzl reasoned that the refuge for the Jewish people should be in a Jewish State where Jews could defend and preserve their national existence.

And so a trickle of Jews began to arrive in Palestine to join the small population of Jews that had resided there since antiquity. Soon the immigration came in waves. The first '*Aliyah*' (Hebrew: 'to go up') between 1880 and 1890 brought some 20 000 Jews and the second '*Aliyah*' (1900-1914) settled approximately 40 000 more. In that time, the Jews commenced some eighteen agricultural settlements (*kibbutz*).[4] Randell notes:

"Most of the land, especially that developed by the Kibbutz movement, was purchased by the Jewish National Fund (later to be owned by the government of Israel). As a result of these operations the wealth of the land increased and the Jews (and Arabs) prospered. For example, the higher standard of living more than doubled the per-capita income of the Arabs in Palestine and improved health standards decreased the rate of Arab infant mortality (from 19.6% in 1922 to 14% in 1939)"[5].

In 1917, the British Government offered the Zionist movement the Balfour Declaration, which expressed official recognition of the right of the Jewish people to establish a national home in Palestine. After the First World War, this agreement was implemented and ratified by fifty two Governments of the League of Nations. Thus the former Ottoman Empire was divided among the European powers, leaving the Jews and Arabs of Palestine under the British Mandatory Government. Under the Balfour declaration, the whole area on both sides of the Jordan river was destined to be the Jewish national home, but in 1922 Britain redivided the land and gave 77% of the mandate to the Arabs as Transjordan (today's Jordan).[6]

The Arabs considered Jewish immigration as a threat to their culture and commenced planned opposition to Zionism as a movement. With the re-awakening of the Arab nation and the growing Jewish efforts at rebuilding the ancient monarchy of Israel on a large scale, conflict was inevitable.

After the First World War, immigration remained the controversial issue that inflamed the conflict between Arabs and Jews. Randall notes that,

"The 1922 census records 643 000 Arabs and 84 000 Jews living in Palestine. Between the two world wars 588 000 more Arabs and 470 000 more Jews made their way to Palestine. The Arab population increased 120% between the creation of Transjordan in 1922 and the United Nations decision to partition the land in 1947".[7]

The majority of the Jewish influx of migrants was the result of anti-Semitism and Hitler's holocaust. *"By 1936 the Jews comprised 29% of the population, held 5.5% of the land area west of the Jordan and only 11% of the area was defined as arable. ...A British Commission in 1936 determined that the claim by the Arab authorities of a shortage of land in Palestine was in fact 'due less to the amount of land acquired by Jews than the increase in the Arab population".*[8]

Between the two world wars the Arabs launched four major riots against the Jews over a shortage of land with fighting breaking out in 1920, 1929 and 1936 to 1939.

On 29th November 1947, the General Assembly of the United Nations voted thirty three to thirteen to set up both Jewish and Arab states in Palestine.

However, the Jews had settled throughout the land and their developments and higher standards of living had attracted large numbers of Arabs to Jewish cities. Segregation of the two peoples was therefore impossible. *"In the end, the Jewish State ended up having a slightly greater Arab population than Jewish (509 780 Arabs to 499 020 Jews), while the Arab State with 749 101 Arabs had only 9 520 Jews. Furthermore, 60% of the land given to the Jewish State was comprised of barren Negev desert. Moreover, the city of Jerusalem, which stood at the centre of the conflict, would belong to neither state, but become an 'international zone' with a population of more than 100 000 in the midst of an Arab state."*[9]

The Jews accepted the plan but the Arabs not only rejected the plan but immediately attacked Jewish settlements in every part of Palestine.

Statehood came by an independent Israeli declaration on the 14th May 1948 and an Israeli victory in a war with the Arabs. International recognition followed with the admission of Israel to the United Nations in 1949, as well as by most nations of the world since.

Almost 50 years after Theodor Herzl had predicted that a Jewish State would exist, his vision became a reality.

Conservative theologians see Israel's miraculous resurrection as a return to the land in unbelief in preparation for the climatic events of the last days and the consummating confrontation with the Messiah. To Jewish minds, it is an entirely different matter. Nonreligious Zionists consider it the fulfilment of their dream to forge a national Jewish homeland in the historical and cultural land of ancient Jewry – a place where Jewish will, dedication, and ingenuity made Theodor Herzl's words a reality: *"If you will it, it is no dream."*[10]

While Israel has now been restored nationally, her existence is under constant threat. She has had to defend her right to exist under international law and has had to fight for the land that has been recognized as hers, for her survival. A day is coming when Israel will be restored spiritually, and when the gloom from Gentile oppression and occupation will end and peace will reign supreme[11]. The Bible talks of a time, yet to come, when the Saviour of the world, Jesus Christ, will come a second time to set up his kingdom and when he will reign on David's throne in Jerusalem for a thousand years. In that day all Israel will *"look to the one they have pierced"* (Zechariah 12:10). They will call on their Messiah and he will forgive their sin, heal their land and *"the Lord will be King over the whole earth"* (Zechariah 14:9).

Today (2012) there are some 5.8 million Jews living in Israel (about 1/3rd of the Jewish world population) but no members of the Temple Society or their spiritual communities. Only the remnants of their original towns and infrastructure, designated of heritage significance, remain.

It is food for thought to observe the return of the Jewish people from their dispersion from around the world to the land of Palestine and their rise to nationhood and, on the other hand, to witness the demise of the German Templers who had answered the call to come to the Holy Land to extend the kingdom of God. After their establishment of highly successful settlements with such admirable religious fervour and personal commitment, they found themselves exiled from the land of Israel and dispersed to Australia and Germany.

Before leaving this chapter I want to include commentary from two other groups of people that lived in Palestine in the first half of the 20th century. I found it helpful, in the context of this discussion, to gain their perspective on how they saw the role and influence of the Templer settlements in Palestine. Their writings were penned before the advent of the Second World War.

Protestant Church Perspective

The first Perspective is from Wilhelm Heinsen, a Bible college lecturer at the Liebenzeller Mission Society in Germany (the German Branch of the China Inland Mission) in the 1930s. Through his travels in the Holy Land and his friendship with Wilhelm Stoll he had an intimate understanding of the teaching of the Bible as well as the Templer history and their settlements in Palestine. In an article *"Die Jerusalemsfreunde"* (Friends of Jerusalem) Heinsen recorded his views about the Templers drive to go to the Holy Land, their beliefs and achievements.

Heinsen writes that in the mid-1800s there was an urgent call among the Pietist movement in Wuerttemberg, Germany, to prepare for the return of Christ, when He would come a second time to set up his kingdom on earth. The appalling social conditions in Germany, the revolutionary political movement of the 1840s and the anti-Christian culture of those modern times, encouraged the emergence of 'enlightened' thinking and new philosophies and ideas were common. Heinsen notes that Christoph Hoffmann, grew up in this environment.[12]

A famine in 1853 and the Crimean war between Russia and Turkey, drew European attention to the Middle East and strengthened the thought in Hoffmann that the establishment of the earthly kingdom of God in Palestine would have to begin.[12]

Hoffmann raised the question about the rightful ownership of Jerusalem and the Holy Land. For a long time (some 1300 years) it had been in Muslim hands. Was it now the time for Turkish rule in Palestine to come to an end? No one had more right to inherit any ungoverned Palestinian territory than the 'People of God' (*Das Volk Gottes*). But such people did not yet live in Palestine in large numbers and so the idea was conceived by Hoffmann among the 'Friends of Jerusalem' in Germany to gather God's people in Jerusalem. From this group of people the Temple Society was formed. Their goal was to start a new world order: that which was prophesied by the Old Testament prophets and founded through Jesus Christ, the establishment of God's kingdom on earth.[12].

In Hoffmann's opinion, the official church of his day was not qualified or fit to establish God's kingdom on earth, so he issued a new call to all true believers to fulfil this God-ordained task to settle in the Holy Land in preparation for the return of Christ[12].

Hoffmann's teaching during the 1850s did not gain wide acceptance in Wuerttemberg. Instead it led to outright rejection and opposition from the State Lutheran Church and, significantly, ultimately also from the Pietist movement which strongly contended that the fulfilment of the Old Testament prophecies to gather God's people in Jerusalem specifically applies to Jews and the Jewish nation. In England and France he failed to recruit leaders for his cause and, at the World Evangelical Alliance conference in Paris in 1855, he found no endorsement.[12]

In fact, a movement among sections of prominent Christians and Politicians in England was gaining momentum at the same time advocating the restoration of the Jewish people to their ancient homeland in Palestine, in contrast to Hoffmann's goal of populating Palestine with multitudes of Christians.

Heinsen notes that from small beginnings and much pioneering hardship the settlements grew and prospered. He describes in glowing terms the beautiful gardens of the German settlements and their economic prowess The First World War was a huge set-back to the numerical and economic growth of the Templers in Palestine but they regathered and persevered.[12]

The individual German settlers did not lack spiritual zeal or genuine devotion to God but its leaders and the organisation as a whole, were plagued with controversy over their spiritual beliefs and practices from its inception. Men like Hardegg, Seitz and Blaich, who formed part of the early Templer movement, identified the spiritual issues, as they saw it that led to the split in the Temple Society soon after their arrival in Palestine.

Christian leaders outside the Templer movement have also expressed their opinions why the Temple Society was not more effective in achieving their spiritual goals.

Pastor Eitel Von Rabenau was one of them. He was a pastor from the Jerusalem Society officiating in the Lutheran Churches in Palestine in the 1930s. In his publication *The German Settlements in Palestine* Rabenau wrote the following in relation to the theological and spiritual development of the Temple Society:

"Pietism was replaced with Rationalism, but not by the usual way of secularisation but significantly under the motto, 'Seek ye first the kingdom of God'. Hoffmann thought he had found in the concept of God's kingdom on earth, the supreme and all embracing idea. From this point of view, his intellect dealt with external and internal political development. He imagined, that the concept of gathering God's people in Palestine, would be beneficial to the circumstances in the Orient. The acceptance of this idea and the execution of it, with all ones strength, seemed for him the pinnacle of all devotion. For Hoffmann the kingdom of God is an idea, an ideal, which man has to turn into reality. It is the ideal of community life, in which all functions

– not only the dogma and pastoral care, but also education, judicial power, the function of doctors, serve the realisation of the moral good, therefore the law of God. Just as in the Old Testament the teacher was at the same time judge and physician, so within the people of God, a pastoral governing power should be at work, encompassing all functions. He therefore wanted to establish an Old Testament theocracy. But the defining criterion was for humans themselves to establish it. For him the seeking of God's kingdom consisted in the indefatigable labour towards the goal to create improved conditions."[13]

Von Rabenau notes that for Hoffmann the sacrificial death of Christ and his resurrection was not central in his teachings. He could not accept that sinful man was incapable of achieving anything of eternal value in his own strength. Instead, he saw Christ as an example to be followed and that it was through humanity's effort that the world, society and governments would become a better place.[13]

Von Rabenau wrote:

"The root cause of the deviation of Hoffmann from that which in the Bible is the kingdom of God, is a misconception of sin. Out of this deficiency, a different dogma of Christ and the road to salvation was developed by him. But the road that Hoffmann took was an error and was revealed as such. All human endeavours cannot establish the Kingdom of God on earth. Only Christ, the Saviour himself, through his word and through his spirit in a community which is receptive to his will in humility and devotion, can accomplish that." [13]

Secular Jewish perspective

The second perspective comes from Professor Alex Carmel (1931 - 2002), one of the foremost scholars on the history of the Templers in Palestine. He is a German Jew from the University of Haifa.

In his book *'Die Siedlungen der wuerttembergischen Templer in Palestina 1868-1918* (The Settlements by the Templers from Wuerttemberg in

Palestine 1868-1918) he records in great detail the history of the German settlers in Palestine.

On the question of land ownership Carmel states that Hoffmann was in no doubt as to who had the right to ownership of the Holy Land. In the early 1840s he had published an article stating that, *"the Holy Land belonged solely and exclusively to the people of God"*. Hoffmann argued that while it was God's original purpose to deed the land to Israel, Israel had forfeited their right to regain the land of their forefathers when they rejected Jesus as the Messiah and the Saviour of the world.[14]

I interrupt Carmel's commentary here to observe that many church fathers throughout history have held a similar view. Today it exists under a number of different names, including Replacement Theology, which is defined as follows:

"God chose the Jewish people after the fall of Adam in order to prepare the world for the coming of Jesus Christ. However, the special role of the Jewish people came to an end. Its place was taken by the Church, the New Jerusalem."[15]

Carmel notes when the Templers established their first pioneering colonies, the question whether the land belonged to the people of God or the people of Israel was not an issue, as both Christians and Jews were an equally insignificant minority among the majority Arab population. This began to change with the arrival of more and more Jews in the 1880s and the progress in land and infrastructure development that followed. When Theodor Herzl founded the Zionist organisation in 1897, and the movement to establish Palestine as the homeland for the Jews gained significant impetus, the Templers were forced to re-examine their belief relating to the rightful ownership of the land.[14]

For the first time they had to face the possibility that what Hoffmann had preached fifty years earlier – the Holy Land filled to overflowing with the people of God – could be wrong. It was the Jews, not the people of God, who began to flood the country from around the world. It happened right before their eyes. The statistics were undeniable. Before the First World War there were some 85 000 Jews in the land, while the Templer population struggled to reach 2000. The Templers' expectation of a great and influential Christian spiritual presence in the land of Palestine was severely dented. Some began to wonder whether they had any future at all in this, their chosen land.[14]

Tensions between the German settlers and the early Jewish migrants started to surface. Each considered the other as an intruder on their patch of real estate. Dialogue between the Templer leaders, the Jewish press and intellectuals became at times antagonistic. A spirit of anti-Semitism and unhealthy rivalry was fostered through some confrontational public dialogue and debate. Nevertheless, relationships between the majority of the Templers and Jews remained cordial.[14]

Fritz Keller, the German Vice Consul of Haifa, unashamedly declared his welcome to the returning Jews. On one occasion he felt it necessary to write to the Zionist movement in Palestine to assure them that not all of the German settlers were in agreement with the anti-Semitic sentiments promoted from time to time through *Die Warte* (The Sentinel), the official publication of the Templers. When the Zionist official, Dr Ruppin, came to visit Keller at his home on Mount Carmel in the early 1900s, he admired the beautiful gardens, trees and parks and how Keller had turned the barren heights of Mount Carmel into a garden paradise.[14]

Keller's response?

"We Germans have done all of this for our friends, the Jews, who have been promised a return to this land."

Keller's words found their fulfilment some fifty years later, when the State of Israel took possession of all German properties.[14]

In time, all the Templers had to accept the reality of the return of the Jews to their ancient land and they also accepted their presence. They learned to co-exist and co-operate with each other. Instead of being seen as a threat to the German settlers, the Jewish resurgence in the land proved to be their economic windfall.[14]

Carmel is very generous in his praise of what the Templers accomplished and lists in detail their achievements in agriculture, construction, business, transport, hospitality and tourism and the contribution of the many professionals that worked as doctors, nurses, architects, engineer, merchants and archaeologists. He readily acknowledges that the successful pioneering work of the Templers encouraged many Jews to return to Zion, in that they proved that settlement by Europeans was possible. [14]

But he remains outspoken in his conviction that,

"When Christoph Hoffmann died (in 1885) his original teaching about the 'Gathering of God's people in Jerusalem' died with him. The effort by Hoffmann since 1845 to secure religious, social and political reform, remains a dismal failure. His teaching did not gain acceptance around the world. There was no trace of the millions and tens of millions of God's people in the land as envisioned by Hoffmann."[16]

Professor Carmel concludes that despite the Templers' many economic achievements, their success in terms of the original goals was minimal.

"The drive for a better world order had to take second place to their survival in the hostile land under a hot Mediterranean sun. The world did not become a better place; redemption of the local people did not eventuate; the first Christian attempt since the crusaders to settle and control the Holy Land was a failure and when the land was eventually transformed from its barren state it was primarily through the efforts of the Jews. Their growth and influence as the so-called people of God, the Temple Society, was non-existent. They did not reach out to Arabs or Jews but expected that they come to them. What the Templers could not achieve through the 'gathering of God's people in Jerusalem', tens of thousands of Jews from all around the world, did"[17]

The Bigger Picture

As I have reflected on our family history in Palestine I see another picture.

A bigger picture! It is not so much about what man has achieved, or failed to achieve, but what God has done and is doing.

Throughout all of these events God has been working out his divine purposes. A belief that God had no plans for the Jews and their land beyond the time of Christ did not stop the return of the Jews and the creation of the State of Israel in their ancient homeland. Likewise, a theology of rationalism did not stop God from fulfilling his promise to build the kingdom of God, His Church, in Palestine and around the world. (Matthew 16:18). God has been building His Church ever since the time of the Apostles by the hundreds of millions of people that have put their faith in Jesus Christ – it is the church universal, past and present.

Jakob Stoll and Wilhelm Mader, together with many of the founding settlers of the Temple Society, believed that God had brought them to the Holy Land for the purpose of extending God's kingdom. Yes, they believed that one day in the future the Messiah would return to this earth to rule and reign from Jerusalem, but in the meantime they would dedicate their lives to share God's good news of salvation with the local population in obedience to Christ's command. (Matth 28:18-20). They did this by word and action: through building close relationships with the local population and the outreach ministries of their church and mission organisations. God used them to bring hope and salvation to people in Palestine and they considered this an honour and privilege.

At age twenty four, in 1889, my grandfather Jakob Stoll could not have imagined in his wildest dreams what lay ahead of him when he left Dornstetten in the Black Forest, in answer to God's call, to help build God's kingdom in Palestine. Nor could he have foreseen the part he was to play in pioneering the Carmel Mission in Haifa when he started to work for the Vice Consul, Fritz Keller, and the positive influence this organisation had on the local population. He would be overjoyed to know that the zeal he and his uncle Johannes had for world evangelisation, was perpetuated through his children and grandchildren.

All of our grandparents' eleven grandchildren have been actively involved in extending God's kingdom by sharing the good news of the gospel. They travelled thousands of miles to many continents of the world and lived and worked with hundreds of indigenous people in diverse countries, including The Gambia and Liberia, Papua New Guinea, Indonesia, Jordan, Syria, Mongolia and Central Australia. Some went as full-time missionaries, pastors and nurses, others as educators, tradesmen, trainers and as friends and helpers. In Australia, Switzerland and North America they worked as volunteers in churches, para-church and missionary organisations, serving God to reach out to all classes of people, from the poor and needy to business and professional men and women, and political and civic leaders.

Right now, Christians and Jews from around the world continue to pray for the peace of Jerusalem. Despite the undeniable weight of evidence relating to the fulfilment of Bible prophecy, so much detail about the future of Israel still remains a puzzle. But when the final piece of the jigsaw puzzle is put in place, the big picture will be complete. The Bible foretells that Jesus, the Messiah, will rule the world from Jerusalem with justice and righteousness. The Jewish temple will be the centre of worship of the one true God. Israel will be the head of the nations. Peace will reign.

Then the expectation of Hoffmann and the Templers, for the spiritual, social and political renewal of God's kingdom on earth, will be realized.

Section III.

The Land of My Youth
(1942-1952)

Zell u Aichelberg 1960

White Christmas

"*Come along boys! It's time to go Christmas tree hunting!*"

The voice of our father beckoned Werner and me to leave the cosy warmth of the living room in search of a brand new adventure.

We put on our warmest winter clothes, slipped on our gloves, donned our beanies and followed our father in great excitement out of the house. We were greeted with the charm and beauty of an amazing winter fairyland. Our first experience of snow! A thick blanket of snow gracefully covered roof tops, streets and meadows. Pillows of pure white snowflakes perched precariously on the tips of tree branches and fence posts, and here and there beautifully sculptured icicles hung glittering from the extremities of roof gutters and fountain spouts. Pure winter wonderland magic! But for us boys, the snow was an invitation for winter fun and games, building snowmen and throwing snow balls. And what fun we had!

The place was Schneeberg, Saxony, in the mid-east of Germany and the time, December 1942. My mother with her children, Werner (6), Herbert (4) and Helga (3) had just arrived as war refugees from Palestine. Grandpa (*Opa*) Ernst Meinel had warmly invited us to make the Meinel ancestral home our home for as long as we needed shelter in Saxony. My mother was eternally grateful for this wonderful provision while she pursued opportunities for a more permanent home base in Wuerttemberg.

View of Schneeberg

The Meinel Family Home, 2nd on left

News from our father at the war front had been scarce. He left Palestine on 31 July 1939, when he was enlisted in the German Army, but was not called up for active military service until 3rd April 1941. His first assignment was with troops of the ill-fated push into Russia. He returned to Germany for a short period of leave in 1942, and was then dispatched to North Africa in early 1943. He remained active in the Rommel Corps until their defeat in May 1943.

My uncle Christian Stoll was also sent to the Russian front, en route to Bagdad as part of the 'Arab Liberation Corps'. When he received news in Stalino in the Ukraine, that his wife and children had safely arrived in Germany from Palestine in November 1942, he immediately applied for a leave pass to visit them for a few days in Coswig near Dresden. On his return from leave he was surprised to find that his company had been directed to withdraw from Russia to Greece and now they were on their way to Italy from where they were to join the war in North Africa. In North Africa he was part of a team that screened and trained Arabs who had volunteered to join the German Army in the war against the Allied forces. Independently and unbeknown to each other, Martin and Christian now both found themselves serving in the war in North Africa.

One has to ask, *"Would Martin and Christian have survived the war had they returned to the Russian Front? What would have been their fate had they been transferred to the equally volatile Western Front?"* Instead, they landed in North Africa in the closing stages of that war after the heaviest fighting was already over. Martin and Christian considered their move to Africa in 1942/3 as divine intervention. The Wehrmacht (German Army) obviously felt that Martin's and Christian's Mediterranean origins and experience would be a better fit in North Africa than Russia. After all, they spoke the language and understood the unique culture and the temperament of the predominant Arab population of that region of the Middle East.

During 1942 and 43 the other members of the Stoll clan were getting accustomed to their status as civilian internees in Australia and Palestine. Uncle Bill and Aunty Tine and their five children, together with some 800 people of German and Italian nationality, were living behind barbed wire in Tatura, Victoria in Australia. Aunty Hulda and Grandma Maria remained interned in Waldheim, Palestine. All keenly felt the separation from one another and their dispersion to distant countries. Would there be a time when they would see each other again?

Dad – first on left

On the 3rd Dec. 1942 my mother rushed to answer the knock at the front door of the Meinel home in Schneeberg. To her utter surprise the person that greeted her was her husband, our father, cutting a dashing figure in his German army uniform. The date was 3 December 1942.

What a surprise! What excitement! Surely, this was the best imaginable Christmas present for everyone. My mother had not seen or embraced her husband since they were so suddenly separated from one another in Haifa some three years and four months before. It was also a great delight for Opa Meinel. A long seven years had passed since his youngest child, Martin, had come to visit Schneeberg.

For us children the reunion was a little less euphoric. Hiding behind our mother's apron, we peeped at this stranger with a great deal of curiosity. After all I was just eighteen months old when he was taken away from us by the war. I had no recollection of a father figure in my life, even though mother had been tireless in keeping his memory alive. She had talked often about him, praying for him, regularly showing us his photo and proudly displaying his image on the mantel piece. For me, getting to know my Dad was a challenge in its own right.

Mum and Dad were so happy. They revelled in each other's company and every day of the twenty two days of Dad's leave was filled with deep and meaningful conversation, lots of activities, laughter, singing and thanksgiving to God for this special time of reunion. Much time was also spent with Dad's extensive family. Friendships were renewed and strong bonds fashioned.

Dad with the extended Meinel Family

Werner and I were in the middle of our snowball fight when we heard his voice calling again: *"Come on boys, we have work to do!"*

We took it in turns to ride on the make-shift cart as our father led us through the town to the edge of a pine forest. In no time a tree was felled and loaded onto the cart and we were heading back towards home again. It was getting late in the day and snow was starting to fall with increasing intensity. The going was tough and cumbersome in the deep snow with the two metre tree on the rickety cart. On more than one occasion our precious cargo tumbled over and frustrated our journey home. By now I was covered in snow; my feet were numb, and my hands were wet and freezing cold. It was almost dark and home seemed a long way away. The fun had gone out of our adventure and, besides, I was not at all comfortable with this semi-stranger called Father. In the end it was all too much for this four year old boy. I burst into tears and babbled in distress, *"I want to go home to my mum!"*

Our first Christmas in Germany turned out to be a wonderful Christmas. The tree we had plucked out of a snow drenched forest now stood transformed in glittering light and splendour in the corner of the room as we celebrated the coming of the Saviour into the world. This was the first time we were united as a complete family of five for Christmas: father, mother and their three children, with Opa Meinel.

The next day we waved our goodbyes to Dad. Our farewell embrace was now a little more enthusiastic than our greetings at his arrival. A realisation had been awakened in me that this man in the army uniform was really my father and that he loved me very much. The love my mother showed for my father was compelling evidence that he really was part of our family. For my mother, the goodbye was excruciatingly painful but she dared not show her emotions too much in front of her children. With God's help she would be mother and father, provider and protector, to all of us.

My Grandparents Ida & Ernst Meinel

Just a few days later we faced another farewell. Our Opa, Ernst Meinel, suddenly passed away, aged seventy seven. For him the last few years, since his beloved wife Ida died after a long illness on 21 February 1940, had proved very difficult. The family home had lost its heart, the joy of yesteryears was gone and the sound of his treasured violin had fallen silent. The gloom of war hung like a dark shadow over his life. He had lost his eldest son in the First World War and the fear of losing his youngest son to another war had become unbearable. He was longing to meet his Lord and Saviour and to be reunited with his beloved wife in heaven.

In early 1943, it was time for Mother and her children to leave Schneeberg. Sadly, to us children, the significance of this wonderful Erzgebirge Region of Germany - its cultural uniqueness and its historic traditions - was beyond our childhood appreciation. Many years were to pass before we gained more insight into the richness of our Meinel heritage.

Typical Schneeberg Christmas Decorations

Now our journey took us south to Wuerttemberg, the area from which my mother's family originated. Our destination was *Zell u Aichelberg.* (Zell).

Zell u Aichelberg

Zell is a small rural village at the foot of the Swabian Alps (*Schwaebische Alb*) some seventy kilometres south east of Stuttgart. It sits comfortably in a landscape of lush meadows, colourful fruit orchards and enchanting forests. A small stream, the Zeller Bach, meanders gently down the slopes of the Swabian Alps. It enters the village on one side, flows underground through the middle of the town centre, and then emerges on the other on its journey to the Neckar. The Aichelberg Mountain forms an idyllic backdrop for the village.

In 1943 approximately 600 people lived in Zell u Aichelberg; the majority were farmers. All of the narrow, winding roads lead to the town centre and market square, and are lined with quaint two and three storey timber framed farm houses. The typical farm house has its living quarters on the top floor and usually sits directly over the cow stable. Next to it, and all under the one roof, is the hay barn. In front of the house, hugging the public road, sits the *Hummelmiste* (dung pit). Its sight and smell identifies it as the typical Swabian farmhouse.

View of Zell from Aichelberg

Zell with Aichelberg in background

Martins Church　　　　　　　Interior Fresco Paintings

The *Martinskirche* (the Martins Church), dominates the village. This Lutheran church is the oldest and most significant building in the town. Its present form dates back to 1386. The peculiar shape of the roof and spire tower is a truncated version of the much taller original tower after it was struck by lightning in 1667 and 1682. The three bells in the tower are inscribed with the first three petitions of the Lord's Prayer. A large collage of extremely well preserved fresco paintings, dating from 1400, decorate the interior of the church walls and have become a significant tourist attraction.

Of special historic significance is the geographic location of Zell. Its northern terrain is dotted with the remains of a now long-disused network of trade routes, dating back to the Roman Empire. This made the town particularly vulnerable to attacks during ancient times, which date back to 435 AD. To the south, the Autobahn gracefully descends the mountain range at the village of Aichelberg. Constructed in the 1930s, it was regarded as one of the great engineering feats in roadway design of its time. It features a massive viaduct standing some sixty metres above ground level where the road bridges between mountains and plains.

The Autobahn Viaduct at Aichelberg

In the spring of 1943, our journey led us to this village. Why Zell?

Back in 1936 Wilhelm Stoll had bought a property there for use by his family. The war had brought an end to his plans so he offered the house for our use. We arrived as complete strangers, war refugees, stripped of home, country of birth and of all possessions except the clothes on our back. But now, as we stood in the *Kirchheimer Strasse* and looked at this house we felt welcomed, secure and at once at home. What an indescribable blessing and relief for our mother. She never ceased to thank God for the foresight and generosity of her brother Wilhelm, who had made all of this possible. While he and his family were living in corrugated huts behind barbed wire as prisoners of war in Australia, we had the comfort and freedom of his beautiful house in Zell.

Otto Mader, the local church deacon and property guardian appointed by Wilhelm Stoll, gave us a warm welcome and showed us through the house. For Werner and me, a new adventure beckoned. It did not take long before we had explored every room. We scampered up and down every stair and poked our faces into every nook and cranny of our new home, which in our eyes, seemed like a huge mansion.

Our Home in Zell

Our apartment was on the first floor and consisted of four main rooms: a lounge, kitchen and two bedrooms. We had running water, electricity and an upstairs toilet. On the ground floor were two large garages, used as store rooms, and next to them a disused bakery. Attached to the back of the house was a large shed stacked high with wood for winter heating.

The house was surrounded on two sides with half an acre of land, cultivated into a vegetable and fruit garden giving much needed produce in time of war. In the very back corner of the property stood a quaint garden cottage. Mother's strict instruction to keep away from it only made us more curious and more determined to explore its secrets.

It was not long before Werner and I discovered a secret door in the main house. A steep stair led us down into a damp, stone-vaulted underground basement with all the mystery and intrigue of a dungeon from the Middle Ages. In amongst the clutter of shelves and vats there lurked dark and intriguing shadows which sent shivers down our spines. The vats were used to store the favoured homemade Swabian beverage called *Most* (pear or apple cider). Just two years later, this dark and eerie dungeon was to become our place of refuge during the bombing attacks at the end of the war.

The Church & Village Centre
R to L: Bakery & Hotel, Town Hall, General Store & Church behind

Our new home was just one house back from the village square, which gave us instant access to the significant civic and community buildings: the town hall, church, general store, bakery and pub.

We shared the house with Otto Mader and another family: Emma Werner (her husband joined them after the war) and her children, Ilse and Karl. Their apartment was located next to ours on the first floor.

Otto Mader (we called him Onkel Mader) lived in a self-contained one room flat in the loft under the roof of the house. He became part of our family and my mother took care of this aged 'uncle' until his death.

As children, we loved Onkel Mader. Two attractions drew us to his little flat on top of the stairs in the loft. He had a parrot perched in a large cage in his room. It was not just any parrot. This was a talking parrot with an amazing array of linguistic skills. He would greet us with *"Guten Tag"* (Good Day) and a whole lot more. We became enthralled with his chatter and taught him to say one or two sayings of our own. The other attraction was the revolving Christmas tree that played carols. Our Christmas Eve celebration always commenced with a visit to the loft to see and hear this intriguing spectacle.

Soon after our arrival, Kaethe Weberruss and her daughter, Elfriede, also came to live in Zell. Kaethe was a close friend of my mother, from Haifa, and came to Germany on the same train we did. We enjoyed the happiest of relationships and Elfriede became like a sister to Werner, me and Helga. Later Uncle Christian and Aunty Christel, Walter and Herta joined us for a short time.

Zell proved to be an ideal country environment for children to grow up in. There may have been a war, tough times and little food but to me and my siblings life seemed good. We had our school friends and plenty of leisure time and space to create our own fun and games. There were enchanting woods to play in, castle ruins to investigate and an abundance of wildlife to chase or capture. We silently slid on our tummies on the soft floor of the woods to observe the elusive deer and her fawns or to follow the distinctive knock of the woodpecker to his nest carved into the hollow trunk of the tree.

Storks Nest in Church

Bird watching became one of our favourite pastimes. We knew every nest in every tree and the number of eggs or newly hatched sparrows, black birds or ravens. Reaching a nest in the furthermost branch of a tree was no obstacle to our climbing skills. We could foretell the weather by the flight of the swallows and predict the start of the summer season by the arrival of the stork to his roosting nest on top of the church roof. In the place called *Brogele*, we sailed our home-made boats down the Zeller *Bach* (brook) in summer, and in winter experienced the thrill of our first toboggan ride on its snow covered embankments.

The pace of the village was laconic. The village news was still disseminated to its villagers by the *Amtsbote* (town crier), a practice going back centuries. In our time Karl Kill rode his push bike to a number of locations in the village and rang his hand-held bell. As locals emerged from their homes or leaned out of the windows of their houses, he bellowed out the latest community news prepared by the Town Hall.

The war depleted the village of the young and able-bodied men; many were never to return. It was not until 1949 that it could be established that fifty of the citizens of Zell had lost their lives. Eighteen were still unaccounted for. The older men and the women left behind made sure that life went on with relative normality. They worked the farms and orchards and tended the sheep. Some of them had help from a number of French prisoners of war that were placed in the village. There was little mechanisation, and harvesting was done manually and transported on mainly cow-drawn carts and wagons. Roads were not bituminised and generally free of cars, except for the occasional motor bike. Transport to Goeppingen was available once or twice a week by bus. As the war lingered on, petrol became scarce. Any car or truck that did appear on the road was fuelled by steam from a wood fired boiler.

Hay Harvest

Zell is not counted amongst the most attractive or historically significant villages in Swabia but it captured my heart. It may have been a small farming village in an obscure corner of Germany, but for nine years of my childhood and early teenage years it was the place I called home. It was my bit of paradise. My German roots and cultural identity are intrinsically linked to this place. My foundations for living were laid here. No wonder my heart has been irresistibly drawn back to Zell, throughout my life.

A Time of War

The events of 20th April 1945 are indelibly etched on my mind. War came to Zell! The American Army besieged the town. By mid-morning they had reduced two houses to rubble. Open conflict began early in the morning at the neighbouring village of Aichelberg when a German plane engaged with the Americans in the air. By nightfall the villagers' worst nightmare threatened to become reality.

Village life in the month leading up to the close of the war had become chaotic. During the night the village was clothed in complete darkness. Every window was shuttered and not a flicker of a light was visible. If there was, the night watchman would be at the door in an instant with a severe reprimand. The piercing sound of the air raid siren was in the air. With its first blast our mother would drag us out of bed, throw some clothes around us and rush us down into the cellar. There we joined the other residents, huddled together, waiting in dread for the drone of aeroplanes and the crash of exploding bombs until the all-clear signal was given. As the raid warnings escalated, the retreat to the cellar became a routine we would carry out in our sleep. After a few months we accepted it as normal.

By mid-1944 more and more enemy planes began to cross our skies in broad daylight. For the children it was an exciting spectacle to look to the heavens and watch the endless columns of those amazing planes fly by. While Zell was spared any direct hits, the main industrial cities and towns, particularly Stuttgart, were bombed mercilessly. We could hear the thud and boom of falling bombs and see the awesome spectacle of the red hot glow of a city on fire some seventy kilometres away.

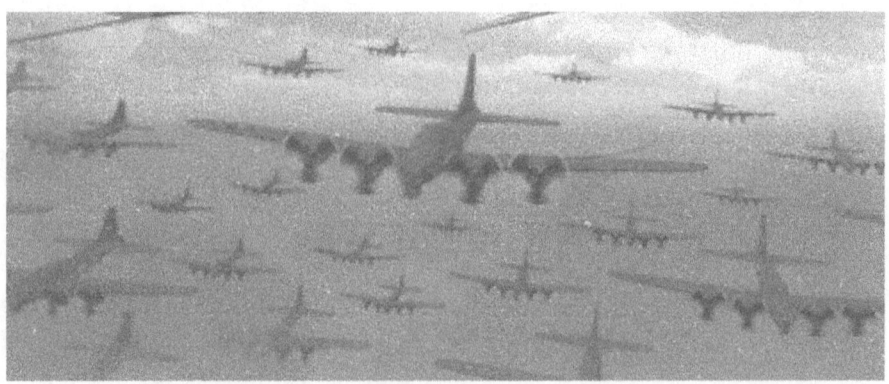

By now any defending German army was nowhere to be seen, except for the remnants of anti-aircraft guns and sachets of bullets and ammunition left behind by the retreating and deflated soldiers. Many deserted the army, seeking anonymity and shelter with anyone who would take them in. There was a small civilian resistance, a 'Dad's Army' of sorts, operating in the village. They were active in building barricades across the main three roads leading into the town centre. They maintained a radio intelligence network and assisted in blowing up the viaduct of the *Autobahn* at Aichelberg in a futile attempt to curb the advance of the Allied forces.

The Americans approached Zell along the disused route of the ancient Roman road via the *Betzgenrieter Wald* (forest) and the town of Pliensbach. There was no time to fortify the town. The road barricades remained partially open and entry into the town centre was unimpeded. As the armoured tanks skirted the village, the Americans pin-pointed the radio network that was operating in the Fritz Rummelspacher house. Without hesitation their tanks turned their guns on it and burned it to the ground.

Further along the Goeppinger road they stopped and set up their base command on a field now occupied by post-war school buildings. The only house within close proximity was the Lutz cottage. When an American soldier suffered an injury to his hand they concluded it came from a shot fired by the German military occupying the Lutz house. The house was quickly surrounded by tanks, fired upon and burnt to the ground.

The entire village had been warned by the town crier the day before to seek shelter as the arrival of the advancing Allied forces was imminent. When dawn broke on 20th April 1945, we had already been bunkered down in the cellar for over twelve hours. By mid-morning my mother decided to do a little reconnaissance. She climbed the stairs to fetch some food (a small piece of smoked sausage) from the loft. Her curiosity got the better of her. She opened the shutter to get a peek at the world outside from the vantage point of the loft.

To her horror she saw the smoke and fire billowing from the two houses the Americans had destroyed along the *Goeppinger Strasse*. As she retreated in haste she felt a 'swish' and heard a 'whistle' rushing past the roof, followed by the sound of an explosion. When she returned to the cellar she tried her best to hide the shock of her roof top experience. She was pale with fright and with her eyes locked in a stare, said, *"It is not safe out there!"* Later we learned what happened. At the exact moment my mother was in the loft, the Americans fired a shot at random into the centre of the village. The tank missile brushed along the roof of our house and exploded in the stable of our neighbour Mr Bazlen's house, killing four cows.

By midday the villagers started to slowly emerge from their shelters. Someone picked up a message that spread like wild fire throughout the town. *"The Americans are going to burn our village to the ground!"* Why? The Americans wanted to take revenge for the death of one of their soldiers whom they claimed was killed by a German civilian. Unless the culprit gave himself up by 1600 hours, bombardment would commence.

Panic and pandemonium broke out among the village population. The situation was exacerbated by the absence of any clear communication between the Town Hall (*Buergermeister*) and the American command. None of the town authorities, nor any of the villagers could speak or understand English. Likewise the Americans must have been without a skilled interpreter. The truth was that the town clerk, Herr Emil Hoyler, was a Nazi collaborator and had gone into hiding.

Werner and I strayed into the village square and saw first-hand the fear and panic. People loaded their cow-drawn wagons, handcarts and bicycles to escape their doomed town with the bare essentials. We ran home to tell our mother and I remember her saying, *"What are they doing? Where do they think they can flee to? I am staying put!"* She was one of a handful of people who refused to panic.

Next we saw an American Army vehicle pull up at our front door with a small delegation of uniformed officers. They had been directed to, *"see Mrs Meinel, the refugee from Palestine. She can speak English"*. After a short exchange with the officers my mother asked our co-tenant, Mrs Werner, to take care of us. She kissed us goodbye and assured us that she would return in a very short time. Werner (9), Helga (5) and I (7) watched as our mother was driven away and disappeared from our view. We probably did have a good cry but I cannot recollect being traumatised in any way. We never doubted that our mother would be true to her word and return to us.

Kaethe Webberruss & Elfriede

What really happened on that day in the village? My mother and her friend, Kaethe Weberruss, were the only English-speaking people in Zell. They acted as interpreters and, on behalf of the citizens, embarked on a long discourse of sensitive negotiations to save the town from destruction. Discussions were made all the more difficult by the fact that this particular day, the 20th of April, happened to be Hitler's birthday. This made the Americans especially nervous and suspicious.

On arrival at the American headquarters the ladies were presented by the American officers with a leaflet, signed by the Fuehrer, Adolf Hitler, which they claimed had been distributed throughout the village. It read: *"The best present any German citizen can give to the Fuehrer on his birthday is the corpse of an enemy soldier!"* The officers wanted to know whether the source of this inflammatory leaflet originated in Zell and whether any German military forces were stationed there.

The ladies returned for a second meeting (this time my mother took Helga with her). They tabled their findings with an emphatic 'no' to both charges, but the commanders remained unconvinced. The threat to annihilate the village was not withdrawn. The Americans had still been unable to establish with certainty how their soldier was injured. The locals, by contrast, claimed to know exactly what happened: the soldier was a victim of 'friendly' fire.

At a third meeting at 10 o'clock at night, the American command was finally persuaded that the ladies had spoken the truth. The officers and Kaethe Webberruss arrived at the house of the *Buergermeister*, Emil Hoyler, who finally showed up, to deliver their verdict. *"The town will be spared from ruin!"* Their only demand was for all weapons and radio transmitters to be delivered to the village square the following morning for confiscation.

In no time the good news spread to every corner of the village. *"The Americans have changed their minds. Our village has been spared. Frau Weberruss and Frau Meinel have saved us and our village from ruin!"*

When some of the farmers wanted to show their gratitude to the American soldiers, they presented them with gifts of eggs and vegetables. Mother was flabbergasted and scolded them. *"Don't you know that there are children in the town who are in far greater need of food than the American soldiers? Don't forget them!"*

What an amazing outcome! Through the efforts of two women, armed with a little charm, a fair grasp of the English language and a good dose of home grown negotiating skills, a village of six hundred inhabitants was spared from a miserable disaster, a fate many other German citizens could not avoid. That night, the weary villagers returned to their houses, unpacked their wagons and carts and enjoyed a good night's sleep for the first time in a long while.

It took many years before I came to understand the enormity of these events and the amazing strength of character my mother showed in this time of crisis. She was not intimidated by the uniformed official of the American Army. Back in Haifa she had already learned the art of diplomacy working with a wide cross section of people from all walks of life and nationalities, including officials of high standing: Vice-Consuls, High Commissioners and high ranking English military officers. She respected all men and women but feared none. She had long before learned the truth that it is more important to fear God than people. *"Do not be afraid of those who kill the body but cannot kill the soul"* (Matthew 10:28,29). She never intended to make a name for herself. Her only purpose was to serve God through the gifts and experience God had given her and to honour His name.

Nevertheless, in my eyes, and that of the villagers, my mother was special. Her comment on what happened that day was, *"No big deal!"* A job was there to be done, and she played her part, particularly as the village authority, the *Buergermeister*, had gone absent without leave.

My mother was generous in praise for the Americans. They were professional at all times and treated her with the greatest respect and courtesy and sometimes with just a hint of curiosity and surprise.

When she was escorted for the first meeting into the army headquarters she was confronted by a soldier who aggressively pointed his gun at her.

"*Don't you point that thing at me!*" she barked as she grabbed the point of the gun and pushed him away.

The first question they asked was, "*Where did you learn your English?*" They were astounded at her fluency and had trouble reconciling how a well-travelled and astute lady came to live among farmers who had rarely travelled outside their own village. She never had a sense that they were really serious about burning the village to the ground. This explains why she decided not to attend the last scheduled meeting. She excused herself on the grounds that, "*My children need me!*"

The American officials kept in touch with my mother during their occupation of Zell. We were always excited to see them. They usually brought some special treats, such as chocolate, chewing gum and even a doll for Helga; goods we could never buy or had not seen or heard of before.

What would have happened to the village of Zell in 1945 had Wilhelm Stoll invested his money in 1936 in Stuttgart and not Zell? Was that purchase, and the subsequent arrival of the Meinels, a matter of coincidence or fate, or was it divine providence? There is no doubt in the minds of the Stoll/Meinel families that only a sovereign God could orchestrate such amazing events for a common good. They were grateful to God that their life in Palestine had prepared them for "*such an hour as this*" (Esther 4:14).

The war came to an end nineteen days later on the 8th May 1945, when the German Reich officially surrendered to the Allies. While this brought unprecedented jubilation around the globe, the people of Germany who survived were about to face their darkest days in their struggle to survive as a people and nation. They did however rejoice that the Nazi regime had come to an end. The people in the West of Germany were free, but the people in the East were about to come under the spell of another oppressive regime: communism.

Herbert, Werner & Helga 1944

When the War is Over!

By the end of the war, much of Europe was devastated. Sustained aerial bombardment had badly damaged most major cities, with industrial facilities particularly hard hit. Infrastructure of railroads, bridges and dock yards had been specifically targeted by air strikes. In 1943 alone, 222 500 tonnes of bombs were dropped on Germany and German-occupied territories. Five million homes and apartments were destroyed, leaving some ten million people homeless by the end of the war[1].

Trade flow was thoroughly disrupted. Food shortages were severe. Millions were in refugee camps living on aid from relief organisations. A flood of evacuees fled the larger cities and moved to the country communities. At the same time, refugees displaced from German settlements in Eastern Europe began to arrive. Although small towns and villages had not suffered as much devastation, the destruction of transportation left them economically isolated[2].

Stuttgart, the capital of Wuerttemberg, with its concentration of the Daimler Benz motor industry and the Bosch auto electrical manufacturing plant, endured some thirty three air raid attacks with over five thousand deaths and many more wounded. Daylight bombing of Stuttgart started as early as 6 September 1943 and culminated with a barrage of fifteen separate attacks in one day on 21 April 1945, just two days before occupation by the French.

Downtown Stuttgart 1946

Of the 63 000 buildings in Stuttgart, 14 370 were totally demolished and a further 9620 had to be demolished. Only two thousand buildings remained untouched by bombing[3]. The Town Clerk, Dr Stroelin, a secret member of the anti-Hitler resistance movement, managed to save Stuttgart from total destruction. He offered the city's capitulation and surrendered it to the French[4].

Post-war Germany was divided into four zones and became occupied by the military governments of Britain, France, America and the Soviet Union. Wuerttemberg became part of the American Zone. While both the French and Americans captured Stuttgart and much of Wuerttemberg, the boundary of the French Zone was moved further west and Stuttgart became the headquarters of the American Military command. With the experience of this dual occupation the local population drew some interesting comparisons between them.

The French, who had fresh memories of the oppressive German occupation in their own country, spread fear and terror shortly after their arrival by the indiscriminate rape of women, deprivation of foodstuff and deforestation. In contrast, the Americans were regarded more as 'liberators', although at first they had no desire to play that role. They concentrated on the vigorous prosecution of the National Socialists and the implementation of their military administration. They were the first of the occupying forces to help the local population with deliveries of foostuff.[5]

Stuttgart will never forget the 'speech of hope' delivered by the US Secretary of State, James F Byrnes, on 6 September 1946. It marked a major change in American Foreign policy toward a just-defeated Germany. It offered the readiness of *"the American people to help the German people to win their way back to an honourable place among the peace-loving nations of the world"* [6].

During the first three years of occupation, the rigorous industrial disarmament program by the UK and USA put the German economy into considerable pain and strain. Living conditions were at an all-time low. Housing and food conditions became unimaginably bad. During 1946 and 1947 the country was also hit with a period of disastrous starvation. This, coupled with an influenza epidemic, cost the lives of millions of Germans and led to huge public strikes. Due to a lack of coal, the primary fuel for heating, schools had to be closed, partially or completely for weeks at a time, particularly during the wintry months of January to March.

Added to those woes was the out of control inflation of the *Reich Mark*. By 1948, it had lost almost all of its value leading to currency reform. On the 20th June 1948, each German resident received 40 Deutsch Mark in exchange for 40 Reich Mark and in August an additional 20 DM. Thereafter Reich Mark balances were only credited in small parts: RM 100 for DM 6.5 (Reich Mark – Deutsch Mark) [7].

In Zell the new notes and coins were delivered by truck to the Town Hall on the day before. The police had to guard it all night as there was no secure money vault to store it [7]. Those who did have savings, effectively lost almost all of it overnight. For some, that was too much to cope with as evidenced by a huge jump in suicides across the country. While I was still too young to understand what the currency reform was all about, I have not forgotten my mother's words to us children from that time. *"Don't ever make money your God!"* The shop owners became shrewd and greedy. Before the currency reform the shops were empty. Thereafter the shop windows were stacked with merchandise. With the new DM almost anything could now be purchased [8].

The punitive occupation of Germany proved to be a huge barrier to its economic reconstruction. This realisation by Washington led to the introduction of the Marshall Plan (officially the European Recovery Program, ERP) in 1948. The Marshall Plan was the large scale program under which the United States sent monetary support to help rebuild European economies after the end of the Second World War. The goals of the United States were to rebuild a war-devastated region, remove trade barriers, modernise industry and make Europe prosperous again. The plan was in operation for four years[9].

In 1949, Germany took back control of their nation. The Federal Republic of Germany was formed and the country subdivided into the States or provinces we know today. The provinces of Wuerttemberg and Baden were amalgamated into the State of Baden-Wuerttemberg. On 12 September 1949, Professor Theodor Heuss, a Swabian, was elected as the first President of the German Parliament.

Rationing of foodstuffs was completely lifted in 1950. By the end of 1952 the economy of Germany had surpassed pre-war levels with output at least 35% higher than in 1938. Life not only improved within Germany but now offered new hope for the displaced persons from the old German territories in the East and refugees from the Soviet Union, resulting in an influx of huge numbers of people by 1951. They came in several migratory waves and initially almost only settled in the American Zone. By 1961, the count of new citizens in Baden-Wuerttemberg, particularly because of refugees from East Germany (the Zone occupied by Soviet Union), rose by 1 620 428, almost a fifth of the total population of 7 759 154 people[9].

The Meinel and Weberruss families were counted among those refugee statistics, together with several others that arrived in Zell. Two of my close German school friends, Otto Antel and Gerhard Guerth, arrived with their families after being displaced by the Russian forces from German colonies in Hungary.

My Aunty Christel, with her children Herta and Walter, lived in Coswig. Coswig was ten to twelve kilometres outside of Dresden, one of Germany's most heavily bombed cities. Fortunately for the Stolls, Coswig itself was not bombed and they survived in the home of Christel's sister and her husband.

But Walter recalls, *"I remember Herta and myself being woken up by our mother at night. We saw the sky above Dresden lit up after allied planes had dropped phosphorous bombs to enable the following bomber pilots to better identify their targets. They levelled large parts of the city and thousands of people perished".* He also saw the terror-riddled people who had survived by the skin of their teeth, streaming out of Dresden to escape to the safety of the country areas as they passed through Coswig railway station.

The post-war period of 1945-1952 coincided with the years of my primary schooling. I started year 1 at age seven, the year the war ended. It turned out to be a disrupted school year. While schools generally remained closed from April to September 1945, we were more fortunate in having a resident teacher in Zell, *Frauelein* Auwaerter. She kept our small school going with minimum disruptions.

Parents had good reason to be anxious about their children's safety during the early post-war years. All manner of army equipment and live ammunition lay scattered around the villages and countryside. As boys, we soon discovered the thrill of hunting for this 'forbidden fruit'. We scoured the ground near and far and built up an arsenal of abandoned live rifle bullets. On instruction from our older peers we quickly learnt the art of disarming bullets. Keeping clear of the detonator, the head was gently extracted from the shell and the gun powder decanted from its casing. When sufficient powder was collected from two or more bullets the home-made fuse was lit. With hearts pounding, we watched as the heap of gun powder crackled, hissed and exploded into an amazing display of fireworks and smoke. Our peers, including my brother, Werner, threatened to inflict all manner of bodily harm if we ever told our mothers.

On more than one occasion however, tragedy did strike. A group of 'invincible' teenagers tried a similar operation of disarming a much larger piece of ammunition, a tank missile, which they discovered along the road near the village of Aichelberg. The aftermath of this explosion left seven young people dead and a community in mourning.

Anti-aircraft artillery became one of our favourite toys. On the outskirts of Zell, on the road to Aichelberg, we found a fully operational artillery gun. We pulled every lever and turned every wheel until this bit of war time machinery was converted into our own merry-go-round. It kept us entertained for many hours and days until the town authorities disabled it. They intervened just in time.

While one of the young boys climbed to the end of the gun barrel, another unwittingly dislodged a lever which turned the gun into an instant slingshot. Fortunately the boy had a safe and soft landing in the tall grass after his ten metre orbit through the air.

The sight of American soldiers was an everyday experience. Many of the villagers, both old and young, tried to exploit the generosity of these friendly soldiers, in an attempt to secure a puff of a cigarette or a bite of chocolate or chewing gum. When this proved unsuccessful the villagers turned to the art of bartering. My friends and I joined their ranks. On one occasion we walked all the way to the *Autobahn* near Aichelberg. Our attempt to solicit some sweets in exchange for a few onions poached from a farmer's field, fizzled. We left empty handed.

Our mother made sure we spent as much time as possible together as a family. Walking in the local woods became one of our favourite pass-times. On one of these excursions, we came across a deserted American Army camp-site at the edge of the *Sonnenweide* forest. As we rummaged through the litter left behind we discovered a 'pot of gold'. It was not real gold, but to us it was just as precious: a small bag of white flour together with other small crumbs of foodstuff. Mother was jubilant. She rushed home and by the end of the day she served up fresh pancakes. With a few drops of lemon juice and a thin sprinkling of sugar, our dinner never tasted better.

That night around the tea table we heard mother give thanks to God for providing for the needs of her family in such a miraculous way.

Father returns Home!

When father had joined the Rommel Corp in North Africa, in early 1943, he faced an uncertain military future. Field Marshal Montgomery had been victorious at the second battle of El Alamein which began on 23 October 1942.

Soon after, Rommel's *Deutsches Afrika Korps* was in retreat, caught between the advances of the British from the east and the mainly US forces from the west. My father was part of the German contingent that surrendered to the Americans in Tunisia in May 1943. They were put on a ship bound for America. The German prisoners were fortunate that they did not fall prey to the German Luftwaffe which relentlessly crossed the skies looking for targets to sink enemy ships. For the next three years he was a prisoner of war in camps near Houston, Texas, USA.

For months on end there was no news from the war front concerning the whereabouts of our father. My mother, like so many wives in Germany, was left pondering, *"Where is my husband? Is he dead or alive? If he is alive has he become the victim of a cruel prisoner of war camp?"* Every day our mother expectantly waited for mail from her husband. Day after day no news came.

But one day, early in September 1943, the post lady rushed into our house and in great excitement shouted up the stairs of our apartment, *"Frau Meinel, come quickly, I have mail from your husband today!"* Mum was beside herself with joy. Her husband, Martin, was alive and safe, in America. That night she sat down and wrote a letter to her husband. In it she poured out her raw emotions and grateful relief.

"Oh Martin, my dearest treasure! Just imagine! When I held those precious pages of your letter in my hands, tears of joy ran uncontrollably down my cheeks. What a relief to know that you are safe."

She also wrote how Helga became caught up in the excitement and ran through the streets telling everybody she met, *"The war is over! My Papa is coming home tomorrow!"* Five year old Helga only repeated what she heard the adults say, *"When the war is over your Papa will come home"*.

What a relief! They may have been separated by thousands of kilometres but now they could communicate with each other again on a regular basis. The only glitch was the unreliability of the mail during and after the war.

Conditions in the POW camp turned out to be exceptionally good. My father spoke in glowing terms of the humane treatment he and his comrades received from the prison authorities. They had a genuine concern for their physical, mental and medical welfare. Because he was a baker he was enlisted in the camp kitchen. The food was rationed but every single day there was an abundance, more than could be consumed by the prison inmates. Christian Stoll wrote in his memoirs: *"The food was not just good, it was exceptional!"* Prisoners from poorer backgrounds were heard to exclaim, *"Never, in my whole life, have I seen so much abundance of food!"* Most prisoners put on weight.

On the other hand dad was appalled by the spiteful behaviour of some of his German kitchen comrades. Again and again they deliberately washed good food and produce down the drain, simply to avoid the possibility of having their ration reduced. While the free citizens in Germany were dying from starvation, the Germans in prison in America complained, *"Not chicken again!"* as they lined up for their daily meals. When the war ended in May 1945, the camp conditions were tightened, food rations were cut and hunger did became an issue. Dad remarked, *"The Americans wanted the prisoners to know that Germany lost the war and that there are punitive consequences for being part of Germany's war machine, which, under the leadership of Adolf Hitler, had inflicted unprecedented evil, death and destruction on the world."*

Dad maintained a journal during his time at Fort Worth. He spent time in the library and recorded in great detail everything he learned about America: the names of the 48 States, its geography, industry, politics, art and culture. He was fascinated by the huge inflow of Germans who had migrated to America from the 1700s onwards. From 1820 to 1920, German ethnicity accounted for the largest group of immigrants, more than any other nationality. Today, about 51 million people, or 17% of the US population, claim to have German ancestry.

Dad became fascinated with those statistics and told us with great enthusiasm that *"there were so many Germans in America that 'German' almost became the official language of the US, being defeated by just one vote"*. It is only recently that I learned that this story, popular in the US and Germany, is in fact called the Muhlenberg legend. Frederick Muhlenberg, a German immigrant and the first ever Speaker of the US House of Representatives, received a petition in 1794 from a group of German immigrants to translate some of the American laws into German. It was defeated 42 to 41[1] on the casting vote of the Speaker.

Dad's journal also gives insight into the deep spiritual relationship he enjoyed with his Lord and Saviour, Jesus Christ. The pages are filled with scripture texts, quotes from Christian devotional books, hymns, prayers and poems. His own reflections speak of God's faithfulness and providence in sparing him from death and injury during the war in Europe and North Africa.

He had a stack of evidence of God's goodness. There was none greater than being re-united with his brother in law, Christian Stoll, in North Africa. Four years earlier Martin and Christian had been enlisted in the German army and had joined different regiments dispatched to different parts of Europe. Later, unbeknown to each other, they were both drafted into the Rommel Corps in North Africa.

The German army surrendered to the advancing American force near Tripoli in May 1943. In among the throng of thousands of surrendered German soldiers Martin and Christian came face to face. They stared at each other in total disbelief. There and then they made a pact to stick together, come what may. Together with tens of thousands of German prisoners of war, they were rounded up for transport to America and ended up in the same contingent, on the same ship, going to the same POW Camp in Texas, America.

Martin relished the friendship of his brother-in-law, Christian. How amazing to be reunited there! The day to day companionship and Christian fellowship they had enjoyed in freedom in Haifa, they could now continue in the confinement of a prisoner of war camp. They looked out for each other and became each other's mentor.

When Christian was transferred from camp Mexia to Fort Sam Houston he asked a favour of the Camp officer to allow Martin to come also. His request was granted and the two enjoyed the rest of their time together in the same POW camp.

Christian's linguistic skills, learned in Palestine, were noticed by the American military and his interpretive services were much sought after. Much of his time was spent in the office of the American headquarters. This did not escape the notice of his fellow prisoners and when Christian voted against a camp strike, they came to the conclusion that Christian had become too friendly with the Americans and that he needed to be taught a lesson. Martin happened to hear of their scheme to 'rough up' Christian, and was able to warn him.

My mother's letters give insight into the heart of a wife and mother separated from her husband by war. She wrote how much she missed him, his presence and his support; how she regretted that he was missing out on seeing the children grow up, and how much the children were missing out on not having a father figure in those formative years of their young lives. She described the first day each of the children went to school and every little detail of their daily lives. She also let him know that the children were no angels, particularly the boys, and that some of their lively and poor behaviour taxed her at times. But when she talked about our early schooling habits, she surprised me.

"Werner", she wrote, *"always does his school work without fuss. But Herbert, he has difficulties knuckling down and I haven't yet quite figured out whether he is just a 'dreamer' or outright lazy!"* Wow! In her letters she assured Martin that she and the children were doing well and that every day was a day closer to his return.

On the 1st April (April Fool's Day) 1946, Werner and I went to school as usual. Our school teacher, *Herr* Friesch, was a good teacher who conducted his multi grade class with a healthy balance of discipline and fun. On this morning he must have been in a particularly good mood. He allowed the village larrikin, Fritz, to interrupt his class.

Fritz burst into the room with irrepressible excitement. Out of breath from running, he blurted, *"Werner... and... Herbert ...your father... has returned from the war ....and he is waiting for you in the village square!"* Was this a cruel joke or was it really true that our father had returned from America? Mr Friesch seemed convinced. Without hesitation he told us to *"hurry up and get going"*.

We had trouble keeping up with Fritz as he ran ahead to the village square. On arrival he pointed to a man, *"There!"* he said, *"It's your dad!"* My head was spinning. Everything was happening so fast. One minute I am engrossed in my school lesson, next I am told that my father was home. He had not been part of our family for seven years and my only memory of him was his short visit to Schneeberg during Christmas 1942. We had not received any notice of our father's departure from America. No mail had arrived for twelve months. This was a total surprise.

As I looked closer, I was confronted by a man dressed in khaki uniform, leaning on a huge sausage bag with POW written all over it. But what completely blew me away was his size. He would have weighed at least seventeen stone! A man of that size, coming home after three years in an enemy prisoner of war camp, while everyone I knew

Dad 1945

suffered from malnutrition, was an equation my eight year old mind could not compute. As my father rushed towards me with outstretched arms and embraced me, I burst into tears, totally overwhelmed by emotions I cannot explain. Was it joy, unexpected surprise, or what?

The three of us, Dad, Werner and I, walked hand in hand to our house, just a few metres up the street. It was Mum's and Helga's turn to fall into his embrace. More tears flowed uncontrollably. For Mum it was all too much. After seven long years away in the Second World War, her husband had come home fit and well. This reality and his out-of-the-blue arrival sent mum into shock. For twelve hours she could not speak.

But then the celebrations erupted without constraint in our family, in our house, with our tenants and in the whole village. With the homecoming of our father we felt that the war was finally over. Now we were united as a family and could face the future together. The house was filled with joy, thanksgiving and song.

When Martin and Christian were released from the prisoner of war camp in America they were first taken to England and detained for a further period of time. Martin was cleared to return to Germany in March 1946 but Christian not until May 1947, two years after the war had ended. On arrival in Germany Christian was fearful of entering the Russian occupied Zone, so Christel took the risk of crossing the border into the West without authorisation to meet her husband after a separation of eight years. Later Christel Stoll with her children was granted permission to leave the Russian Zone. After spending several weeks in a transition camp in Plauen, East Germany, they travelled to Wuerttemberg to join us, and her husband, in Zell.

Now that our father was home, his immediate task was to find work, any work, no matter how menial. He started labouring in a stone quarry just a few kilometres outside Zell. A few short weeks of hard manual labour on a post-war diet was all that was needed to reduce this overweight returned soldier to our 'look alike' of skin and bones. Two months later he was pleased to get his first job as baker with Karl Heinzelmann in Kirchheim (1 July 1946 to 15 February 1948). He pedalled the eight kilometres there and back on his pushbike every day. Other employment opportunities followed; all of which took our Father further away from home. He first worked as master baker with Otto Mehner in Stuttgart (1 March 1948 to 15 July 1950), then as labourer with Alfred Karle in Heiningen (17 July 1950 to 23 June 1951) and master baker at the *Roessle* in Stuttgart (25 June 1951 to 19 April 1952). For most of these times our dad would only be home for part of the weekends.

On 28th February 1948, our family increased by one with the arrival of Ingeborg (Inge), a healthy baby girl. My parents were overwhelmed with joy and grateful to God for this special gift, a post-war daughter, born to them in their mature years (my mother was forty six years old). My sister Helga was delighted to have a new sister and a playmate. Werner and I, now aged twelve and ten, were fascinated by the new baby but preferred to keep ourselves occupied doing 'boy things'.

Inge's Baby Dedication with Family and Friends 1948

Dad with Inge

A Childhood to Remember

My memories of life in Zell are of a very happy and exciting childhood. The life style and the conditions we experienced during the war we accepted as normal; we knew no different. For nine years this was our home, our childhood playground. And from this playground emerged stories of unforgettable fun and adventure and a deep appreciation of the importance of a good education, regular church attendance, good friends to play with and a home filled with love. Life centred on school, the home, church and play.

Primary School

When we first arrived in Zell I went to kindergarten and at the age of seven started primary school education. School started at 7.30 am and finished around midday, Monday to Saturday.

By today's standards school was regimented. I liked all of our teachers: *Fraeuline* Auwaerter, *Herr* Liebler and *Herr* Friesch. As far as I can remember, I received the cane only once from *Herr* Liebler. The education system had however not yet reached that enlightened stage where children were permitted to write with their natural left hand. I was forced to write with my right hand. When it came to drawing I could only do it with my left hand. This left me with the lifelong legacy of being ambidextrous and with almost unreadable handwriting.

Herr Friesch (left), Werner (back row 1st on left) and
Herbert (front row 3rd from right)

At school I developed an appetite for learning. Every so often *Herr* Friesch would stray from his regular lessons to recite one of his many war time stories. We sat on the edge of our seats as we listened with rapt attention to his life and death adventures: how he managed to escape, both from the clutches of the Russian soldiers, and arrest by the German authorities, when he deserted the German Army in the closing stages of the war. *Herr* Friesch was not Swabian but came to Zell in 1937 when he was appointed head teacher. In the post-war years he was instrumental in resurrecting the Zeller *Turn-Sport-Gesang Verein* (Gymnastics, Sport & Choral Club). In 1949, he started the post-war town choir *Liederkranz* and the football club. On his retirement in December 1967, after thirty years of service, he was made an honorary citizen of Zell for his tireless contribution to education and service to the local community.

My best subjects in my final year (seven) were reading, singing and music. In our geography and physics lessons we completed some amazing projects. I revelled in the sketching and drawing required for this work. Later, this passion led me to pursue a career in Architecture. I felt good when I topped my class in arithmetic, having scored one hundred percent in times tables. My parents and *Herr* Friesch wanted to groom me for higher education. The process required enrolment in the Middle or Grammar School (Year six to ten Gymnasium) in Goeppingen. For better or worse this never eventuated, as my parents were undecided at the time whether to migrate to Australia or remain in Germany.

But it was the school sporting activities that really aroused my passion. Two afternoons were dedicated to sports lessons. As we had no sports grounds in Zell we walked the four kilometres to Bad Boll twice a week to play football (soccer), handball or compete in athletic competitions. This was our routine for five years until the football pitch was completed at the *Zeller Berg* (Hill of Zell). In summer, we walked five kilometres to the nearest swimming pool in Weilheim, where I learned to swim the breast-stroke. We never regarded walking these distances as a chore. Any sport was stimulating and such fun but, for me, football topped it all. I became a founding member of the Zeller junior football team. In the *Bundesliege*, I followed the State team, VFB Stuttgart.

May Day Celebrations

May Day celebrations were always a lot of fun and the school played a major part in the annual carnival. Young and old participated in the march through the village streets, led by my brother, Werner. As he was the tallest and strongest in the school, he carried the maypole tree surrounded by a circle of girls holding streamers flowing from the apex of the pole. In the town square, the school performed gymnastic feats, games and tricks to the enthusiastic applause from onlookers.

Lichtenstein Castle

School excursions were rare during the post-war years. I do have vivid memories when, during our senior years, we visited the Lichtenstein Castle on an all-day bus tour. This romantic castle of Neo-Gothic design sits on a cliff face overlooking the Echaz Valley near Honau in the Swabian Alps. It contained a large collection of historic weapons and armour. I was mesmerised by this fairy-tale castle with its moat, draw-bridge and extravagant fit-out of weaponry dating from 1200 to 1850 when the Counts of Wuerttemberg completed the building in its current form. It is one thing to see drawings of these castles and read stories in children's books, but quite another thing to see the real thing when fantasy becomes reality.

Family Photo 1949

When I think of our home life, I think first and foremost of my mother. She was the heart and soul of our home and was the most significant influence in my childhood and early adolescent years. After our father's return from the war in 1946, his work kept him away from home for much of the working week. The day to day care and nurture of us children still rested firmly in mother's capable hands.

At every breakfast and evening meal we would sit around the kitchen table and eat the meagre meals our mother had prepared with love and ingenuity. The meal would not be complete without family devotion. She would reach for her Bible and *Andachtsbuch* (devotional book) and read a short portion, closing with a heartfelt prayer. When Dad was at home he would lead these family devotions. He considered this a privilege and divine responsibility as head of the family.

As soon as we could read reasonably fluently our parents gave us a Bible – the real Bible, not a children's Bible – and encouraged us to read a chapter each night before we went to sleep. Much of what we read did not make a lot of sense but we persisted under sufferance. To make this ritual more exciting, Werner and I decided to turn it into a competition to see who could read the allocated chapter the fastest. Our motives may have been misplaced but our parents knew the importance of making us familiar with the truths of the Bible.

While there were some Nazi collaborators in our village their influence was minimal. Our mother had already formed her own strong convictions that what Hitler was doing to the Jews, to Christian leaders, as well as disabled and disadvantaged people, was wrong. When her school friend from Haifa, Ludwig Beilharz, came to Zell on one of his regular visits, he presented her with two Swastika flags for us boys. He also encouraged her to enlist us in Hitler's Youth movement when we were old enough to join. That never happened. Ludwig was informed, firmly but politely, of her view on that matter and while she accepted the flags, we were prohibited from displaying them outside of our house.

From very young we were taught the value of a good work ethic. There were always chores to do: chopping wood for the stove and heater; making our beds; washing dishes; helping in the garden; washing the kitchen floor; sweeping the front yard and footpath. Later, we earned pocket money for washing out the huge *Most* (cider) vats for a number of the local farmers as well as our own. I was small enough to crawl through the small trap door to scrub the inside of the vat with warm water to remove the slimy and smelly coating. Adults supervised this task because of the very real risk of being overcome by the toxic fumes. We may have complained about our work routine from time to time, especially when it interfered with our playtime plans, but on the whole we accepted it.

Saturday was compulsory bath time. Once a week the large metal bath tub was placed on the kitchen floor and filled with warm water from the kettle. One by one, each of us children were thoroughly scrubbed from head to toe. Other non-negotiable chores included the shoe cleaning ritual on Saturdays. Woe betides the child who had misbehaved during the week. His or her punishment became shoes cleaning for the whole household. Like her parents before her, our mother wanted to keep any necessary work on Sundays to an absolute minimum.

Christmas always brings back the happiest of childhood memories. Here is an account of what celebrating Christmas in Germany means to me.

It is Christmas Eve, 24th of December 1944. The Second World War was slowly grinding to its tragic and painful end. Times were tough; food was scarce. Our mother prepared Christmas Eve celebrations for us children, aged five, six and eight. There was no money to buy Christmas presents for the children, but on this occasion, three parcels arrived from friends and relatives in Saxony, totally unexpected.

Winter came early; snow was falling and 1944 would be a 'White Christmas'. After the Christmas Eve service at the village church our mother walked us three children back to our home in the cold and falling snow. She lit the wax candles on the pine Christmas tree, cut fresh from the local forest just two days before. We peeped through the key hole to get a glimpse of what was in the lounge room, but we could not see anything; the key hole had been blocked up. Then we walked in suppressed excitement into the cold, sparsely furnished lounge room, singing our favourite Christmas carol, *Ihr Kinderlein Kommet* (Oh come all ye children), with eyes glued on the three small parcels nestled below the Christmas tree. As we sat on the floor our mother reached for the well-worn Bible and read the Christmas story from Luke chapter 2.

"Do not be afraid. I bring you good news of great joy that will be for all people. Today, in the town of David a Saviour has been born to you; he is Christ the Lord (Luke 2: 10, 11)."

Mother asked us children to close our eyes. She folded her hands, bowed her head and prayed. She thanked God for sending Jesus as Saviour into this world to bring hope where there was despair, love where there was hatred, peace where there was pain, and joy where there was sadness. She thanked God for His protection and for providing for all the family needs during the dark years of war and she prayed for the safe return of her husband and the father of their children.

Then, and only then, it was time for us children to be presented with our gifts. What a joyful celebration it was! The brown paper wrapping was neatly folded and put aside for further use.

But more surprises awaited us. We heard the sound of bells in the street and then it entered our house. Our mother opened the door and in came Saint *Nickolaus* (St Nicholas), accompanied by *Knecht Ruprecht* (Servant Ruprecht). Our joyful expectation turned to fear; we knew what was coming next.

According to legend, Ruprecht threatens to put badly behaved children in a sack to take them away to the dark, dark forest. And sure enough Ruprecht asked, *"Have you been good children?"* To which we truthfully answered, *"Not all the time"*. As Ruprecht moved toward Werner and me, we fled to the safety of our mother. Ruprecht only let go of us when we promised to be very good.

Then *Christkindle* entered the room bearing gifts. (Christkindle was promulgated by Martin Luther during 16th-17th century Europe, explicitly to discourage or replace the legendary figure of St. Nicholas. Many Protestants changed St Nicholas to the Christkindle, or Christ Child, as the giver of gifts and the date was changed from December 6 to Christmas Eve) [1]. We took a deep breath but were still not sure whether the presents were really meant for us. Once we were allowed to handle them, our mood changed and we sang our Christmas song to all with their enthusiastic applause. Before St

Nicholas, Servant Ruprecht and the Christkindle left, they favoured us with a number of Christmas carols sung in beautiful harmony. By 9 pm we were very tired and Mother put us to bed. We were the happiest children in the world. I will never forget the Christmas of 1944.

For our mother this happy Christmas Eve was not yet over. So much was on her mind. The next morning she sat down to share her innermost thoughts in a letter to her beloved husband.

"I stayed up a little longer last night after the children went to bed, read a bit and my thoughts drifted back to Haifa while we were still all together. I thought back to 2 years ago when you came home from furlough and we celebrated Christmas as a family in Schneeberg. How glad and thankful I was that you could spend this brief time with us all and how wonderful it was that we could see each other again. These beautiful memories I shall keep close to my heart and never ever forget."

Many more great Christmas celebrations followed after Dad returned home from the war. Our parents made many sacrifices and surprised us with gifts that they could not afford, practical gifts that would help us to enjoy life as children. I shall never forget the year when Werner and I, in our early teenage years, were presented with a pair of ice skates each. They were the early model skates that clamped onto the heel and sole of our everyday winter boots. They brought us many hours of fun.

Three major events were celebrated over the German Easter season: the Christian Easter, the confirmation of year seven school students, and their graduation from primary school. It was in our family celebrations at home that we first became acquainted with the Easter tradition of homemade multi-coloured and hand-painted Easter eggs and sugar bunnies. Our large garden provided the ideal setting for our egg hunt early on Easter Sunday morning.

I could never quite decide whether I should loathe or love my brother, Werner, for being the eldest in the family. With the benefit of hindsight I now know that there are distinct advantages in being the second child. When mum was not around she made Werner my guardian. As I was too young to play with Werner's older friends, he was forced to make some huge personal sacrifices to keep me company while I played with my friends. Even today my class mates consider Werner as much a part of their class year as that of his own older class.

There were times when Werner showed his displeasure at having to be his brother's keeper. On one particular day his frustration boiled over and he threw a rock-hard cake of soap at me. He wasn't really concerned at my screaming – he was used to that – but when he saw blood shooting from my forehead like water from a drinking fountain, he panicked. *"What have I done? I have just killed my brother!"* Mother was outraged and grounded him for several days. Werner was conscience stricken and irreconcilably remorseful. As for me, I felt Werner did me no harm. I can barely remember the incident and there certainly was no permanent damage.

More often than not Werner and I were partners in crime. As the swarm of aeroplanes darkened our skies, we were inspired to conduct our own make-believe war games. We grabbed the forbidden swastika flags and, starting at opposing ends of our bed room, advanced toward each other. As we walked we punched a small hole in the soft plaster ceiling with the pointy end of the flag pole. Each hole represented one aeroplane from opposing squadrons: one from the RAF Fighter command and one from the German Luftwaffe. By the time we came face to face in the middle of the room the ceiling was covered with hundreds of 'planes'. We had such fun that we repeated the exercise starting from the opposite side of the room. Mum was not impressed with the new 'decoration' of the bedroom ceiling. The damage we had caused left her numb. She threw up her arms in hopeless despair and mumbled: *"I wish your father was here!"*

Several months later, when we were perfectly well behaved and the memory of our aerial battle in our bedroom was long forgotten (but the evidence remained for all to see), a big male figure, Pastor Berg, a friend of the family from Haifa, appeared in our house. As we listened from the room next door and heard our mother's description of our frequent mischief, we knew we were in trouble.

Pastor Berg commanded our presence and took the trouble to explain that all bad behaviour has consequences. Not only had we inflicted costly material damage but we had put our mother through considerable emotional pain and suffering. In the absence of our father, he was here to inflict the punishment we deserved. The fact that we tried to trick him by disappearing under our beds did not help our cause. When he did find us he gave us such a thrashing, which we thought was not only disproportionate to our deed but totally inappropriate, coming from a complete stranger and long after the event. Our only consolation was our mother's unspoken reaction. Her body language told us she thought that her well-meaning friend had overstepped the mark.

When I was about eleven or twelve, my parents thought I should learn to play the piano. We did not have a piano but we did have a harmonium. I started harmonium lessons with my junior primary school teacher, *Fraeulein* Auwaerter. Later, *Herr* Friesch continued my tuition. When Mother explained that she had trouble raising the fee, he still gave me lessons.

For a year or so I had my lessons on the piano in the school principal's lounge room and practised on the harmonium at home. Later my parents found a friendly neighbour who allowed me access to her piano for one hour a week. I never felt comfortable in her house. The lady was a cleanliness fanatic. Before I could enter the spotlessly clean room I had to remove my shoes and tip toe across the highly polished floor boards to reach the piano. However, my emotions soon turned from fear to rapture as I discovered the joy and satisfaction that comes from playing and listening to music. I hasten to add that my tuition was not in the classical repertoire; it simply consisted of basic lessons in learning to play the scales and German folk songs and hymns.

Our latent musical talents were further stimulated when Werner and I were loaned a brass instrument to practice. We had only just commenced our introduction to the German *Oompah* sounds when it was time to leave our village. But a seed had been sown that was to lead us into the world of Brass Band playing in the not too distant future.

In Haifa, my parents enjoyed the rich and diverse cultural life of the Temple Society: choirs and instrumental performances, live drama, plays and recitations of poetry. In Zell, after the war, there was little opportunity to attend public performances of any kind. Dad made sure we listened to the radio when one of his favourite classical pieces was playing. We had our first taste of live theatre when mother took us to Goeppingen to see a play about *Max und Moritz*: a magical story of two boys bent on causing mayhem. On another occasion we saw a play of the Christmas story in the neighbouring town of Eckwaelden. It's funny, the things you remember from your childhood!

At home we felt loved and totally secure. Our parents expressed their love by action but rarely, if ever, verbally. This was typical of that generation of Swabians. But their way of life spoke louder than words. They were strong and their care of us was such that we never felt deprived. Mother, in particular, had an astonishing grasp on the practical realities of life. She was unflappable through the highs and lows of life in the 1940s and endowed with a strong sense of conviction. She knew right from wrong, good from bad, and lived her life with a real sense of purpose.

I felt out of my depth when, on one occasion, Mother broke out of that typical Swabian/Stoll mould and began to verbalise her feelings. She spoke gentle, kind and meaningful words to me, not sloppy sentiments but words of conviction and love. The two of us had spent a very enjoyable time together on a beautiful summer's day. As we were walking home from picking pears on our *Wiesle* (small meadow) on the Goeppinger Road to Bad Boll, Mother stopped, looked at me and said, "*Herbert, I love you very much. You make me proud. You have the ability to make something special out of your life.*" I looked to the ground, a little embarrassed at her words, but I felt really good. I have never forgotten that day or those words of love and encouragement from my mother.

Central to every Sunday was going to church and Sunday school.

Fresco paintings - Interior of the Martin Church

Two aspects of church life left a lasting impression on me. As a small boy, the church building felt gigantic and the nave was cold and full of mysteries. Church, however, was never boring. It was not the order of service that captured my attention, but the large coloured fresco on the walls dating back to 1400 AD, over 100 years before the Reformation. Staring down at me in graphic, uncompromising life-size reality were scenes depicting the life, death and resurrection of Christ.

In these paintings little is left to the imagination. The Apostle Peter stands at the pearly gates of Heaven, key in hand. The devil, replete with horns and tail, props open the jaws of the dragon at the gates of Hell, poised to snap up his prey. There is the manger scene, the flight to Egypt, the dedication of Jesus and the cruel massacre of innocent babies by the sword of King Herod.

They all left me spell-bound. I saw cruelty and fear in every picture, including the suffering and death of the saviour of the world and the martyrdom of the apostles. But I also heard the words of my parents that it was God's greatest expression of love that took Jesus to the cross. I wished the man-made expressions on the cold stone walls were not so scary and a little more cheerful.

As I lowered my glance away from the frescos my eyes caught the small frame of *Pfarrer* (Pastor) Knapp. This kind gentleman carried out his parish duties despite suffering serious war injuries. We were taught to always close our eyes for prayers. *Pfarrer* Knapp prayed with his eyes wide open, gazing at an imaginary spot on the floor in front of him. Because of his head injuries he could not close his eyes without the risk of losing his balance. Of course, we boys made it our duty to also keep our eyes open, just in case he did fall. But something else caught my attention.

As the pastor faced the congregation I could only see one hand protruding from the end of the sleeves of his pastoral gown. The hand on his right arm was missing - another war legacy. I watched in amazement as he conducted the service. With his left hand he held his prayer and liturgy book and with the fleshy stump of his right arm he gently flipped the pages as efficiently as any able-bodied person. I wondered when the books would slip from his grasp and crash to the ground. That never happened!

A church deacon asked Werner and me if we were interested in learning to ring the church bell. Our mother agreed and off we went. Our lesson began with a climb up the tower steps until we reached the belfry. It used to accommodate three bells but only one was now left; the other two had been confiscated for war use.

The size of the bell dwarfed us and left us awestruck. The whole experience of climbing the rickety stairs to the lofty heights, while dodging timber trusses and cobwebs, made it a real life adventure.

Back on the ground floor the deacon continued to shout out instructions. *"Hold the rope firmly with both hands, pull and then loosen your grip!"*

Then it was our turn to put theory into practice. Werner clasped the thick rope firmly and pulled it down with all of his strength. When he succeeded in making the bell ring he was so excited that he forgot to let go of the rope. The next minute his feet were off the ground and he was sailing towards the ceiling before he remembered to let go of the rope. When it was my turn I fared no better. We learnt two things that day: bell ringing takes a lot of skill and a joy ride at the end of a bell ringing rope is good fun.

At the age of 13 I was introduced to the pipe organ. The organ tuner had arrived in town and he came to our school looking for a volunteer to assist him. When *Herr* Friesch chose me, I was pleased for the opportunity to skip classes but very nervous at what was expected of me.

Herr Friesch cheered me up. *"Relax Herbert, I know you know your scales and you will do a great job."*

For a whole day I sat at the console and pressed every key and foot pedal the organ tuner asked for. Every now and then he invited me around the back into the amazing forest of organ pipes and associated mechanics. I stared in amazement at the array of hundreds of organ pipes, each one skilfully crafted to a different shape, length and diameter. I listened with curiosity to the breathy sound they made, from the deep rumble of the bottom octaves that set the floor boards vibrating, to the high-pitched clarity of the top notes. To this day I love the unique sound of the pipe organ. Nothing evokes the emotions more than the majestic sound of an organ played to full capacity.

Bad Boll Academy

Pietism had strong roots in our district as a result of the presence of the Blumhardts in Bad Boll and the subsequent work of the Christian Academy there. A small group met on Sunday afternoons in Zell in a hall built by the Reuter family specifically for Bible study, fellowship and prayer (*Die Stunde*). Mum and Dad loved the fellowship of these Christian brethren. The Bible teaching made such an important contribution to their spiritual growth during their stay in Zell. I often heard them talk with great enthusiasm about those meetings.

Once or twice a year a special guest speaker came to hold evangelistic meetings or seminars on prophecy. One of Dad's favourite speakers was Pastor Wilhelm Busch. Dad read his books and went to his meetings when his itinerary brought him to Stuttgart. At home Dad would recall in great detail what he had learned. I liked everything I heard about God. On more than one occasion I chose to sacrifice an outing with my school mates in preference to going to these Sunday afternoon meetings, especially when the subject related to what the Bible taught about the end times.

Dad was keen for all of us to hear the best of the pastors and Bible teachers that came to our district. On one particular sunny Sunday afternoon we embarked on a trip to Kirchheim, eight kilometres away, to hear this special preacher. Our means of transport was one bicycle between five people. Dad, ferried us one by one a kilometre or so closer to our destination, while the rest kept walking. We never made it to the meeting but we had lots of fun and laughter, except for Mum. She had decided that the project was doomed before it started.

My interest in spiritual things was cultivated further through my confirmation in the Church. Everyone in my school class was Protestant and confirmation lessons were compulsory. Regrettably I remember very little about Luther's Catechism, taught to us by Pastor Knapp. Werner was confirmed the year before. On Palm Sunday 1952, at the age of fourteen, it was my turn.

We all received a Certificate of Confirmation inscribed with our own personal scripture verse. Mine came from Psalm 27 verse 1: *"The Lord is my light and salvation; whom shall I fear? The Lord is the stronghold of my life; of whom shall I be afraid?"*

My parents took the time to make us aware of the significance of confirmation. They explained that it marked the end of primary schooling and the commencement of our working lives (unless pursuing studies in higher education). But, just as we are now at an age where we must take responsibility for forging our own careers, so we must accept responsibility for fostering our spiritual lives.

My parents assured us that they would always support us in our spiritual journey and pray for us, but emphasised that becoming a Christian was a personal choice based on ones understanding of the truth found in the Bible. It was not until I was much older that I recalled their words: *"Going to Church, being baptised and confirmed is in itself no guarantee of going to heaven, but believing that Jesus is the Son of God and died for our sins, is."*

They asked me to memorize my confirmation text and make it my personal truth for life.

Confirmation Class – Herbert, 2nd from left, middle row, with Pastor Knapp in the middle of the back row

The quality of the social life I experienced with my school friends was second to none. In the 1940s and early 50s we were inseparable. We did everything together; from harmless pranks to high adventure, through every season of the year.

On the 11th of June 1988, after an absence of thirty six years, I was back in the company of those friends. I had accepted an invitation of my school friend, Wilhelm Rummelspacher, to come to Germany for a reunion of the Class of '38' for a 50th celebration (*50er Feier*).

Almost the whole of my class turned up (thirteen out of sixteen) as well as ten of Werner's classmates, plus their wives: a total of thirty six people. We went on an all-day bus trip to the Black Forest starting at 6.30 in the morning, and concluding with a grand dinner at the *Panorama Hotel* in Aichelberg. It was a day charged with high emotion as we revelled in each other's company and reminisced about our childhood experiences in Zell. What made it special was that my wife Margaret could share this moment with me and so gain some insight into what this place, my friends and culture, meant to me. There was just one set back: my German was a bit rusty and I struggled to express myself fluently.

During winter, the sledge, the skate and the ski became our treasured possessions. Between the ages of ten and thirteen we graduated from riding our sledges down the gentle slopes of the *Brogele* to the more challenging rides on the steep inclines of the Aichelberg. Riding down this course required not only courage but a high degree of skill to navigate this obstacle course of trees at high speed. The exhilaration was indescribable as we flew down the steep slope head first, lying flat on our stomachs with our legs acting as steering rudders. We never seemed to tire. We scampered up the slope again and again, to get as many rides as possible before nightfall.

Werner, Herbert, Mum, Helga & Elfriede

Accidents were inevitable. One of my school friends, Gerhard Guerth, became a victim of this winter sport. He crashed head first at high speed into one of the many tree trunks. We found him lying unconscious in the snow. None of us felt particularly good as we rushed him to his home on his sledge in a semi-conscious state. At our reunion dinner he told us that this accident has left him with a permanent health problem!

Ice skating is normally associated with the graceful glide over the smooth surface of frozen ice. For us it was a more hazardous experience. Our ice rinks were the roads. When the slushy snow surface turned into ice we learned to skate on the uneven and unpredictable surfaces. Soft snow patches and exposed steel manholes were the bane of our lives, resulting in many spills, pain and bruises. The nearest lake was in Bad Boll. We visited it on the rare occasion when a sustained winter snap froze it over and made it safe for skating. Skating on ice became an effortless delight, in comparison to our skating on snow.

But, we never thought our manoeuvres were too risky. On the rare occasion we did, the thrill of adventure dulled any sense of fear. A group of us had a creative idea to go speed skating. We had previously experimented with clutching on to a horse-drawn sleigh to glide over the frozen road at the galloping speed of a horse. Our next target became the public bus. We knew that it picked up passengers in the town square at midday. As the bus began to move out, about six of us lads emerged from the shadow of our hiding places, latched on to the bumper bar at the back of the bus, careful not to be spotted by the bus driver in his rear vision mirror. The challenge was to see who was 'the last man standing'.

To this day I can feel the sensation that rushed through my whole body as I hung on for dear life: the beating of the heart, the rattle of the skates, the vibration of my legs building until my whole body shook uncontrollably. At my first attempt I only lasted a few metres before I released my grip. It was only when we crashed and came home bruised and bleeding that our parents found out what we were up to. That put a quick end to this venture.

My first and only attempt at snow skiing was during a winter excursion organised by Willy Mannal, the newly appointed youth leader of the Church. He managed to borrow several sets of skis. We took our first tentative manoeuvres on the mainly flat snow terrain and gentle glides down some shallow slopes. However, the real purpose of this outing was not to learn to ski but to find, identify and document the footprints of birds and animals embedded in the freshly fallen snow. This relatively minor event is one of my favourite memories.

Willy Mannal (right, back row) with Youth Group.
Herbert, centre, front row

Summer and the long midyear vacation offered the most excitement for us children. Hiking, biking and camping became our favourite holiday activities.

A year or so after the war had come to an end I observed a new phenomenon: groups of people marching through our town with rucksacks on their backs, their walking sticks swinging and voices singing. I asked mother, *"What are they doing? Where are they going?"* It wasn't long before we became part of this healthy lifestyle. Pushbikes were rare, so we went walking and hiking everywhere. We hiked to the woods, through meadows, up the mountains and along the small streams that flowed all year round. We explored the castle ruins on the *Turmburg* (Castle Hill) at Aichelberg; quenched our thirst from the crystal clear waters of streams; picked wildflowers and cherries when in season, and revelled in the swimming pool in Weilheim.

Werner and I did not have a bicycle until the late 1940s. For the first time this gave us the freedom to travel further afield and explore the many attractions this region afforded. I saw my first drag race in Kirchheim and Willy Mannal organised camping trips on which I had my first experience of sleeping overnight in a tent. When I became a teenager, my parents allowed me to attend a Summer Camp with the Templers in Maulbronnen. Each of these outings away from home left a very positive impression on me. I became fascinated by the many enchanting old buildings, churches and castles and made my first attempts at sketching them.

When the soccer pitch on the Zeller Berg was completed in 1949, the school principal, *Herr* Friesch, set about recruiting and training a junior football team. He picked the required number of lads from the senior school, including me, to play in the district competition. Everyone was nervous. This was the first post-war football team in Zell. It was a first for our coach and team manager, *Herr* Friesch, and certainly a first for all the members of this fledgling team. At the end of our first season *Herr* Friesch was pleased with our effort, which exceeded even his own expectation. We competed against much stronger teams from much larger towns but still managed to bag a number of wins. Being left footed, I played up and down the left wing and became the leading goal scorer. When we played out of town we had to forfeit our matches on more than one occasion for lack of transport. There just were not enough cars available in town to take the full team to our destinations.

The home also provided the setting for us to play with the children of our tenants, Ilse and Karl, and school friends. Werner and I were generally too absorbed with boy things to take much interest in our younger sister, Helga. She, on the other hand, wanted to attach herself to her older brothers and their activities, much to our displeasure. Nevertheless, I like to think that her exposure to her older brothers had something to do with the energetic, robust and adventurous person Helga has become.

Helga had her own circle of close friends. She had a special connection with Elfriede, Kaethe Weberruss's daughter, who spent much time in our house and became like a sister to the whole family. The arrival of baby Inge changed the dynamics of our family. Helga had a little sister to play with and helped Mum to look after her. Inge is ten years younger than me and, regrettably, shared experiences during our time in Zell are harder to remember.

I do recall the time when the three of us were put in charge of our little sister, Inge. The idea was to introduce her to our favourite pastime, a visit to the *Brogele*, where we had spent many happy hours when we were younger. We had forgotten how inquisitive and lively a three and a half year old child could be. As Inge rushed towards the water's edge, she stumbled and we only just managed to stop her from falling into the stream. What we could not do was stop her from getting mud and dirt all over her new dress, recently tailored by Mum.

Inge at the *Brogele* in 2012

From late 1951 we started to pick up signals from our parents that our time in Zell was coming to an end.

Looking to the Future

The decision was made. We were going to Australia! The passports were ready, immunisation was completed and the basic living essentials were packed in wooden crates, ready for dispatch a month before our departure in May 1952.

Werner had completed one year of his carpentry apprenticeship. I had just turned fourteen and was in the throes of finishing my primary schooling. Helga was in year six and Inge was just four years old. For months and months my parents had wrestled with the question of whether to migrate to Australia or spend their future in Germany.

It was my uncle Wilhelm Stoll and his family who encouraged my parents to move to Australia. In 1941, he and his family were exiled from Palestine to the 'land down under'. After the war they were offered Australian citizenship and by 1948 they had settled near Nuriootpa in the Barossa Valley in South Australia.

Things were looking up for them. There was plenty of work and a good education system for the children. So much of their new country reminded them of their homeland of Palestine. There was the Mediterranean climate, the diverse mix of arid and fertile landscape, and the large plantations of oranges, apricots and vineyards. Even the eucalyptus tree was common to both countries.

But they also felt a strong connection between the Barossa Valley and the country of their national origin, Germany. Much of that beautiful valley was pioneered by settlers from Germany during the 1800s. They came in pursuit of religious freedom and established Lutheran parishes in Tanunda, Bethany, Marananga, Light Pass, Neukirch, Ebenezer and other locations throughout the Barossa. For many, German remained their first language (*Barossa Deutsch*). These Christian people had sponsored the Stoll family and supported them with housing, work and practical help. The Stolls began to feel at home in this beautiful land, among these kind and generous people who had such a strong and vibrant faith, and rich German heritage.

Wilhelm Stoll had no hesitation in hailing Australia, and the Barossa Valley in particular, as the new 'Canaan'; the land flowing with 'milk and honey'. He was enthusiastic for us to join them. But his was not the only voice that beckoned us. Large numbers of Templer people, residing in Germany after the war, had begun to go to Australia to rejoin their relatives and friends. They wrote with equal enthusiasm about this privileged land of Australia and the opportunities it offered for a better life. My parents were persuaded and plans for saying our farewells were in full swing.

To me, going to Australia was yet another invitation to a new adventure and more excitement. So much was happening in the months leading up to our departure that I had little time to think and reflect on the significance of being uprooted from the place that had been my home for nine years.

First, there was my graduation from primary school. I was happy with my school results and the completion of this milestone. For all of my classmates it meant the start of their working career at age fourteen.

Next, one of our play times in the *Sonnenweide* woods turned sour. A school mate accidentally smashed a piece of fallen oak branch into my face and messed up my mouth. It resulted in an emergency visit to the dentist in Boll and left me with the legacy of a black front tooth.

My confirmation took place soon afterwards. The whole family, including Uncle Christian and Aunty Christel celebrated the occasion over afternoon *Kaffee und Kuchen*. Late in the afternoon Werner and I, with our cousin Walter and a number of other graduating boys, went for a walk down to the *Brogele* to let off some steam. The next minute a cigarette was lit up and I was asked to have a puff. This threw me into a dilemma. My parents had prohibited smoking and made it clear that it was a filthy habit. The solemnity and spiritual significance of my confirmation, which we were celebrating as a family on this very day, was still foremost in my mind. But now these older boys insisted that smoking was an act of initiation to prove that I was now a man. I gave in, took the cigarette and had several big puffs. I did not feel good about it. In fact I was ashamed of myself. I became violently sick and threw up. That was the first and last cigarette I touched!

A week later, my family and I were sitting on the bus in the town square waving our farewells to our many friends and the villagers that had gathered to say goodbye. Mum and Dad held back their tears but Helga cried her eyes out. She couldn't bear the thought that she might never see Elfriede and her other school friends again. Inge was too young to appreciate what was going on. She laughed and squealed, just happy to be going on a bus ride. I didn't know how I should feel. I was certainly a little sad but also excited. My teacher, *Herr* Friesch, had given me (and my brother) a brand new pair of football boots, as a farewell present. He expressed the hope that I would make good use of them in Australia.

Our journey took us by train through Switzerland to Italy. In Genoa, the 12 000 tonne Lloyd Triestino passenger ship, the Oceania, awaited us. We found our six berth cabin on one of the lower decks of the ship and settled in for our four-week, 20 000 kilometre passage to Australia. The excitement had been building and now we were finally aboard this amazing ship. Werner and I quickly found our bearings and in no time at all we knew our way to the dining rooms, lounges, deck, the swimming pool and many more of the intriguing features of the ship.

Our journey commenced with a land trip to Mount Vesuvius, seven kilometres inland from Naples. In school we had learned about its volcanic eruption in AD 79 and the destruction of the Roman cities of Pompeii and Herculaneum. Now we saw with our own eyes the excavated ruins of the licentious Roman city of Pompeii and learned about the people of that day. My parents bemoaned the depravity of these citizens and their lifestyle, so shamelessly exhibited in the ruins.

Our ship finally left Naples and after we crossed the Mediterranean Sea, it docked at Port Said in Egypt. The strange sights, smells and sounds in the streets and bazaars, over-crowded with people and beasts, were bewildering and just a little scary. We made sure to stay close to our parents.

Our Ship, the Oceania, on its way to Australia

We watched in awe as our ship skilfully navigated through the Suez Canal and then unwound as we travelled down the calm waters of the Red Sea and the Gulf of Aden into the Indian Ocean on our way to Ceylon (Sri Lanka). In Colombo the heat was stifling and a cautious sip of the sickly sweet drink we bought in the stalls did nothing to quench our thirst. The endless sea of humanity that confronted me left an indelible impression on my teenage mind, of a country steeped in poverty, misery and sickness.

Life on board ship quickly established its own routine. For the first few weeks it was dominated by my daily dash to the open porthole of our cabin, where I emptied the contents of every meal into the ocean waters. Life for me was miserable. I couldn't shake off the constant discomfort of sea sickness, or the severe ear infection for which the ship doctor couldn't find a cure. In stark contrast, the rest of the mainly Italian passengers were living it up. Their passionate singing could be heard until the early hours of the morning on every day.

On the long open sea from Colombia to Fremantle we experienced a pleasant diversion. We celebrated the long standing tradition of the 'Line Crossing Ceremony' on the 11th of May 1952. The ship was decorated and everyone gathered around the swimming pool in front of King Neptune and his court, who were dressed in their most splendid regalia. As the ship crossed the equator selected passengers were playfully interrogated by King Neptune and his entourage. Proceedings dragged on as everyone joined in the fun. At the end of the ceremony each one was initiated as a 'Son of Neptune' and received a certificate to that effect.

Helga & Inge in the Ship's Swimming Pool

Further into our journey excitement built as the word spread. *"We are nearing the west coast of Australia!"* Finally, our destination was within reach. Every deck of the ship was crowded with passengers and we all scanned the horizon for our first sight of Australian soil.

"I can see it!" someone shouted as they pointed at the faint outline of land appearing in the distance. Spontaneous jubilation erupted all over the ship and people began to celebrate the near end of a long journey. For others the mood changed to silent contemplation. I wonder what went through the minds of my parents. For them the reality of coming to a new country at the

age of fifty to raise four children in a new culture weighed heavily on their minds.

The first impression of our first port of call in Australia, Fremantle, was decidedly negative. After a casual stroll around the dock and a look at the town, hearts sank. Many expressed their sentiments openly. *"What have we come to? This looks like the end of the earth!"*

For me, the best of the ship cruise was just around the corner. As the Oceania turned east to face the notorious storms of the Great Australian Bight my sickness vanished. I finally discovered my sea legs. When everyone else fell sick and retreated to their cabins, I thrived in the elements on the open decks. What fun to roll with the ship through the gigantic waves and to stagger from rail to post while the spray and waves rolled over the planks. For the first time on the journey, I had no trouble keeping my food down.

At the end of May 1952 we disembarked in Melbourne. After staying with friends from Palestine for a few days we travelled to Adelaide on the overnight train. Around midday we boarded the train to Nuriootpa in the Barossa Valley, where we were picked up by members of the Wilhelm Stoll family and taken to our new home at Ebenezer. We received the warmest of welcomes.

After a separation of 13 years, three of the four Stoll siblings, Wilhelm, Hulda and Maria were now together again, in Australia.

Section IV.

The Land of New Beginnings
(1941 – 2004)

Tanunda 2004

Exiled to the Land Down Under

To understand our coming to Australia more fully, I need to briefly explore the connection between the German Templers from Palestine and their journey from exile, to internment, to freedom, to citizens of Australia.

My uncle Wilhelm and his family were part of the group of German Nationals from Palestine that were brought to Australia by the British authorities and interned in a camp for German and Italian citizens at Tatura, 12 kilometres from Rushworth in the State of Victoria. They arrived at Tatura on August 25th, 1941 and spent the next five years in the camp behind barbed wire.

Aerial View – Tatura Camp

There were four internment camps able to accommodate 1000 people each. The Germans from Palestine were in Camp 3 which was divided into four compounds surrounded by a four metre high barbed wire fence. The newcomers, 667 Germans (including 613 settlers from Palestine) and 178 Italian citizens were allocated to compounds A, B and C[1]. They adapted to the internment lifestyle as best they could and enjoyed a reasonable amount of autonomy. Children were given a high level of education in German and the Australian

Education Department offered evening classes in English, French, Japanese, Russian, Spanish and Italian. In their leisure time the Germans cultivated their cultural and scientific interests, hobbies and social life. Instrumental ensembles and choirs were established, plays performed and church services and Templer meetings conducted regularly[2].

Dormitory Huts at Tatura

Wilhelm did voluntary work as a baker in the camp kitchen. His five children – Ruth, Wilhelm, Theodor, Gerhard and Siegfried – went to a school which was taught in German by the internees, including trained teachers from the Templers and German missionaries from New Guinea.

Fortunately, the Australian Government moved away from the destructive 'friend-versus-enemy' thinking, very soon after the end of the war. A judge of the High Court, the highest court of the country, was commissioned by the government in 1946/47 to examine the political past of the Germans from Palestine. At question was their allegiance to German National Socialism. The results of his detailed investigation went a long way towards their political exoneration. His report concluded, *"In general, they are practical, morally sound and peaceful people...any thorough, unprejudiced examination of their previous history will essentially confirm this, in my opinion."* In the end the judge recommended that only 70 of the 504 men, women and children from the Templer communities then in Australia be repatriated to Germany[3].

From the beginning of their internment, the Germans expected to return to Palestine after the war was finished. As late as April 1946 this remained their stated wish. When political circumstances made it clear that this was not possible, Justice Hutchins gave the internees the choice of either remaining in Australia or agreeing to repatriation to Germany. In the event that they decided to stay in the country, he held out the prospect that the Australian authorities would support the transfer of the internee's assets from Palestine. Furthermore, he would raise no objections should the Templers already in Australia wish to send for their relatives at their own expense. (The Meinels came to Australia on that basis.) At a meeting on the 17th June 1946, the majority of men in Camp 3 voted to stay in Australia. The internees in the other camps reached similar decisions[4].

The Australian Government estimated the value of the property left behind in Palestine by the Templers now in Australia to be 5 000 000 pound sterling, and that of the other Templers also interested in settling in Australia, at 15 000 000 pound sterling. It recognised that without access to these resources, successful settlement of this religious community could not be guaranteed. In a Treasury memorandum of 2nd October 1946, it was described as being in the interest of Australia to have the abovementioned assets of the Temple Society and of its members, transferred[5].

This permission by the Government for the settlers to become permanent residents of Australia happened at a time when the wounds suffered by the Australian people in the war had not yet healed. Thousands of other German prisoners of war, and civilian internees, were sent back from Australia to Germany and Germans in general were still excluded from immigration to Australia[6].

For Wilhelm Stoll, the decision to stay in Australia was not so much driven by financial considerations, as the conviction that Australia could offer much greater opportunities for his children than Germany, which was struggling for survival in the early post-war period.

By mid-August 1946, the first of the internees were permitted to leave the camp. By October 30th, 1947, 455 had been released. Of those, 263 found accommodation and work in Victoria, 89 settled in South Australia, 90 in NSW and 13 in Queensland.

For the internees who had been transported to Australia in 1941, and the refugees from Palestine who followed them after the war, the early stages of economic recovery were extraordinarily difficult. Having been cast out of the Holy Land, they had literally nothing. Successful entrepreneurs, prosperous tradesmen and hard-working farmers who had owned large areas of land, had to start again at the bottom of the social ladder as labourers or small wage-dependent employees. In the case of the younger refugees, this painful re-adjustment to totally new and different circumstances succeeded without too many complications as there was no lack of employment opportunities. However, it was very difficult for the older ones who could not make use of their years of professional experience. They found it hard to adjust[7].

In spite of these difficulties, Wilhelm Stoll strongly believed that God would help his family to make a successful new beginning in Australia. On release from the camp in late 1946, the Stoll family travelled to South Australia and settled on a farm in a place called 'World's End', near Burra. Wilhelm, through contacts with the Lutheran Church, was offered a job as a farm labourer by the Heinrich family. They were given an old house 1.5 kilometres from the farm with sufficient bedding and other furniture to live in, and a cow for their daily milk supply. Ruth helped with the farm housework, milking cows and doing childcare, while Wilhelm (Bill) was old enough for farm work. Theodor (Ted), Gerhard (Gary) and Siegfried (Fred) went to school in Burra. They were encouraged to earn pocket money from after school activities. Reducing the rabbit population in the area became one of their favourite income activities. The local congregation of Point Pass, led by their Pastor, provided extra assistance to the family during the initial stages of settling in.

Ted Stoll, reflecting on those times, writes: *"My father had been seriously injured during World War I. He'd lost the sight in one eye and could not drive. We still think being given this job as a farm labourer was more due to the kindness of the Heinrich family for fellow Christians in need of housing and work, than their own need for farm help. My father found being a farm labourer at that stage of his life very hard work."*[8]

After one year in Burra the family moved to the Barossa Valley. In the Lutheran congregation of Neukirch, several kilometres outside the town of Nuriootpa, they found a very caring group of people who helped them set up home in the old church school house. A year later, the Stoll family was able to rent a large old farmhouse near Ebenezer, approximately 8 kilometres from Nuriootpa. Later, in 1954 they moved to Nuriootpa. Wilhelm worked as a labourer in orchards, vineyards, the Barossa Cannery and home gardens until his retirement.

Ted said, "My father's status from a business owner and employer in Palestine to labourer in Australia was not easy for him. Once, when pruning vines at a time when he was feeling low, he told the son of the vigneron with tears in his eyes that 'even the kookaburras are laughing at me'."[8]

However he persevered and his faith was strengthened through those difficult years. Wilhelm Stoll accepted his circumstances of coming to Australia as part of God's plan for his life. He could not have foreseen in 1946 that this plan was to culminate in the reunification of all of his siblings and their families in the beautiful Barossa Valley.

Wilhelm Stoll was a living testimony to the truth of the words written over the doorway of the ancestral Stoll home in Haifa. *"Great peace have they who love your law and nothing can make them stumble* (Psalm 119: 165)."

Wilhelm Stoll & Family at Ebenezer 1952

Back Row: Bill, Ruth, Aunty Hulda, Ted
Front Row: Tine, Fred, Wilhelm, Gary

Ebenezer

It was just over a week after our arrival at Ebenezer, and barely three weeks since we put our feet on Australian soil, when my brother Werner and I arrived at Nuriootpa High School on the 1st day of the start of the 2nd term in 1952.

We were ushered into the school yard for general assembly. The Australian flag was hoisted and everyone paid their allegiance to Queen Elizabeth of England. They sang, *"God save our gracious Queen"*. Straight away I got this funny feeling in my stomach and I was overcome with strange thoughts; thoughts of inferiority!

I was a German.

I belonged to the nation that inflicted intolerable evil, death and atrocities on the world; a nation that was defeated by England and the Allies; a once proud nation now without honour and respect. What reception could I, a lonely German migrant boy, expect from this crowd of English speaking Australians? Right then I wished I could make myself invisible.

My brother and I found ourselves in the front row of the class room. We sat, observed and listened but understood nothing. The teacher talked and wrote on the chalkboard. The class responded, laughed and sang and I did not have a clue as to what was going on. I wondered what in the world I was doing here.

Boys and girls cast curious looks at us from all corners of the room. I blushed with embarrassment as I realised that, not only did I speak a different language, but I also looked different. My shoes were of a different design and the clothes I wore had a distinct European look, unlike anything the local boys were dressed in. The bell rang and I was swept along by the stampede of students racing to the next room for another lesson.

I awoke from my melancholy thoughts when the teacher walked in and greeted the class with: *"Guten Morgen!"* (Good Morning). I had landed in a German class! But why was I, a German national, enrolled to learn to speak German? Before I had time to unravel the logic of this question the teacher approached our desk. She explained in exemplary German:

"The School thinks that your attendance at German Classes is possibly the best way for you to learn how to read, write and speak English!"

This made no sense to us at the time but proved to be right. It certainly provided a very welcome connection with our homeland and allowed us to be active participants in class at least for a short period of each school day. The teacher introduced us to the class and we received a roaring applause of welcome.

My spirit lifted. The class roll was called. I listened in amazement at the names of my fellow students: Schmidt, Mattner, Schulz, Schrapel, Munzberg, Saegenschnitter…all German names. In the school yard we were surrounded by students doing their very best to talk to us in Barossa Deutsch, learnt from their parents and grandparents. Many of them still spoke German at home. Their warmth and enthusiasm began to ease my fear and apprehension. It slowly dawned on me that, probably, there was no better place in the whole of Australia for a German migrant boy to be than right here in the heart of the Barossa Valley.

The Physical Education and Woodwork classes gave further opportunity for active participation. Werner, who had commenced his apprenticeship in Joinery in Germany, became the star pupil of Mr Rodney Pike, our Woodwork teacher. I struggled with my first project, a set of timber bookends, but relished the advantage of having an older experienced brother by my side.

At my first PE session we played a game of football. But it was not the game of football I knew. They called it "Australian Rules". The game of football I knew they called "Soccer". My brother and I knew absolutely nothing about this Australian football game. All we knew were the rules and tactics of the round ball game, the game we had played since we could walk. But this was something else!

How any sensible game of football could be played with such a curiously shaped ball with its unpredictable bounce was beyond our comprehension. The game began and somehow we worked out that our task was to chase the ball all over the paddock and put it through the sticks at one end. But which sticks? There were four: two tall and two shorter and no cross bar. I ran like mad but the ball eluded me time and time again.

Then my moment arrived. The ball bounced around my legs right in the goal square. I was in a dilemma. What should I do? Pick up the ball with my hands first and then kick it, or was I allowed to soccer it off the ground through the sticks? I had worked out that heading the ball was not a wise option. I picked up the egg-shaped ball to kick it but by the time I interpreted the signals and shouts from my team mates, the ball had been ripped out of my grasp and cleared by the opposing team. The soccer skills of this schoolboy champion striker made absolutely no contribution to a winning score on the occasion of my very first Aussie Rules football match, in the very first week of my high school education in Australia.

Before long I felt accepted. The teachers went out of their way to offer help and support in the class room and outdoor activities. I was constantly surrounded by boys who talked to me, protected me and asked lots of questions about life in Germany. I understood some of it but, at that stage, I had no hope of communicating with any degree of intelligence. I knew they finally considered me as one of their own when they gave me a new name. They called me 'Herb' and I felt good and honoured. My soccer boots, brought with me from Germany, never saw the light of day. They remained unused in the bottom of our wardrobe. Instead, I wore a pair of Australian football boots which, almost subconsciously, became a symbol of my ambition to become integrated into the Australian culture as quickly as possible. I have never played competitive soccer since.

Every day, through sunshine, wind and rain, Werner and I peddled our borrowed pushbikes the eight kilometres each way between school and our home at Ebenezer. When it was wet the dirt road turned to slush and the clay mud clung to the tyres like glue and made progress frustratingly cumbersome. During the winter months we often became soaking wet. Turning back was never an option. Shivering all over, we placed ourselves in front of the open fire in the class room before the first lesson began, in a desperate attempt to warm up and dry out. We wondered about the logic of having a blazing fire with the doors and windows propped wide open!

Helga was enrolled in grade 7 at the Lutheran Primary School at Neukirch: a one room school for years 1 to 7. She struggled with the new language the same way Werner and I had. She was not impressed when placed in the entry grade levels for reading, writing and arithmetic. She felt isolated. When just a few of the girls made fun of her, going to school became more than a chore; she hated it. The truth is that Helga mastered the English language better and quicker than any of us. We admired that, with just a small dose of jealousy. Inge was at home with mum, waiting to turn five before she could start school.

Our first home on the property at Ebenezer was an early Australian farmhand cottage. It had three rooms, a rusty galvanised iron roof and verandah on one side. It was very old and falling to bits. Uncle Wilhelm and the local Lutheran congregation had lovingly restored it. The mud walls had been whitewashed and the dirt floors covered with linoleum. For us children, the flickering light of the kerosene lamps at night, the creak of the rusty windmill outside, and the rowdy scramble of the resident possums in the roof, filled our house with intrigue and adventure. However, after a while, the novelty of our visits to the outside 'drop-loo' lavatory – in all weather conditions, day and night – lost its attraction.

Our first Home in Australia at Ebenezer

For Mum and Dad these living conditions were a huge step back in time. They brought back memories of similar primitive living conditions Mum had experienced forty years earlier as a teenager in Haifa, and of the internment camp in Waldheim, when we lived in a single room above a chicken coop for three years (1939-42). None of these sentiments were expressed openly. There was work to be done to transform this humble dwelling into a home filled with love, laughter and singing. And, that is how I remember it.

Mum was busy as mother and homemaker and Dad was out looking for work. He couldn't afford to be fussy. He was offered work as a farm hand by the Kleinig family from Neukirch, who were co-sponsors of our immigration permit. They also offered income opportunities for the whole family picking olives from trees no one had harvested for years. Dad found this type of work frustrating and unrewarding but it was necessary to survive.

Fortunately, opportunities for work in the 1950s were good and Dad found employment in the Kowald Bakery in Murray Street, Tanunda. He struggled with the circumstances that confronted him in the bakehouse. His English was very limited and he had to deal with baking methods and machinery not familiar to him. To Dad, the bread and other baked goods lacked flair and taste. However, in the early 1950s the local owners were not yet ready for the introduction of Continental and Middle Eastern breads, pastry or specialist cakes. It was in later decades that Martin's baking reputation and influence were to leave their mark in the Barossa Valley.

Dad's only means of transport from Ebenezer to Tanunda, a distance of sixteen kilometres, was by bicycle. For almost twelve months he pedalled his bike for one hour in all weather conditions to get to work by three am, five days a week; and another hour to get home again. Dad (and Mum) carried their burdens silently. But we were not spared his bouts of frustration and anger when he had to face howling head winds or severe cloudbursts. Under those conditions each journey took him much longer and drained every bit of energy from his body.

He did not allow such events to dull his sense of humour and spirit of adventure. In summer, he loved to stop at the half way mark of his travel home to cool off in the swimming pool in Nuriootpa. On those occasions when he found the pool closed, he took matters into his own hands. More than once he scaled the chain wire fence, stripped down to his under pants and made himself at home in the refreshing water of the pool. The fact that he may be trespassing, or the embarrassment of getting caught, barely crossed his mind. He pedalled his bike for the rest of the journey with renewed enthusiasm, laughing and singing all the way home. Dad never seemed to grow old.

For us teenage children, the property at Ebenezer became our playground and introduced us to the Australian rural landscape: stands of mature gum trees, lots of native plants, a dam with yabbies, and a cavernous creek with wildlife and steep brown-red cliffs. The first winter and early spring transformed the dry, brown earth into a carpet of lush green grass with an amazing display of rich blue flowers. Our euphoria was somewhat deflated when we learned that this unique plant, called 'Salvation Jane', is a weed and one of the farmers' worst nightmares.

We got to know our Stoll cousins well; in particular, Fred, Gary and Ted. They lived in the main farmhouse on the property with their parents. The eldest two children, Ruth and Bill, boarded in Adelaide. Ruth was studying to become a teacher and Bill, a Lutheran Pastor/missionary.

The Stoll Farmhouse Home at Ebenezer

By 1952 they had lived in Australia for eleven years and they became our role model for everything Australian. We spent a lot of time together. We played football and cricket in between the alleys of the tall gum trees and had our first attempt at shooting rabbits under Fred's guidance in the dry creek bed. Uncle Bill's milk cow grazed on the property. Helga and Inge kept their distance while Werner and I took it in turns to see who could squeeze the most milk out of the udder. At other times we watched a spectacle we thought belonged to a past farming era: a team of twelve horses harnessed to a huge ploughing machine, cultivating the ground in the adjoining paddock.

First Attempt at Cricket   On the Hunt for Rabbits

In late 1952, the whole Meinel family vacated the cottage at Ebenezer and moved to Light Pass. We had been offered accommodation in the manse while August Simpfendoerfer, the Pastor of the Immanuel Lutheran Church in Light Pass, went to Germany with his wife for long service leave, leaving their children behind. Mum and Dad became their house parents in exchange for free lodging.

To everyone's delight, Uncle Christian and his family arrived in Australia in November 1953. They moved into the cottage the Meinels had vacated at Ebenezer. Christian was employed by Bert Boehm, an orchardist in Light Pass, for a number of years. Later he worked for a builder, C O Juncken in Nuriootpa. Christel and their daughter, Herta, worked in the Cannery in Nuriootpa for a while. Later, Herta moved to Adelaide to work at the Royal Adelaide Hospital as a nurse. In February 1957, she left for Indonesia to marry Hans Wyler. They and their family later settled near Zurich in Switzerland.

Walter started work with his father, Christian, in the orchard in Light Pass until Paul Wieland, a fellow German Palestinian, having heard about Walter's engineering background, offered him a job in the garage he was operating in Truro. Gary, who originally was a farmhand, joined him there soon after. When Paul Wieland obtained a Volkswagen franchise, he moved the business to Nuriootpa.

At Ebenezer, our cousins gave Werner and me our first lessons in driving a car. The Ford buckboard was put through an enormous amount of pain before I could master the art of double-declutching to change gears.

Walter and Gary gave Werner preliminary instructions on how to ride a motor bike. All of a sudden Werner takes off. I watched, petrified, as I saw the bike and rider shoot across the ground at breakneck speed heading straight for the stone walled shed next to our house. My heart sank to the bottom of my stomach. I could see Werner and the bike splattered against the wall. Catastrophe! Once again, my imagination got the better of me. To my great relief, Werner took control of the bike and brought it to a standstill just short of the wall.

When we weren't playing in the grounds outside, we entertained ourselves in Uncle Wilhelm's house. I took a liking to the harmonium and tackled playing through the hymns of the *Reichs-Lieder* book from cover to cover. Wally played the violin and he inspired Gary to learn. Dad had inherited Grandpa's antique violin and was keen for one of his children to keep the tradition going in the family. I got the parental nod and Gary taught me the basics. Much to Dad's disappointment I did not persevere with it and the precious violin was put back into mothballs.

Wally & Herb

Our family mixed freely with the local community from the Lutheran congregations of Ebenezer and Neukirch who had befriended us. We attended church and participated in its various activities. They were wonderful and generous people, who went out of their way to make us feel welcome and part of their Barossa community.

The Mickan family heard about Dad's love of the sea, which was ingrained in his psyche from his days swimming in the Mediterranean Sea in Haifa. They invited the whole family to an all day picnic on the beach at Brighton. We boarded the truck early in the morning. The adults squeezed into the cabin, the children parked on the open tray at the back and we all endured the 80 kilometre ride over the bumpy road to the beach. We made ourselves at home under the shade shelter at Brighton and had the best of fun all through the day.

For us it was our first experience of swimming in the sea. In Germany in summer, boys were used to running around all day in the sun with no top on. So we took little notice of Mr Mickan's warning to cover up. The journey back home was less fun. The effect of sunburn began to make its presence felt. Nursing its painful consequences for several days taught us an important lesson never again to expose ourselves for long periods of time to the Adelaide sun and sea breezes.

Helga, Inge & the resident cow

Helga & Inge

The Barossa Valley is synonymous with vine growing and this industry is the primary employer of the people who live there. Max Grope was one of a number of Lutheran vine growers who offered employment opportunities to our family. Max part owned and managed a mixed farm, which included vineyards, apricot and peach orchards, and a small acreage of wheat and barley. Fred already worked for him on a casual basis and soon after our arrival Max also offered Werner and me work, on an as-need basis, during our high school days.

Saturdays found us three cousins learning the hard yakka of the wine maker. We had to spade the weeds away from the trunks of the vines until it felt as if our backs broke. After pruning, we dumped the vine cuttings into the horse-drawn fire furnace for burning. Occasionally, we helped with the hand picking of grapes during the harvest season. During lunch we rested our weary bodies on the grass edge of the vineyard, ate our homemade sandwiches and drank the cool water from the hessian waterbag, while Max practiced his best German 'Barossa Deutsch' on us. Fred jumped in as interpreter whenever we gave him the blank stare.

In the summer school holidays, we picked apricots and peaches in the heat of the summer sun. Or, we cut apricots, stacked the trays into the sulphur box and laid them out in the sun for drying. We helped with the construction of farm sheds made from the trunks and branches of the eucalyptus tree, and a roof from thatched straw harvested direct from the field. Mr Grope was insistent that the best way to securely anchor the posts into the ground was with rammed earth, not concrete. We quickly learned that the blunt end of the crowbar was a handy way to consolidate the dry clay around the bottom of the post and that the quickest way to get blisters on your hands was to not wear gloves.

We got involved with the tractor and discovered why it had replaced the hitherto reliable horse. Its capability and versatility extended from ploughing the soil of paddocks and vineyards, to drilling post holes, to powering the blade of the wood saw. We felt like kings when Max let us sit behind the wheel of the tractor for the first time.

Of all the memories I have of our association with Max Grope one stands out. It was the hay season. The stacked hay bales were ready to be collected from the field. Fred, Werner and I joined Max at Light Pass after school and started loading the bails onto the Bedford truck. It was hard work and Max said we needed to have a break. We sat on the bales of hay and Max produced a flagon of claret. He filled our glasses to the brim. We raised them to the sky and shouted in good Barossa fashion, *Prosit.*

I had never tasted wine before, so I took my cue from Werner and Fred and emptied the glass. We got on with the job in high spirits and finished loading the truck. I wondered why my head was spinning and my feet were no longer steady. When the last bail was loaded we patted ourselves on the back for a job well done. Surely there was nobody else in the Barossa that could do a better job!

I opened the paddock gate and watched as Max gently manoeuvred the truck over the sloping ground towards me. I stared in disbelief as I saw the truck lean sharply and then dump half its load unceremoniously onto the ground. Our hilarity vanished. We reloaded the truck and got home well after dark. My teenage mind rationalised, "*It's the wine that is to blame!*" I have never had a drink of alcohol since.

Max must have been frustrated out of his mind at times with the farming ignorance of his immigrant boys. On rare occasions he did lose his temper. He shouted, "*Dummkopf*" (ignoramus) at us and threw his hands up in the air. But I remember him most for his friendliness and great sense of humour. He was motivated by his love for helping fellow Lutherans and we will be forever grateful for him taking us young teenagers under his wing.

Every pay packet we received was handed to our parents in full as our contribution towards the costs to migrate to Australia.

Today I have come to recognise the value of those humble beginnings in Australia at Ebenezer and Light Pass. The events and circumstances my siblings and I faced in making a new beginning, in a new country, in a mud house in the back-blocks of Nuriootpa in the Barossa Valley, helped to shape our character for life. Now we look back with a great deal of pride and joy on what those days of hard work taught us and what we achieved. The values our parents instilled in us from a young age were reinforced: values of labouring and learning, of family, faith, friends and fun.

We also learned something about the challenges that migrant children have to deal with. Inge, as a five year old, started her schooling in the one teacher Lutheran primary School at Light Pass. It was not a happy introduction to learning for Inge. Some of the students openly expressed their dislike of this German migrant, labelling her a Nazi. On another occasion our parent's house, at 10 Elizabeth Street Tanunda, was pelted with eggs. While my school experiences were positive, these incidents brought to light the anti-German sentiment that still lingered in isolated pockets of the Australian society in the early 1950s, even in the Barossa Valley.

It was not something that bothered me much at the time, but on reflection, I have come to recognise that the challenges and conflicts a migrant child faces are very real and personal and they certainly left their own unique emotional footprints on my life and personality. I was fearful, shy and at times withdrawn as I struggled with the adjustments to become integrated into the Australian way of life. I could not wait to shed the migrant tag. It was never an intolerable experience but it did stretch my comfort zone. Living under the umbrella of loving parents, and the extended family at Ebenezer, cushioned the impact of any permanent negative outcomes.

However, for our parents it was altogether different. They carried the full burden of making a new start in a new country. They did not complain. Dad recognised the opportunities that life in Australia promised for him and his family. His robust faith, strong work ethic and the support of the Stoll families gave him the confidence to succeed. But the obstacles he faced, and the responsibility he placed upon himself as head of the family, were like a huge mountain. They tested his faith and sapped his strength and will to their very limits.

For Mum it was equally hard but she coped better. Her fluency in the English language, and having all her siblings around her, gave her a head start. By contrast, Dad's relatives were a long way away, back in Germany, inaccessible behind the "Iron Curtain" from 1961 onwards. When it came to raising a family, Mum could also draw on the coping mechanism she had developed through the difficult internment and war years. Those experiences had made her stronger and better equipped to deal with the challenges of change and new beginnings.

Dad and Mum did not consider it a coincidence that their very first home in Australia was located in a place called Ebenezer. Their mind went back to the story in the Bible where the people of Israel erected a stone memorial as a reminder of how God had delivered them when they were in great distress and in fear of their lives. They called that memorial, Ebenezer, which means, *"Thus far has the Lord helped us"* (1 Samuel 7:12). The place in Australia called Ebenezer reminded them that just as God kept them safe and secure through the tough times of Haifa, Waldheim and World War II, so He would help them in the future. The memories of God's help in the past gave them confidence and strength for the present and the future.

Ebenezer was also the place in Australia where the four Stoll siblings were reunited as a family. When they were scattered to opposite corners of the world at the commencement of World War II in 1939, they had no guarantee that they would ever see each other again. Yet, by 1953, all the descendants of Jakob and Maria Stoll – Wilhelm, Hulda, Maria and Christian, their spouses and their 11 children, an extended family of eighteen people – found themselves reunited as a family in the Barossa Valley in South Australia. What a blessing! What a miracle!

Despite war, displacement, internment and prisoner of war camps, not a single life had been lost or injured and a whole family was safe in Australia. From this point onwards the Jakob Stoll dynasty would be perpetuated in Australia.

The Stoll Family re-united at Ebenezer at Bill Stoll's engagement to Daphne Roennfeldt

Barossa Living (1953-1957)

In 1953, the Meinels said farewell to Ebenezer and Light Pass and moved to Tanunda. At Ebenezer we served our apprenticeship in the Australian way of life and culture. In Tanunda we graduated as fully-fledged Australian citizens. After fifty years of struggle and turmoil, and thirteen years of being uprooted from their home in Palestine, Mum and Dad put down fresh roots in Australia in the fertile soil of the Tanunda community. Here they nurtured their children to adulthood and became part of the local community. From humble beginnings they carved out a new life. For over thirty years they reaped the benefits of living in the "lucky country" enjoying what had eluded them for so long: national peace, security and economic stability.

For all the Stoll/Meinel children, the Barossa Valley became the springboard that launched them into their careers, marriages and community life.

When Mum and Dad first arrived in Tanunda they rented a small cottage in Elizabeth Street. It was a quaint old building with a detached kitchen/dining room and outside toilet. The backyard was covered by a huge pepper tree. Right across the street was the town swimming pool, the Tanunda Oval and next to it the Show Hall.

Our 1st Home in Tanunda

Tanunda meant no more tiresome bike rides for dad. He slowly learned to adapt to the traditions of the Australian bakehouse. However there was no pressure on him to improve his English. Wherever he went the locals happily conversed with him in German.

Werner commenced work with Burley and Mader in Nuriootpa, doing his Australian apprenticeship in joinery and carpentry. I was in my second year of high school, Helga in her first year. Both of us caught the bus to school each day. Inge attended the Lutheran Primary School in Tanunda with a much more positive and friendly learning environment. Dora Renner, her teacher, went out of her way helping Inge with after-hours tuition.

Mum poured all her energy into creating a warm and welcoming home. Any spare time was spent in the garden growing vegetables all year round. There were always flowers to decorate the home. During the fruit season Mum did shift work in the cannery in Nuriootpa and Dad also worked there for a while as a second job, to raise some extra income. My parents had a strong conviction they learned from the Bible. "Owe no man anything" (Romans 13:8). They lived frugally and were determined to pay off any debt as quickly as possible. On weekends and during holidays, Werner and I did odd jobs for a builder, Heinz Gartner. I learned how to paint and can proudly point to a number of houses in and around Tanunda whose roofs I painted.

Hard work was offset with lots of fun. Every spare minute during summer we rushed across the road to the swimming pool. We swam, chased, dived and played all manner of teenage tricks with our new found friends in the pool. (There were no safety restrictions.)

Nothing could keep Dad away from the pool, either. With childlike exuberance he mounted the one and three metre diving boards, testing the leverage of the board to its limit, before launching his seventeen stone frame into the air. He hit the water with varying degrees of precision, always unleashing a gigantic splash that threatened to empty the pool. Everybody watched and applauded whenever Martin mounted the board for one of his dives.

On March 1st, 1954, I was woken from my sleep by the thunder of an approaching train. The knob on the end of my steel bed frame began to rattle, the light bulb swung like a pendulum from the ceiling and everything around me shook and swayed as the noise reached its crescendo. Everyone woke and instantly jumped out of bed. We heard our father shout, "Dive for cover!" Then, in a moment, everything went quiet again. We were all shaken! We had just experienced our first earthquake. We went back to bed but none of us went back to sleep.

The next morning we learned that a 5.6 Richter magnitude earthquake had hit Adelaide at 3.40 am. There were no reported fatalities but sixteen people were injured and extensive damage occurred, including many of the early buildings in the central business district of Adelaide, with an estimated cost of damage of $500 million. This earthquake was Australia's most destructive, only eclipsed by the 5.6 Newcastle earth quake in 1989, which caused $4 billion damage, killed sixteen people and injured a hundred and sixty. Our home in Tanunda developed severe cracking but remained structurally sound[1].

One day, as we sat around the dinner table, Mum and Dad said, "We are moving!" By 1955 they had saved enough to put a deposit down to buy number 10 Elizabeth Street – the first home in Australia they could call their own. The house was just a few hundred metres from where we had lived, much closer to the main street, yet still within sight of the Tanunda oval and other sporting facilities.

The Meinel Family Home in 10 Elizabeth St, Tanunda

Before we moved in we turned the place upside down. Werner assumed the role of foreman/tradesman and we went to work stripping out each room, repairing cracks and painting throughout. The house had mains water, electricity and an outside toilet with septic tank. A few years later the town was also connected to a mains sewer. Werner fitted out the kitchen with new cupboards and the bedrooms with built-in wardrobes. Later our German family friend, Mr Rippert, built a new bathroom and large pantry. Dad established a spacious chicken coop and yard, while Mum turned the back yard into a vegetable garden and flower nursery.

The home became a hive of activity. Saturdays were bedlam. Dad turned our humble kitchen into a commercial bakery. He was awake at four am kneading the yeast he had prepared the night before and systematically created a menu of bread rolls, pretzels and continental bread, followed by an array of specialty pastry and cakes: Bienenstich, Torte, Apple, Cherry and Apricot Kuchen; all cooked in the kitchen's domestic oven.

Mum & Dad in the Kitchen 'Bakery'

After breakfast Mum helped Dad in the kitchen and by lunchtime the large pantry was stacked to capacity with food. The smell of freshly cooked breads and cakes was mouth-watering. Mum, Helga and Inge helped clean up the mess Dad had left in the kitchen. By evening everything was restored to normality and Mum was in charge of her kitchen again as she prepared the Saturday night special meal: potato salad and Vienna sausages with crusty freshly cooked rolls. My all-time favourite meal!

Dad's home-baking was just a hobby, at first. He did it for the enjoyment of his family and friends. He always had spare stock in the pantry or fridge throughout the week. Any visitors, including strangers, were welcome and offered *Kaffee und Kuchen*. Nothing made him happier than a positive response from a satisfied customer.

But Martin also thought of the widows; people that were not so well off; the sick, and the elderly in hospitals or nursing homes. On Saturday afternoons he jumped on his beloved pushbike and made a personal delivery to their homes and rooms. When appropriate, he shared a Bible verse and prayed with those he visited.

People soon queued up for Martin's Bienenstich which developed legendary status in the Barossa and beyond its borders. People placed orders for special celebrations and Martin found it hard to say, 'no'. The kitchen was now chaotic, Mum 'tore her hair out' and Werner and I learned to keep our distance.

Langmeil Church with Grave of Pastor Kavel in foreground

On Sunday, the church bells rang across the town and the locals flocked to the four Lutheran churches in the town. Mum and Dad were members of the Langmeil Lutheran Church. It is a historically important Lutheran Church in the Barossa Valley because of its association with Pastor Kavel, the first Lutheran Pastor to arrive in the colony in 1838. The church was usually full. We worshipped there as a family every Sunday.

At home we sat around our kitchen table and enjoyed our special Sunday meal lovingly prepared by Mother. At the conclusion, Dad reached for the Bible and daily devotions book (*Andachtsbuch*). He asked one of us children to read the designated Bible verses, and then the devotional before praying. Everything was conducted in our native German. We held hands around the table and sang, *So nimm denn meine Haende* (Take Thou my Hands and lead me). Werner sang base, Dad tenor, Mum alto and the girls and I, the melody.

> Take Thou my hand and lead me, choose Thou my way!
> "Not as I will," O father, teach me to say.
> What though the storms may gather, Thou knowest best;
> Safe in thy holy keeping, there would I rest. [2]

Around the Kitchen Table
L to R: Werner, Inge, Margaret, Herb, Dad & Mum

Once a month, on Sunday afternoons, in the tradition of our Pietist forefathers, relatives and invited German-speaking friends met for the *Stunde*, (home Bible study), led by one of the men in one of the Stoll/Meinel homes. More intimate fellowship was shared as we all squeezed around the table, decorated with a white lace table cloth and flowers from the garden, enjoying a rich feast of *Kaffe und Kuchen*.

Kaffee und Kuchen with Family and Friends

How we enjoyed those quintessential German moments. But, when anyone visited our place they were always treated with the same hospitality. Cousins Gary, Walter and Fred would come to say hello but more often than not their motivation was to get their fill of Uncle Martin's specialty cakes. Our home drew many local, interstate and international missionaries and preachers, as well as travelling salesmen. They came for Christian fellowship and always left with a smile and a full stomach.

The Michelmore family was one of Dad's Barossa customers. They raved about his Bienenstich. One of my architectural colleagues in Adelaide, Doug Michelmore, remembers how his uncle and aunty froze a portion of Martin's Bienenstich. They travelled to England and, shortly after their arrival, shared this Barossa delicacy with their friends in London over a cup of tea.

Martin introduced Bienenstich and other continental pastries in the bakeries where he worked. These products are popular in the Barossa today. But what is sold over the counter cannot match what Martin produced in the domestic kitchen of number 10 Elizabeth Street. He kept his recipe close to his chest. Even his children could not replicate the special taste that made it so palatable.

Our home was never a quiet place. Overriding the busy household activities were the animated voices of Mum and Dad; the squeals and squabbles of four teenage children, and the greetings of visitors at the back door. Opinions were voiced, arguments refuted or endorsed in a mixture of German, Arabic and English. Our parents broke into Arabic when they didn't want us to follow what they were discussing. When I observed Mum and Dad in animated conversation, I wondered how much of the Arabic temperament had rubbed off from their time in Palestine.

In the early years the family conversation in the home was strictly conducted in German. But slowly, almost imperceptibly, English words crept into the conversation between us siblings. When English dominated, our parents remonstrated and reminded us not to forget our native language. Today, struggling to speak fluent German, we appreciate our parents' wise counsel. Then, our primary goal was to be integrated into the Australian society as quickly as possible. To speak good Australian English was the key to achieving that objective. It did not take long before we competed with each other to see who could speak with the least trace of a German accent. The outcome was never in doubt: Inge, Helga, Herb and Werner, in that order, from youngest to oldest.

On 31st of January 1958, Werner and I rushed back from the Riverland where we had been working with Heinz Gartner on a building project. We could not afford to be late, for we had a very important appointment in the Tanunda Town Hall: the naturalisation ceremony to become Australian citizens. We cleaned up and dressed, and next moment, the whole Meinel family, with Bible in hand, declared the oath of allegiance.

"I swear... to Her Majesty Queen Elizabeth the Second that I will observe faithfully the laws of Australia and fulfil my duties as an Australian Citizen, become entitled to all political and other rights, powers and privileges, and become subject to all obligations, duties and liabilities to which an

Australian Citizen or a British subject is entitled or subject, and have to all intents and purposes the status of an Australian citizen and British subject."[3]

We sang the Australian National anthem by heart, "God save our gracious Queen", and were presented with our Certificate of Naturalisation as an Australian Citizen by the Chairman of the District Council of Tanunda, Mr F A Garrett.

At the conclusion we were swamped with people congratulating, welcoming and wishing us the best. I smiled, with an inward glow of pride: at last I could call myself Australian. It was just five years and eight months since we arrived in Australia.

Academically I was stretched during my four years at Nuriootpa High School by the language barrier. During my final year I had to repeat my Intermediate English. I failed Leaving English but passed it the following year by correspondence with Muirden College in Adelaide, while working full time as Storeman with the Barossa builder, C O Juncken.

In my second year (just twelve months after arriving in Australia), my class teacher, Mr Marcus Krieg, recorded in my diary, "Herbert's English has improved so much that next term his results will be counted and he will be classified. He is a very good student and tries hard".

Some of my school mates had fun at my expense. Brian Hurn sat next to me in the class. I asked him to help me with my spelling. He was more than willing but I didn't trust his mischievous grin when he dictated the letters for me to write down. So I was not altogether surprised to find, on return of my assignment, that my teacher had to correct a rude word on more than one occasion. Brian Hurn became a Sheffield Shield cricketer (fast bowler) and later Mayor of the Barossa Valley Regional Council.

I held my teachers in high regard: Mr Krieg, Mr Bentley and Mr Maynard and headmasters Mr McPherson (52-54) and Mr Noblett (55). They helped to motivate me with their words of encouragement. Bill Bentley wrote, "His popularity and the confidence which his fellow students have in him, testify to the esteem in which he is held by them."

I was selected in the school football, cricket and athletics teams. Nuriootpa High competed with schools such as Brighton High, Woodville High, Gawler and Stirling. All of this gave me a real impetus and built my confidence with every competition.

School Cricket Team, Herb in front row, 1st from right

Bill Bentley was a keen cricketer. He coached me and was convinced that my left hand orthodox leg break was special. I was persuaded that it must have been really good when I kept bowling him out at practice. On one occasion we played cricket against a team from Adelaide on our home turf. Bill called on me to bowl and said, *"You know what you have to do. Just put the ball in the hot spot!"* (The spot from which I bowled him out.)

I bowled accurately, but on my fifth delivery the opposing batsman swung his bat and I watched the ball clear the fifteen metre high pine trees at the perimeter of the oval, landing in the front garden across the main road to Truro. I was somewhat relieved when I learned, much later, who humiliated me: Neil Hawke. He later enjoyed a very successful career playing in the Australian Cricket team. He also played league football.

In athletics, I enjoyed middle distance running, especially the 880 yards. For weeks I ran multiple laps around Tanunda Oval, every morning. On the school sports day, I gained first place and my name was inscribed on the Honours Board as the school champion for the year.

School Athletics Team. Herb in middle row, 2nd from left

On another occasion, our school was invited to compete in the Inter-school athletics competition in the Adelaide Hills. My team mate and I hatched a tactical plan for the 880s race. He decided to lead the field at a hot pace and wanted me to conserve my energy for the finish. I watched him sprint away to the front of the pack at a crazy speed, only to see him standing exhausted on the sidelines, retired from the race, at the half way mark. With half a lap to go there were five runners ahead of me. As I passed one, two, three runners I became conscious of the boisterous barracking from the school team on the sidelines. I pushed myself until there was just one runner ahead of me. The noise was deafening. I was in pain. I reached out and fell over the finishing line, exhausted. The race was over. As I looked up I stared into the face of the adjudicator and heard him say, "*You came 2nd!*" I was beaten by the smallest of margins. What a race!

While still at high school I became a member of the Tanunda Football Club. Werner and I played in the Reserves in the Barossa and Light Football Association. At the beginning of the 1956 football season I rolled up in the club change rooms ready for play, only to discover to my bitter disappointment, that my name was missing from the Reserves team. I was ready to go home when the team manger approached me and said: "Congratulations, Herb, you are playing in the A's today!"

I could hardly believe it. Just four years ago I played schoolboy soccer in Germany, now I was playing Australian Rules football at the highest level in the Barossa and Light competition. What a thrill; what an achievement! Sadly my football career ended in the following year when I moved to Adelaide to study.

During the final year at high school our teachers discussed the subject of our future. *"What will you to do when you leave school? Are you going to work in a trade or planning further studies?"* They presented me with a list of jobs and professions. As I scanned the pages "teacher" and "architect" caught my attention. I liked the idea of teaching but excluded it as I still struggled to master English.

I chose Architecture with a little hesitation at first. Initially I was motivated only by my love of drawing, but as I familiarised myself with the role of an architect and the job opportunities it offered, my enthusiasm and commitment grew in confidence. Architecture also fitted comfortably with my interest in the Fine Arts, particularly music and drawing. I saw Architecture as a Fine Art with a utilitarian purpose. For me there was a tremendous appeal in the fact that an architect could exercise his creative skills and produce a design that would not only bring aesthetic enrichment to its environment but also would serve the practical needs and functions of people, organisations and communities.

Sounds of the Barossa

In the month of December, Murray Street, the main street of Tanunda, came alive with Christmas shopping, decorations and street activities. The Tanunda Brass Band played carols up and down the street and Werner and I were part of it. It was the first time we played in public. We were very excited but the thought of blowing a wrong note in public petrified me. Our confidence grew with every carol and the friendly encouragement from the older Band members. People gathered around, sang along and applauded enthusiastically. By the end of the evening, I was left in no doubt about the very real love affair that existed between the Tanunda Town Band and its audience. I soon learned what an institution this band was in the Barossa Valley and what an honour it was for me to be part of it.

The Tanunda Town Band has been part of the Barossa culture since its settlement in the mid-19th century. The early settlers expressed their gratitude to God, for freedom and new opportunities in their new land, through music, particularly brass. They played at religious events, town events, Barossa Festivals and competitions. The Tanunda Town Band is the oldest continuously operating brass band in the Southern Hemisphere and one of the oldest in the world. The Tanunda Band Competition was instituted in 1910. To this day, the competition at Tanunda remains legendary and is remembered with fondness by all who participate, be it band personnel or onlookers. The Band received its A Grade status in 1927 – the first South Australian band to receive this achievement.

Werner and I were introduced to the Band by Ian Rothe, our next door neighbour at 22 Elizabeth Street. The conductor, Galvin John, took us under his wing and tutored us when we arrived in Tanunda. After our basic lessons on the tenor horn, Gal John introduced Werner to the baritone and, ultimately the base trombone, and me to the euphonium, to fill those vacancies in the ranks of the band. From playing Christmas carols in the main street of Tanunda we graduated to the Tanunda Band competitions. We practised every week and during pre-competition two or three times a week.

Those were exciting times. Dressed in the full regalia of the band uniform we competed in the "Street March" up Murray Street, the "Quick step" on the oval and the "Own Choice" and "Test Piece" on a platform on the oval, or in the Hall. When the adjudicator's bell rang, the Band warmed up by playing a hymn.

Werner and I marching with the Tanunda Town Band at the Band Competition 1956.

I played when the band won the A-grade competition in 1955 and 1956. During those years the band performed at many local, country and Adelaide functions. For us migrant boys, still struggling to get a firm grip on the language, custom and culture, these events helped to expand our knowledge and social inclusion more than any formal education. Gal John tested our comfort zone further by entering us both in the South Australian Eisteddfod Solo Champion competition in Adelaide. Werner and I both returned with a winner's trophy. Our parents were so proud of their sons.

My career with the Tanunda Town Band ended in 1957 when I moved to Adelaide to study Architecture. Werner played on for several more years until he also left the Barossa, but not before the band claimed one of its highest achievements in 1957: winner of the Australasian A-Grade Championship.

Over the decades the band has competed on the national and international stage and recorded the soundtracks for the movies, *Breaker Morant* and *Reunion*. In 1967 the first *Melodie-Nacht* concert took place. This phenomenally successful annual two night sell-out concert to audiences of 3000 people, was based on the concept: A program of music that everyday people want to hear – NOT band music. The popular melodies from the band and guest artists have spellbound audiences ever since. For their 150th Anniversary Celebrations in 2007 they issued a CD, *Ein Prosit*, as a tribute to the German tradition of *Oompah* music. They have also ventured into the classical repertoire by staging the works of the great composers[4].

I remember my association with the Tanunda Town Band with a great deal of nostalgia and pride. To play in one of Australia's best and most highly celebrated brass bands within two years of our arrival, is an opportunity only Australia could have given.

The Barossa Valley is more than vineyards and vine. To me and our family it is synonymous with the sound of brass music, and the male voice choir, the Liedertafel.

Dad joined the Tanunda Liedertafel soon after we arrived and remained a member until his death in 1984. In his thirty year association with the choir, Dad rarely missed a practice held every Tuesday night for eleven months of the year. He relished singing the traditional German songs and Lieder, and took great pride in the choir's performances to Barossa audiences, the Adelaide public, and in regional areas of South Australia, as well as interstate.

The Liedertafel, like the Town Band, is a cherished institution in the Barossa Valley. The fifty two member male voice choir was founded in 1861, drawing its four part singing material from traditional popular German culture. The choir was re-organised in 1920 and, despite an interruption by World War II, has been active ever since. Along with third and fourth generation German-Australians, the group includes singers from many European backgrounds.

Many of their performances are for charity. The annual *Kaffee-Abend* in mid-November is always a popular drawcard for lovers of male voice choirs. The Australian Broadcasting Corporation has recorded the Liedertafel several times since 1932 and the choir first performed on television in 1961 for its centenary. It has also appeared on programs broadcast in Germany. Dad talked with great enthusiasm about the day the Liedertafel performed for Queen Elizabeth II in Elder Park, Adelaide, in 1963.

At Dad's funeral service the Liedertafel sang one of his favourite hymns and formed a guard of honour during the procession from church to cemetery. For Dad, the transition from Germany to Australia was more difficult than for Mum and the rest of our family. His association with the Tanunda Liedertafel lifted his spirit. The singing and camaraderie with the men of German background was food for his soul and helped to make him feel accepted in his adopted country.

In Search of Purpose

The events of 1956 changed my life.

The first four years in Australia were past. I finished my secondary education at Nuriootpa High School at the end of 1955 but still struggled with English. I passed intermediate English and all my Leaving subjects, except English. This forced me to defer my University studies while I repeated Leaving English by correspondence with Muirden College in Adelaide. At the same time I started my first full time job with the Barossa builder, C O Juncken, in Nuriootpa. I considered myself very fortunate to find work in the construction industry. My studies in Architecture may have been delayed a year, but I gained valuable practical experience with a builder.

C O Juncken is a highly respected builder in the Barossa, winning major contracts throughout the Barossa and South Australian country areas. When the contingent of Palestinian Germans settled in the Barossa in the fifties and sixties, the company offered employment to many of them. These included the architect Theo Wieland, Mr Pross, my cousin Ted Stoll, and later Uncle Christian, and the design draftsman Mr Rippert. Theo Wieland became the Managing Director and Ted Stoll followed in the seventies and eighties. I joined the company as a storeman apprentice. My boss was Mr Pross. Prior to World War II, Mr Pross was a very successful hotel proprietor in Haifa and he exercised his considerable skills of bookkeeping and customer service with equal enthusiasm and precision in the builder's store.

This was my first full-time job. I stumbled nervously through racks and stacks of hardware, sanitary ware, electrical fittings and every product necessary to construct a building. Every item that left the store was methodically recorded against a specific job sheet. Mr Pross insisted that every nut, bolt and washer be counted and entered in meticulous hand writing by its correct trade name, catalogue or serial number. He was a hard task master. There was no room for error. He led by example. I quickly learned that every job, no matter how big or small, was equally important and had to be carried out well, to the very best of one's ability.

The annual stock-take was a major event, but also a somewhat boring activity. Just when I had become overwhelmed by the drudgery of the endless 'bean counting', the building foreman, Les Stelzer, asked me to help him load his delivery truck. I was ecstatic when he asked me to get behind the wheel and take the small truck for a drive through the streets to a building site. I had only just received my driver's licence and it made me feel so good and special that Mr Stelzer showed such confidence in me.

Weekends were jam-packed with playing sports, doing the occasional job for Heinz Gartner or going out to special events, including the Mallala car races and the Hill Climb near Angaston. My parents followed the scriptural injunction to *"Keep the Sabbath holy"* (Deuteronomy 5:12). The most important activity of every Sunday was going to church to worship God with fellow believers. Dad and Mum and all of us four children became members of the Langmeil Lutheran Church and were active in the various activities of the parish.

My focus during 1956 was to prepare myself for going to Adelaide the next year to study. I worked hard to save money during the day. I studied Leaving English by correspondence at night and enjoyed playing in the Tanunda Town Band and competing in the Barossa and Light Football Association.

But there were also other things that occupied my mind. I was eighteen years old and the internal dialogue I was having with myself day by day seemed to grow in momentum. I was struggling to understand what it all meant.

Questions about my past confronted me. What took my grandparents to Palestine and why did my parents have to leave their native home and country? The tough years during the war in Germany and the death and destruction I saw all around me left many more unanswered questions. And now, as a new immigrant, I still struggled with the inner conflict of my national identity. I loved my new country, Australia, but my heart was still strongly attached to my German roots. Persistent voices within me became stronger every day.

Up to this point in my life, in my boyhood innocence, I had accepted all these happenings as normal. But, was travelling half-way round the world by the time I was fourteen years old and living in three different countries through the turmoil of war, really normal? I was not yet aware of the extent to which those dramatic events had impacted me during my young and impressionable childhood years, nor of the emotional scars that left their imprint on my mind.

I was fearful, struggling with a sense of inadequacy and insecurity. I had a pre-occupation with death and dying. I longed for peace and stability. But, I also had many positive, but competing feelings about my school friends and parents, particularly my mother, whose strength, faith and love inspired me.

Soon my internal dialogue switched to other topics. *"What is the purpose of life? Is there any purpose beyond mere existence?"*

I had lots of questions about God. I went to church and Sunday school. I was baptized and confirmed in the Lutheran Church. I even read my Bible. Surely I was a good enough person to call myself a Christian? But, I still remained miserable. I lacked peace and assurance.

I looked at nature: the beautiful Swabian Alps in Germany and the intriguing landscape of Australia. I looked at Architecture: the beautifully crafted cathedrals and the magic looking castles. I looked at the aeroplane: the modern flying machines that covered the sky during the war years. I concluded that where there is design there is a designer, and where there is creation there is a creator.

I did not question the existence of God, but I did wonder, *"Is it possible to know God?"*

My search to find peace with God continued. I was puzzled when my sister Helga came home from work one day - a changed person. As a teenager, Helga was often a source of irritation to Werner and me. My parents struggled to direct Helga's natural energy and enthusiasm into positive, constructive behaviour. Helga's change in conduct was dramatic. It begged an explanation. None was forthcoming; at least none that made any sense to me. Instead Helga invited Werner, Cousin Fred and me, to a youth rally in the Adelaide Town Hall, organised by Youth for Christ and founded by Billy Graham in America.

The Town Hall was packed with young people. The music was bright and joyful, but it was the speaker that held my attention. He said some amazing things which spoke directly to me and to my questions. He said that peace of heart and mind was not found in religion or good works but through a relationship with the master designer, God. He explained in detail that the historic events that took place some 2000 years ago relating to the death and resurrection of Jesus Christ, made it possible for me to find peace and purpose in life through knowing God personally. He said that this relationship was offered by God as a free gift and was available to all that were willing to place their faith and trust in him. When he said that trusting Jesus was not a leap in the dark, but accepting one of the most authenticated facts of history, it all made sense. I bowed my head in prayer and by an act of my will invited Jesus Christ to come into my life. I asked him to forgive all my sin and failure and to take control of my life.

Instantly peace flooded my heart. My life was overcome with joy and contentment. I knew without a shadow of doubt that I had become a Christian that day. In the words of scripture, I was "born again" (John 3:3) and I now had assurance about my eternal destiny.

Little by little, step by step, I learned that God had a unique plan for my life. The Bible came alive and spoke directly to my needs.

"For I know the plans I have for you (declares the Lord). Plans of welfare and not calamity, plans to give you the future you have hoped for." (Jeremiah 11:9)

In the ensuing months and years, God did an amazing work of grace across the whole of the Stoll/Meinel families. It started when Jenny Grocke, a local Lutheran girl, befriended my sister Helga while working at the Tanunda Hospital. In a relatively short time, my brother Werner and our cousin Fred, also came to faith in Christ. Other older cousins had taken that step of faith in earlier years. Of all the blessings our parents had enjoyed in Australia, this most precious to them. It was a far greater blessing than any material prosperity. God answered their prayers. All of their children had discovered God's chief purpose for man: to glorify God and enjoy Him forever.

This spiritual renewal spread beyond the family circle. Many from the local community, young and old alike, found new life and purpose in Christ. We had an insatiable appetite for God's word, the Bible. A Saturday night Bible study and prayer meeting commenced; evangelistic meetings were held in the Band Hall, and car loads of people were taken to Adelaide, to Youth for Christ rallies, Bible and Prophetic conferences and Missionary meetings.

But, so much more was yet to come.

L to R – Herb, Fred, Werner, Helga & Jenny

Leaving Home

Eventually it was time for me to pack my bags and leave home for Adelaide to study Architecture at the School of Mines, North Terrace. I found lodging at the Luther Seminary in Jeffcott Street, North Adelaide. The Seminary trains men as pastors and missionaries in the Australian Lutheran Church. It is also a University College for non-theological students like me, attending higher education institutions.

I left home in late February 1957, nervous and wondering how I would cope. I had never been away from home, from my parents' guidance and protection. I still regarded myself a migrant and had been to Adelaide only twice. As I said my goodbyes I was comforted by my plans to come home to Tanunda on free weekends. My new-found faith inspired and encouraged me every day.

My parents were grateful to the Church for finding board for me at the Seminary. It was important for them to know that their son was safe in a Christian community while newly exposed to big city life. I had my own concerns about being accepted by the professors of theology and the academic staff at the Seminary. Back in Tanunda, in the enthusiasm of my new found-faith, I and my friends, had questioned the pastors on some of the teachings and practices of the Church.

I need not have worried. The Principal, Dr Hebart, made me feel welcome. Matron Nitschke and her staff looked after our daily needs with love and compassion and I shall never forget the camaraderie of the student community. I was invited to become the artist for the Seminary's annual magazine, *The Bond*, and I made a number of artistic contributions in this publication.

Herb with Fellow Students   Artisitic Rendering

My five years at Luther Seminary proved to be a very enriching experience. It was my introduction to the intellectual forum of the typical student environment and the enlightenment of Higher Education. It forced me to examine what I believed. Was the Bible really the word of God and entirely trustworthy? I wanted to have a strong grasp of its truth for myself and not what my parents and others told me or believed. As I began to read and study the Bible I quickly discovered that the Bible was much more than an academic book of theology: it was a blue print for life and eternity. It not only showed me how to receive eternal life but how to live well in this life.

During my first year in the class room and drawing studio of the School of Mines (later renamed The University of South Australia), I felt disadvantaged. Most of my fellow students were from privileged backgrounds with a college education. Some were the sons of architects, and most had studied 'Drawing' in high school. I pressed on to make the most of my study opportunity.

At the end of the first year I ran out of money. I found a job with Carodoc-Ashton-Woodhead & Beaumont-Smith Architects while I studied part time. Their office was in the Savings Bank building in King William Street. I caught the tram from North Adelaide or, on a nice day, walked, but most of the time I pedalled my bike to work. I leaned it against the Bank building in the adjoining laneway and after work picked it up again, without fear of it being stolen.

The next year, 1959, was a repeat of my study/work routine but two events stood out. On the very day of my twenty first birthday (6 January 1959), I was called up by the Commonwealth of Australia for national service training (CMF). For three months I did basic training in the Australian Army at Woodside in the Adelaide Hills. I had been drafted into the catering corps, presumably because my father was a baker.

The second event was life changing. My sister, Helga, came to my work at the Savings Bank building and introduced me to her new friend, Margaret Bridges from Stansbury, Yorke Peninsula. They met while nursing at the Royal Adelaide Hospital. I was preoccupied and took little interest in Helga's new friend. However, Helga arranged for Margaret to come to Tanunda for a weekend and enlisted my help to escort her by train to our home. On our one and a half hour train ride to Tanunda, Margaret and I engaged in playful banter and shared a good laugh. I felt very comfortable in her presence, but the thought of any future relationship never crossed my mind. I had to finish my studies before I could consider any romantic attachment. At least, that was the advice my parents gave me and it seemed perfectly reasonable to me.

Those plans came undone when Margaret invited the whole Meinel family to her twenty first birthday party in Stansbury. In amongst the buzz of people and party celebrations our eyes met. A soft glow of love and affection was kindled in my heart and with every day it gained an unstoppable momentum. Our romantic relationship was off and running and I was less than half-way through my studies. Oh dear!

In Stansbury. L to R – Dad, Margaret's Mum Gwen, Mum, Herb, Helga, Margaret, Jennifer (Margaret's sister) & Inge (front)

I felt the need to accelerate my study and to tackle all of my third year subjects full time during 1960. Every holiday period I was back in the office of Caradoc-Ashton to earn my keep. By the end of that year I switched offices seeking the experience of working in another architectural practice.

When I joined Woods-Bagot-Laybourne-Smith & Irwin in Melbourne Street, North Adelaide in 1960, at age 22, I could not have foreseen the opportunities this practice offered me during our 30 year association. The company grew from a single office of about thirty people to over two hundred in Adelaide and then into one of Australia's largest architectural practice with offices in Melbourne, Sydney, Canberra, Darwin, Launceston and overseas. I advanced through the ranks of the company and became a partner and director at the age of forty. A position I held for 12 years.

In 1960 I struggled to balance study, work and my deep love for Margaret. The Lutheran Seminary was still my Adelaide home and my trips to Tanunda were getting fewer. On March 2nd, 1961 we announced our engagement and on February 3rd, 1962 we were married in the Unley Park Baptist Church by Margaret's minister, Brian Simonds.

Our 1st Home, 31 Corunna Ave, Col Light Gardens

We wanted to put God first in our lives and our marriage. We inscribed our wedding rings with the words, *"Glorify the Lord with me; let us exalt His name together."* (Psalm 34: 3) By the end of 1961 we bought our first home with money borrowed from my relatives. I left the Lutheran Seminary and after our wedding took up residence at 31 Corunna Ave, Colonel Light Gardens.

I was still two years away from finishing my Architectural degree. Margaret had plans for a big family and was keen to start sooner rather than later. Our first child was born in November of the same year.

I was now working and studying to support a family. Margaret suffered a lot of sickness during our first three years of marriage and times were tough. To give myself the best chance of finishing my study well I took three months off from work to complete my last year. The subject for my thesis was, 'A Lutheran Seminary and University College'. Most of my research and inspiration came from my live-in experience at 104 Jeffcott Street, North Adelaide.

At home Margaret and I literally ran out of money and we were down to our barest food essentials. My energy was sapped and I suffered severe tonsillitis. Had we been foolish to get into such a predicament? We desperately called out to God to help us and the very next day a parcel of food arrived with a sizable cheque. This was the first of many instances where we have seen God respond to our prayers in a miraculous way.

I received my Diploma in Architecture on June 9th, 1965 and shortly thereafter I was registered as an architect.

For Mum and Dad their children's welfare was foremost. Like any parent they wanted their children to grow into mature adults with successful careers, happy lives and good marriages. They were overjoyed. Australia has indeed given each one of their children the very best opportunity in life. They are amazed and proud of each of their children in their chosen careers and lives.

For Dad, having two sons, both Directors during their working lives, had a special meaning. When Werner wrote home that he had been appointed a Director of the ATA Mission Company in PNG, Dad saw this as a pinnacle of great achievement and he knew exactly what to do. He took Werner's wedding suit out of the wardrobe in Tanunda, where it had been moth-balled; dry cleaned it and posted it to PNG. After all, to be a Director, one has to wear a suit! Werner chuckled when the suit arrived. He was the last person to place importance on position or title but understood Dad's sentiments and valued it.

But it was the children's spiritual welfare that was of highest priority for Mum and Dad. From the day each child was born they prayed they would find peace with God and serve Him with all of their heart in mission, here or abroad. They lived long enough to see how God answered their prayers.

One by one, each of Mum and Dad's children made their exodus from the parental home in Tanunda.

I left in 1957, on a part-time basis and permanently after my marriage in 1962. I practised as an architect for 38 years. Margaret and I have four children: Marianne, Philip, Andrew and David.

Helga left home after completing 2nd year high school in 1955. She became a nurse, studied at the Melbourne Bible Institute and at the age of twenty eight commenced a missionary career spanning over forty years that took her to Africa, the Middle East and Australia.

Inge, after completing her intermediate certificate at Nuriootpa High School, also started a nursing career. She left home in 1956 and worked in a number of hospitals in Australia with overseas stints in Germany, West Africa and New Zealand. In 1979 she married Dr Paul Cowie and moved to Whyalla. They have four children: Michael, Katherine, Sonia and Megan.

Werner was the last sibling to leave home. He was a carpenter/joiner and worked for Burley & Mader in Nuriootpa for seventeen years, studied at the Sydney Missionary Training College and in 1972, aged thirty six, he married Christine Basedow of Nuriootpa. Chris and Werner moved to Papua New Guinea, where they served as missionaries for seventeen years with the Alliance Training Association. All their children were born in PNG: Steven, Helen, Tim and Martin.

We may have left home, but through the years our hearts and feet were irresistibly drawn back to No 10 Elizabeth Street, Tanunda, in the Barossa Valley. While Mum and Dad were alive, the Tanunda home was the family hub and anchor for us all.

In Their Footsteps

It is Christmas Eve, 1974. Three of Mum and Dad's children are in Tanunda to celebrate Christmas with them. Inge still lived at home while working at the Tanunda Hospital, Helga was home on furlough from the Gambia, and Margaret and I with our four children – Marianne (12), Philip (10), Andrew (8) and David (3) – had come from Adelaide. Werner and Chris could not make it home this Christmas; they were in Mount Hagen, PNG.

The temperature had reached 40 degrees Celsius. The Barossa hills were brown; trees and gardens parched; everyone was thirsty and wished they had air-conditioning. After the Christmas service in the Langmeil church finished we all rushed home to celebrate our family Christmas. Mum and Dad lit the candles on the Christmas tree and from the youngest to the oldest we marched in single file into the lounge room, singing in German, *Ihr Kinderlein Kommet* (Oh Come all ye Children). The grandchildren had to be restrained from plundering the parcels that were piled high beneath the Christmas tree. Dad asked me to read the Christmas story from Luke chapter two, in English.

"Do not be afraid. I bring you good news of great joy that will be for all people. Today in the town of David a Saviour had been born: he is Christ the Lord." (Luke 2: 10, 11)

Christmas 1974

Then Dad prayed in German, followed by us in English. We thanked God for sending the Saviour into the world to offer hope and salvation. We thanked Him for his providence in reuniting the Stoll/Meinel families in Australia. We thanked him for providing a safe and prosperous new country and home for us all in this beautiful region of Australia, called the Barossa Valley.

Then it was time for the presentation of the gifts. Oh what a party! The room overflowed with gifts and was littered with fancy Christmas wrappings that were destined for the rubbish bin.

Every year I had celebrated Christmas Eve just like this. During our married life, Margaret and I and our children spent Christmas Eve with my parents in their home in Tanunda. This pilgrimage continued until they moved into a retirement village in 1982.

For all of those twenty years our children experienced the wonder and delight of the true meaning of Christmas in the sanctity of the family home; a tradition passed on from one generation to the next.

It has been my unique privilege to celebrate Christmas on different continents, in different cultures and languages. I've celebrated it in the depth of wintry Germany and in the middle of a heatwave in Australia. I have celebrated it in pain and poverty, and in plenty and prosperity. Times change, societies transform, and circumstances fluctuate, but the story of Christmas remains the same. The unchanging truth of God's coming to this earth to bring salvation to all mankind, has remained the same. Recognition of this truth has made Christmas special, every year.

The Christmas celebration is just one example of the Christian world-view that has been the hallmark of the Stoll/Meinel families.

My grandfather Jakob Stoll was a young man when he migrated from Germany to Palestine in 1889. He had a love for God and a commitment to be part of a people whose highest purpose in life was to build and extend God's kingdom on earth. He exercised his godly influence as a baker and small business owner, was missionary-minded and brought much blessing to Jews, Arabs and Christians during the fifty years of his stay in the Holy Land.

Jakob & Maria Stoll aged 74 & 72

Jakob and Maria's four children – Wilhelm, Hulda, Maria and Christian – followed in their footsteps. While they lived in Palestine they invested their adult lives in reaching out to the local people through their work as bakers and gardeners and their involvement in their local church and the Carmel Mission. When their work and influence in Palestine came to an abrupt end, they rebuilt their lives in Australia. They continued to serve their Lord and master, Jesus Christ, with unabated dedication in their work places, their local community, the Lutheran Church and a number of interdenominational mission societies.

Jakob and Maria Stoll had eleven grandchildren. Their prayer for their grandchildren was the same as for their children: that each one would come to know Jesus Christ as Lord and Saviour and become ambassadors of God's kingdom. Jakob and Maria died in 1940 and 1945. In their lifetime they never knew how life turned out for their children and grandchildren after they left Palestine. Did God answer their prayers? Did the grandchildren follow in their grandparents' and parents' footsteps? What were their opportunities to share the message of hope and salvation in their lifetime? I am one of those grandchildren and want to record something about each of them. So, here they are, from oldest to youngest, by family.

The children of Wilhelm & Tine Stoll

L to R – Ted, Gary, Ruth, Fred, Bill
Front – Tine & Wilhelm Stoll

Ruth Stoll: Teacher

Ruth became a teacher, Senior Mistress and Deputy Principal at a number of large high schools in Adelaide, Nuriootpa, Elizabeth and Stirling. For some two years she also taught in Stuttgart, Germany. Ruth was active in a number of church and missionary activities: leader of Vocational Bible Schools,

Scripture Union Camps, Interschool Christian Fellowship Camps and Beach Missions. She was a much loved Aunty to eight nieces and six nephews, and was the chief organiser/host of the Wilhelm Stoll clan and their family gatherings. Ruth was an avid prayer partner and financially supported a number of missionary organizations. She died on April 4th, 2001, aged 71.

Wilhelm (Bill) Stoll: Pastor, Missionary, Educator

Bill became an ordained Pastor of the Lutheran Church of Australia. For thirteen years he was a missionary in PNG serving as teacher, headmaster and principal of a teacher training school and a seminary. On returning to Australia he became a senior lecturer at the Lutheran Teachers College/Lay Training Centre in Adelaide. The Centre prepared lay and ordained people for missionary service in PNG and amongst Aboriginals in Australia. Bill married Daphne Roennfeldt from the Barossa Valley. They have four children: Anne-Marie, Peter, Jane, Timothy. Bill died on November 19th, 1997, aged 66.

Theodor (Ted) Stoll: Accountant, Business Manager.

Ted left school at fifteen, in December 1947, and continued his education by correspondence and night school. His early working experience was with local farmers before he found employment with the builder, C O Juncken, in Nuriootpa. In over forty nine years of service, he advanced from Junior Clerk to Managing Director of the company. Ted was involved in many activities and leadership roles at St Petri Lutheran Church in Nuriootpa, including Vice Chairman and Chairman of the congregation. He was Secretary and/or Treasurer of a number of church and community based organizations. Ted is the custodian of a comprehensive collection of the Stoll Ancestry family records, as well as the early history of the Templers in Haifa. Ted married Joyce Kruger from the Barossa. They have four children: Mark (d.1982), Karen, Stephen, Jeanette. After the death of Joyce in 2000 Ted married Elaine Scott (nee Williams) in 2011.

Gerhard (Gary) Stoll: Farmhand, Mechanic, Missionary.

Gary's career started as a farmhand in the Barossa Valley. After suffering from polio he decided to become a motor mechanic. His three month visit to the Hermannsburg Lutheran Mission in Central Australia in 1958 turned into forty three years of continuous service with the Mission. He started as motor mechanic, then became Superintendent of the Hermannsburg Mission (1962-84), which led to his appointment as Superintendent of the whole of the Finke River Mission Field in Central Australia (1985-2001). Much of the latter role entailed Bible translation and the training of Aboriginals for ministry. He married Elizabeth Simpfendorfer and they have four children: Kathryn, Robert, Heidi, Julie. Following the death of Elizabeth in 1992, Gary married Roma Scholz (nee Lange) in 1996. Since his retirement in 2001, Gary and Roma live at Woodcroft, serving in their local Lutheran Church.

Siegfried (Fred) Stoll: Motor Mechanic, Missionary, Purchasing Officer.

After finishing his final year of high school at Immanuel College, Fred trained as a motor mechanic in Tanunda. He completed his missionary training at the Melbourne Bible Institute and served for nineteen years with the Sudan Interior Mission (SIM) in Liberia, West Africa, doing mechanical maintenance, working in the radio follow-up department and Mandingo outreach by radio, and visiting listeners. On moving to America in 1985, he worked in the SIM home office, in Charlotte, North Carolina as mission purchasing agent in the Purchasing and Shipping Department (affectionately known as the "Buy and Bye Service"). Fred married Goldie Hewitt and they have two children: Esther & Jonathan. Since his retirement in 2002 Fred and Goldie live in the SIM retirement village in Sebring, Florida. Fred has been active in many roles in the churches he attended in South Australia and Victoria in Australia, Liberia in West Africa, and in South Carolina and Florida in America. Fred has a love for preaching and had many opportunities to speak in churches during mission furloughs and more recently in the local jail in Sebring.

The children of Maria (nee Stoll) and Martin Meinel

L to R: Herb, Margaret (Herb's wife), Inge, Werner
Front Row: Martin, Helga, Maria

Werner Meinel: Joiner/Carpenter, Missionary, Manager.

Werner commenced his joinery apprenticeship in Germany and finished it in Australia. For seventeen years he worked with Burley & Mader in Nuriootpa. After two years at the Sydney Missionary Training College he served for seventeen years as a missionary with the Alliance Training Association (ATA) in Mount Hagen, PNG. He managed a timber and hardware business, and trained nationals in joinery and building skills. On returning to Australia Werner worked as Timber Salesman for Otto & Co for eighteen years. Werner married Christine Basedow from Nuriootpa and they have four children: Helen, Stephen, Timothy, Martin, all born in Mount Hagen. They have served in many capacities and leadership roles in the churches in the Barossa Valley, Mount Hagen, PNG, and at Clovercrest Baptist Church, Adelaide.

Herbert (Herb) Meinel: Architect FRAIA, Facilities Manager.

Herb graduated from the South Australian Institute of Technology in 1964. In his thirty years with Woods Bagot Architects he was a Director of the Company for twelve years. He joined the Buildings & Property Division of Flinders University in 1991 as University Architect and became Head of the Division for eight years (Facilities Manager of the Campus). Herb was involved in many church activities and leadership roles at Southern Christian Fellowship and Edwardstown Baptist Church in Adelaide. For twenty six years he was active in CBMC (Christian Business Men's Committee), an international organization reaching out to business and professional people with the gospel. For four years he was National Chairman. Herb married Margaret Bridges from Stansbury, Yorke Peninsula, SA. They have four children: Marianne, Philip, Andrew & David.

Helga Meinel: Nurse, Missionary.

Helga, as a double-certificated nurse, has worked in hospitals in Tanunda, Adelaide, Gawler, Melbourne and Tasmania. From 1965 to 1967 she studied at the Melbourne Bible Institute In her 40 plus years as missionary Helga has worked in The Gambia, West Africa, (for 21 years), Sydney (as Assistant National leader of WEC for 10 years), and Jordan and Syria in the Middle East (10 + years). She has travelled extensively around the world and in particular in the countries of our roots – Israel, Germany and Australia. Since taking up residence in Adelaide in 2006, she has assumed leadership roles at Grange Baptist Church including Prison Ministry Outreach. She still visits Jordan for short term ministry trips.

Ingeborg (Inge) Meinel: Nurse.

Inge, as a double-certificated nurse worked in various hospitals in Adelaide, Tanunda and Tasmania, including overseas at a Surgical Hospital in Bad Cannstadt, Germany (1972) and the WEC Medical Clinic in The Gambia. She worked in her husband's Bunyarra Medical Clinic in Whyalla for twenty one years as the practice's nurse. Inge has been active in Christian outreach and ministries all her life through the activities of her churches and other groups such as School Crusaders, WEC Youth camps and Navigator Ministries. In the Whyalla Baptist Church she contributed to the Craft Group, Bible Study and Visitation Program. Since returning to Adelaide she has been active in Edwardstown Baptist Church ministries. Inge married Dr Paul Cowie and they have four children: Michael, Katherine, Sonia, Megan.

The children of Christian and Christel Stoll

L to R: Wally, Christel, Christian & Herta

Herta Stoll: Medical Technician, Nurse

Herta received her diploma, which included twelve weeks of nursing training as Medical Technical Assistant, in the Karlsruhe Hospital in Germany. From 1952-53 she was employed at an X-RAY Institute in Bruchsal, Germany. When the family moved to Australia at the end of 1953 she trained at the Royal Adelaide Hospital to become a nurse (1954-56). In 1957 she married

Hans Wyler in Indonesia and their three children – Christoph, Andres, and Dieter – were born there. Hans was a Swiss citizen and worked for the Basel Mission in Banjermasin, Indonesia, as administrator/treasurer. In addition, he lectured at the Geredja Theological Seminary, teaching English, German and Accountancy. The family returned to Zurich, Switzerland, in 1964 where they attended the Evangelical-Reformed Church. For twenty years Herta was a team member of the Basel Mission shop. The proceeds funded projects in under-developed countries. Herta also had a passion for visiting the local Aged Care institutions.

Walter Stoll: Motor Mechanic, Service Manager.

Walter qualified as a motor mechanic in Germany, specialising in the Volkswagen brand. In Australia he worked for nineteen years at the Truro Service Station and then as General Manager for Wieland Motors in Nuriootpa. Since 1974, Walter and his family have lived at Bowral, NSW, where he worked as Services Manager for Bill Worners Motors, Mittagong. Walter has participated in Christian ministries in the Lutheran Church and Bible study groups in the Barossa Valley, in Young Adults ministry at the Bowral Church of Christ. At Moss Vale Community Baptist Church he served as elder, worship leader and lay preacher. He has also had a close association with Capernwray Fellowship, Creation Ministries International and the Southern Highlands Christian School. He married Brigitte Wieland and they have two children: Tania & Rolf.

A Tribute

Mum and Dad's health deteriorated in the latter years of their lives: Dad suffered from Alzheimer's disease and Mum's mobility was in decline. They found wonderful care and support in the Lutheran Rest Home in the years preceding their deaths. I was leading a Home Bible Study in Adelaide when I received word that Dad had passed away peacefully in the Nursing Home at Tanunda on August 13th, 1986. He was laid to rest in the Langmeil Cemetery, in a double plot he had purchased, just metres from the front door of the Langmeil Lutheran Church.

Two years later, on November 9th, 1988, Mum's journey on this earth also came to an end. Diagnosed with cancer of the pancreas she underwent surgery at the Royal Adelaide Hospital. As she lay in the Intensive Care ward the doctors advised they could do nothing more for her. She knew her time had come and now she was inwardly preparing herself to meet her Lord and Saviour. With eyes closed, she quietly began to sing, in German, one of her favourite hymns that we often sang around the kitchen table as a family: *So lang mein Jesus lebt.*[1]

Because my Jesus lives, and daily strength He gives,
All fear and sorrow flee away, my heart with love aflame.

Helga had rushed back from the mission field in The Gambia. She and Inge were at her bedside and quietly joined Mum, singing:

My shepherd-guide is He, who safely leads His sheep.
To pastures green and waters fresh, my deepest thirst He quenches.
When clouds obscure the sun and lions around me run,
I know that in my darkest night, my Jesus holds me tight.

With each verse mother's voice grew stronger and louder. Helga and Inge whispered, "Not so loud mum! You are in hospital." They apologised to the nurses for disturbing the quiet of the ward. The nurses smiled and reassured them. "Don't worry! It is rare to hear singing in an Intensive Care Unit!" The crescendo built until all five verses had been sung.

And should my feet grow weak, the world bring me to grieve,
I quickly flee to Jesus breast, He gives me perfect rest.

With unshakable faith, she declared what Jesus meant to her as she sang the last verse.

So only look to Him; that surely is to win.
My Jesus loves me of that I am sure, my heavenly home's secure.

Mum opened her eyes, looked into the tear-stained faces of Helga and Inge and whispered, "Am I still here or in heaven?"

Her body had failed but her spirit was alert. All her life she considered herself a pilgrim on this earth. Finally, she stood at the threshold of her eternal home, which God had prepared specially for her. She longed to be in the presence of her Lord. She was ready!

Just seven days later our mother, Maria Magdalene, passed away. After eighty six tumultuous, but blessed years on this earth she entered into her heavenly rest She was buried next to her beloved husband, Martin Gottfried, in the Langmeil Cemetery.

Our parent's graves with backdrop of Langmeil Lutheran Church

Mum has a special place in the heart of each of her four children. In her lifetime she showed us how to live courageously, and in her death how to die with confidence and dignity.

After Dad's death Mum directed the family home to be sold. As their executor I gained valuable insight into the principles that governed Mum and Dad's giving to God's work. Mum specifically directed that the first ten percent of the gross proceeds from the sale of the home be distributed to five Church and Mission organizations, locally and overseas. They had practiced this principle of giving to God all their lives, only known to the recipients.

There were other occasions when Mum and Dad's legacy was publicly applauded by the Tanunda community. Dad's Bienenstich was much talked about and received special acclaim by such culinary luminaries as Maggie Beer, in her book, *Maggie's Table*. Bienenstich, translated literally, means "bee sting". This yeast cake has a honey and almond crust on the top and is filled with cream or custard. The cake was well known in Germany but not generally in Australia at the time of our arrival in 1952.

Angela Heuzenroeder in her book, *Barossa Food* explains: "Anyone who lived in Tanunda in the 1960s can tell you how the cake really came to be known there. It was because of a baker called Martin Meinel, who worked in various bakeries in Tanunda. A recent immigrant from Germany, Mr. Meinel introduced to his customers some of the recipes he knew from living in Europe, but the one that immediately became popular was the Bienenstich. Members of the Liedertafel choir remember especially the slabs of cake that he took along to the choir practice. The few bitter almonds included in his recipe made it different from any other versions that have been made since."[2]

Angela knew Martin personally and she was keen to record some of his other heroics. She writes:

"How could anyone forget Mr Meinel? He and his wife were very much part of the town community and the local children all knew him because he loved swimming. On lazy, hot afternoons down at the pool, he swam with the youngsters out from school. He could use his hands like a siphon and squirt water meters into the air. He was also impressive when he projected his

*large, doughy form off the diving board and did 'honey pots', spraying the pool with water droplets. Honey pots in the pool and bee-sting topping on the yeast cake; these were the achievements that made Mr Meinel famous in the town."*²

Martin at the Tanunda Pool with Herb & Grandchildren
Andrew and Philip

Jakob and Maria Stoll, my grandparents, reached the ages of 76 and 77, and they are buried in the German Cemetery in Haifa, Israel. Their four children, with their spouses, lived their last thirty plus years in Australia, most of them well into their eighties. Their graves can be found today in the Lutheran Cemeteries of Nuriootpa and Tanunda.

Aunty Christel Stoll was the last of that generation of the Stoll/Meinel families to pass away. She died 3rd May 2004, aged ninety seven.

All of them left an incredibly rich heritage of faith, family and culture to their eleven descendants: me, my brother, sisters and my cousins. We are the beneficiaries of the values and beliefs of our parents and grandparents, the foundations of which were fashioned in the crucible of the day to day life in the Stoll family bakery in the German settlement in Haifa. None of us automatically inherited our Christian faith from our parents or grandparents. There are no grandchildren in God's family. Each of us, by an act of will, personally accepted God's gift of salvation at different times and places. But all of us are forever grateful for Christian parents and grandparents who modelled genuine Christian lives.

As I closely studied the lives of my ancestor's, seven symbols come to mind that accurately represent and summarize the values, beliefs and priorities they lived by.

The Bag of Flour: They were diligent and thorough. They worked hard long hours industriously in the bakery, garden, nursery and home. They believed that the head of the family had a God-given responsibility to provide for his daily needs and that of his entire family. *"If anyone does not provide for his immediate family, he has denied the faith and is worse than an unbeliever."* (1 Timothy 5:6)

The Bible: They read it daily, meditated on it, studied it, taught and shared it in their weekly fellowship meetings. They believed the Bible is the word of God, completely trustworthy and relevant for every age, including the present and that *"Man does not live by bread alone, but on every word that comes from the mouth of God"* (Matthew 3:4).

The Daily Devotional Book (*The Andachtsbuch)*: They conducted family devotions around the meal table, read from the Bible and a devotional book and prayed. They believed that *"the family that prays together stays together"*.

The Sunday Suit: They attended Church services faithfully in their best attire with fellow believers for worship, teaching and fellowship. Sunday was very special. The bakery was closed and the entire day was spent in rest and recreation with family and friends. They followed God's instruction to *"Keep the Sabbath holy"* (Deuteronomy 5:12).

The Tithe: They tithed, giving generously to support the local church, mission societies, orphans, the poor and needy. They believed that *"God *loves a cheerful giver"* (2 Corinthians 9:7) and it was their privilege to give to others out of the material goods with which God had blessed them.

The Hymn Book (*The Reichslieder Buch*): They loved to sing, especially the revival inspired hymns from their German *Reichs-Lieder* hymn book, as well as the treasures of the Lutheran Hymnal. They sang the favourite hymns in beautiful four part harmony. They believed in *"making a joyful noise to the Lord"* (Psalm 98:4) and that music from the heart is a great way to express worship and praise.

The Christmas Tree: They made the most of every opportunity to celebrate life as a family and community. Public holidays were set aside for outings, fellowship, fun and recreation. Christmas celebrations in the German tradition at home and at Church formed the pinnacle of the year's celebrations. They believed that *"the joy of the Lord is your strength"* (Nehemiah 8:10).

Nothing Can Make Them Stumble has traced some 150 years of the Stoll/Meinel family and, in particular, the story of our grandparents and parents from 1854 to 2004. They left their homeland of Germany during social, economic and spiritual turmoil to pioneer a Christian Community in Palestine. They did not stumble when faced with the many obstacles that they confronted: the hardship of the pioneering years; the challenge to their personal beliefs and the historic Christian faith; the set-back of World Wars I and II; the expulsion from Palestine during World War II; and migration to Australia. Their eyes were not fixed on circumstances but on God, His Word and the promise of an eternity with their Saviour. They chose not to follow the pursuit of fame and fortune but to seek the kingdom of God first and foremost. They lived by the motto of the missionary statesman, C T Studd: *"Only one life, twill soon be past, only what's done for Christ will last."*[3]

Aged eighty two, Uncle Bill, just prior to his death, no longer able to write, recorded on tape for his Stoll relatives in Germany an account of his life in Australia and the difficulties he encountered. He concluded his reflections with the following words:

"The Lord is faithful. He never forsakes his own. He keeps on giving overflowing joy, so we never lack anything. And He will surely take us to our eternal home, where there is no more suffering, no more tears, no more pain, but everlasting joy at who Jesus is and what he has done. Our joy will be in Him and we will join in the chorus of praise and thanksgiving with all the saints, forever and ever."

Annie Johnson Flint expressed her faith and attitude of living through tough circumstances in words that match the sentiments of my ancestors:

> He giveth more grace when the burdens grow greater.
> He sendeth more strength when the labours increase.
> To added affliction He addeth His mercy.
> To multiplied trials He multiplies peace.
>
> His love has no limits. His grace has no measure
> His power has no boundary known unto men
> For out of His infinite riches in Jesus
> He giveth and giveth and giveth again
>
> When we have exhausted our store of endurance;
> When our strength has failed ere our day is half done.
> When we reach the end of our hoarded resources,
> Our Father's full giving has only begun.[4]

Our generation has observed the lives of our forebears in awe and admiration as they navigated threat, loss and hardship, without bitterness and lived happy and contended lives in diverse communities in different parts of the world.

How did they do it?

It is my hope that the stories of their lives recorded in these pages will provide hope, inspiration and answers to this question for succeeding generations of the Stoll/Meinel families and all who read it.

Footnotes

SECTION I

The Stoll Genealogy

1. Verlag fuer Standesamtswesen, Gmbh, Berlin, 1933/34, *Der Ahnenpass*, German State Department
2. Larson, Bob, 1980, *Your Swabian Neighbours*, Schwaben International Verlag, p.144
3. Johannes Woessner & Karl Bohn, 1968, *Dornstetter Heimatbuch*, Stadt Dornstetten, p.456

Political & Economic Environment

1. Larson, p.73
2. Larson, p.74
3. Larson, p.76
4. Larson, p.83
5. Larson, pp.85-86
6. Larson, p.87

The Spiritual Climate

1. Anders, Max E & Lundford, Judith A, 1991, *30 Days to Understanding Church History*, Wolgemuth & Hyatt, p.222
2. Anders & Lundford, p.254 -Deism denied the supernatural aspects of Christianity – the role and work of Jesus, the inspiration of scripture, prophecy, miracles, and prayer – but maintained that the Bible had ethical and moral value for society."
3. Anders & Lundford, p.255

4. Troll, Thaddaeus, 1968, *Deutschland deine Schwaben*, Hoffmannn & Campe Verlag, Hamburg, p.66
5. Anders & Lundford, p.259
6. Linder, Robert D, 2000, *The History of the Church, Essential Bible Reference*, Three's Company, pp.17-21

The Cultural Heritage

1. Larson, p.7
2. Larson, p.7
3. Larson, pp.12-14
4. Larson, p.45
5. Larson, p.25
6. Larson, p.21
7. Larson, p.139
8. Larson, p.114

Dornstetten

1. Woessner & Bohn, p.755
2. Woessner & Bohn, p.274
3. Willi Bidermann, Extract from article *Vom Schwarzwald ins Heilige Land*

The Templers

1. The Temple Society, p.2
2. Sauer, p.20
3. The Temple Society, p.2
4. The Temple Society, p.3
5. Sauer, p.25
6. The Temple Society, p.4
7. Yossi Ben-Artzi, 2008, *The German Colony,* Haifa Tourist Board

8. The Temple Society, Extracts from *Footprints of the Templers*

SECTION II

The Pioneering of the German Colony in Haifa

1. Price, Randall, 2003, *Fast Facts on the Middle East Conflict*, Harvest House Publishers, p.23
2. The Temple Society, p.5
3. Wassermann-Deininger, Gertrud, 1965, *Here we have no lasting city...*, Wassermann-Deininger, p.9
4. The Temple Society, p.64.   Sauer, p.50
5. Sauer, p. 50
6. Woessner & Bohn, p.693

Shaking Foundations

1. The Temple Society, p.5
2. The Redemptive work of Christ refers to Christ's sacrificial death on the cross as the atonement for the sin of the whole world and as the only way of salvation for mankind
3. The Temple Society,
4. Wassermann-Deininger, Gertrud, 2008, *Band I- Wir haben hier keine bleibende Stadt*, EUSEBIA-Missionsdienste, Stuttgart, p24. (translated from German by H E Meinel)
5. *Die Warte*. Death Notice 12.5.1877

Give Me this Mountain

1. Wassermann-Deininger, Band I, p.24
2. Johannes Seitz, 1919, *Erinnerungen und Erfahrungen* (Recollections and Experiences – Translated from German by H E Meinel), Verlag der Liebenzeller Mission Bad Liebenzell.

3. Wassermann-Deininger, 2008, pp.36-37

A Childhood to be Cherished

1. Marcinkowski-Schumacher, *When it Rains out of a Blue Sky*, R Brockhaus Verlag Wuppertal, (English translation by Martin Stoll 1995) p.26
2. Sauer, Paul, 1975, *Beiharz Chronik*, Sueddeutsche Verlagsgesellschaft Ulm, p.114
3. Marcinkowski-Schumacher, p.33
4. Marcinkowski-Schumacher, p.34
5. Marcinkowsky-Schumacher, p.16

A Healthy, Happy & Wise Community Life

1. Temple Society, p.7
2. Sauer, p.74
3. Temple Society, p.7,8
4. Marcinkowski-Schumacher, p.20
5. Marcinkowski-Schumacher, pp.21-22
6. Marcinkowski-Schumacher, p.26
7. Beiharz Chronik, pp.115-116
8. Marcinkowski-Schumacher, p.43
9. Sauer, p.96

A Troublesome & Uncertain Future

1. Wassermann-Deininger, Band I, p.37
2. Heinsen, Wilhelm, from Article written to the Wilhelm Stoll family in the 1930s, *William Mader – Gardener from Winterlingen near Ebingen.*
3. Wassermann-Deininger, 1965, p.29
4. Wassermann-Deininger, 1965, p.24
5. Christian Stoll Family Memoirs
6. Christian Stoll Family Memoirs

7. Wassermann-Deininger, 1965, p.26
8. Wilhelm Stoll War Dairy 1914-1918
9. The Temple Society, pp.9-10

Brothers, Sisters & Spouses

1. See http://www.liebenzell-mission.org
2. Christian Stoll Family Memoirs
3. See http://www.echt-erzgebirge.de

The Fabulous 1920s & 30s

1. The Temple Society, p.11
2. The Temple Society, p.12
3. Bill Stoll Family Memoirs

The Winds of Change

1. The Temple Society, p.12
2. Wassermann-Deininger, 1965, p.38
3. The Temple Society, p.13
4. Christian Stoll Family Memoirs
5. The Temple Society, pp.13-14
6. See http://www.historyplace.com/worldwar2/holocaust
7. Christian Stoll Family Memoirs
8. See http:/www.en.wikipedia.org/wiki/Atlit_detainee_camp

Behind Barbed Wires

1. Christian Stoll Family Memoirs.
2. The Temple Society, p.14
3. Wassermann-Deininger, 1965, pp.56-57
4. The Temple Society, p.14

The Exchange

1. Wassermann-Deininger, 1965, p.59
2. Wassermann-Deininger, 1965, p.60
3. Friends of Israel (FOI), Workers Together Publication, 10/2009
4. http://en.wikipedia.org/wiki/Bergen-Belsen_concentration_camp
5. Wassermann-Deininger, pp.60-61

The End of the Templer Settlements in Palestine

1. . Wassermann-Deininger, 1965, p.57
2. . The Temple Society, p.15
3. . Wassermann-Deininger, 1965, pp.68-74 (Eye witness account by
   Kurt Seidler, brother in law of Gertrud Deininger)
4. . The Temple Society, p.15
5. . The Temple Society, p.15
6. . Bitzer, Karl, Article *Rueckschau ins Gelobte Land*, p.64
   (Translated from the German by H E Meinel)
7. The Temple Society, p.17
8. Martin Rinkart/Johann Crueger, Hymn 556, Word Music 1986

The Bigger Picture

1. Price, Randall, 2003, *Fast Facts of the Middle East*, Harvest House Publishers, pp.46-48
2. Price, p.51
3. Woods, Dr Deane & Smith, Geoff, 9.10.2010, Conference Lecture Notes, *A Day in the Prophetic Word*
4. Price, p.20,
5. Price, p.27
6. Price, p.31,32
7. Price, p.36

8. Price, p.28
9. Price, p42
10. Elwood McQuaid, *Zwi*. Friends of Israel, p. 161
11. Woods & Smith
12. Wilhelm Heinsen, 1930s, *Die Jerusalemsfreunde,* Article written for the Wilhelm Stoll Family, p.1-10
13. Von Rubenau, Eitel Friedrich, *The German Settlements in Palestine.* Article to celebrate 100 years of the Jerusalem Society.(Translated from the German by Klaus-Peter Hoffmann 2001)
14. Alex Carmel, 2000, *Die Siedlungen der wuerttembergischen Templer in Palestina 1868-1918*, W. Kohlhammer Verlag Stuttgart, p.295 (Translated from the German by H E Meinel)
15. Soulen, R. Kendall, see http://www.theologicalstudies.org/article
16. Carmel, p.295\
17. Carmel, p296
18. Carmel, p.298

SECTION III

When the War is Over

1. Larson, p.92
2. Wikipedia, Free Encyclopaedia, *The Marshall Plan*, http://en.wikipedia.org/wiki/Muhlenberg_legend
3. Larson, p.107
4. Larson, p.93
5. Wikipedia, Free Encyclopaedia, *History of Baden-Wuerttemberg*, http://en.wikipedia.org/wiki/Baden-Wuerttemberg
6. Larson, p.96
7. History of Baden-Wuerttemberg

8. Wolfgand, Gueth, 2007, *Geschichte und Geschichten aus Zell am Aichelberg II*, Gemeinde Zell unter Aichelberg, p.43 (Translated from German by H E Meinel)
9. History of Baden-Wuerttemberg

Father Returns Home

1. Wikipedia, Free Encyclopaedia: *The Muhlenberg Legend* http://en.wikipedia.org/wiki/Muhlenberg_legend

A Childhood to Remember

1. Wikipedia, Free Encyclopaedia. *Christkind*, http://en.wikipedia.org/Christkind

SECTION IV

Exiled to the Land Down Under

1. Sauer, p.237
2. Sauer, p.241
3. The Temple Society, p.16
4. Sauer, p.287
5. Sauer, p.291
6. The Temple Society, p.16
7. The Temple Society, pp.16-17
8. Ted Stoll, Family Recollections

Barossa Living

1. Wikipedia, Free Encyclopedia, http://en.wikipedia.org/wiki/Great-Adelaide-Earthwork
2. Julia Sterling/Ira D Sankey, *Take Thou my Hand and lead me, Hymn 532,* Sacred Songs & Solos, Marshall, Morgan & Scott

3. Naturalisation Certificate, 31.1.1958
4. Barossa Band Festival 2007, Celebrating the Tanunda Town Band 150th Anniversary

A Tribute

1. C Gebhardt, *So lang mein Jesus lebt,* Reichs-Lieder hymn 272, Verlag G Jhloff & Co., Evangelische Buchhandlung, Neumuenster i. Holst,1953. (Translation from German by H E Meinel)
2. Angela Heuzenroeder, *Barossa Food,* pp.278-279
3. From poem written by C T Studd
4. Annie Johnson Flint, Poem

PHOTOS

Photos included in this book are sourced from personal and family collections and the following publications:

1. Dornstetter Heimatbuch, p.1, p.18, p.20
2. Beilharz Chronik, p.33, p.36, p.74
3. The Holy Land Called, p.40, p.45, p.62, p.70, p.73, p.143, p.237, p.238
4. Wir haben hier keine bleibende Stadt..., p.131
5. Martin Kirche, p.173, p.217, p.218
6. Your Swabian Neighbors, p.182, p.190, p.191
7. The Bond 1960, p.283, 284
8. Die Siedlungen der wuerttembergischen Templer in Palestina, p.32, pp.46, 47
9. Geschichte und Geschichten aus Zell am Aichelberg, p.177, p 178, p.205

www.ingramcontent.com/pod-product-compliance
Lightning Source LLC
Chambersburg PA
CBHW070622160426
43194CB00009B/1347